CHINA

A History

VOLUME 2

CHINA

A History

VOLUME 2
FROM THE GREAT QING EMPIRE THROUGH
THE PEOPLE'S REPUBLIC OF CHINA
1644–2009

Harold M. Tanner

Hackett Publishing Company, Inc.
Indianapolis/Cambridge

19 18 17 16 15   2 3 4 5 6

For further information, please address
  Hackett Publishing Company, Inc.
  P.O. Box 44937
  Indianapolis, Indiana 46244-0937
  www.hackettpublishing.com

Cover design by Abigail Coyle
Interior design by Elizabeth L. Wilson
Maps by Tracy Ellen Smith
Composition by Agnew's, Inc.

Every reasonable effort has been made to contact the rights holders of copyrighted materials in this book. The author and the publisher would be grateful for any additional information and will address any errors or omissions in subsequent printings of the book.

Library of Congress Cataloging-in-Publication Data
Tanner, Harold Miles.
  China : a history / Harold M. Tanner.
    v.   cm.
  Includes bibliographical references and index.
  Contents: v. 1. From Neolithic cultures through the Great Qing Empire
(10,000 BCE–1799 CE) — v. 2. From the Great Qing Empire through the People's Republic
of China (1644–2009).
    ISBN 978-1-60384-202-0 (v. 1 : paper) — ISBN 978-1-60384-203-7 (v. 1 : cloth) —
ISBN 978-1-60384-204-4 (v. 2 : paper) — ISBN 978-1-60384-205-1 (v. 2 : cloth)
  1. China—History.   I. Title.
  DS735.T34   2010
  951—dc22   2009048040

CONTENTS

Acknowledgments

My education in China's history, language, and culture has been a long journey —both real and metaphorical—a journey in which this book marks only a milestone, not an end. It has taken me from my home in New Jersey to Taiwan and China, to London and New York City, and to my new home in Texas. The many people who have helped me along the way have enriched my knowledge and transformed my thinking, though perhaps not as thoroughly as they would have liked. Their teaching, advice, and support have made this book possible. The list of those to thank begins with my teachers: Parry Jones, who introduced me to the study of China's history at the Princeton Day School in New Jersey; Stuart Schram, Paul Chen, and Ian Nish at London University's School of Oriental and African Studies; and at Columbia University, Madeleine Zelin, Andrew Nathan, Tom Bernstein, Gari Ledyard, Bob Hymes, Wm. Theodore de Bary, Irene Bloom, Morris Rossabi, and Hans Beilenstein. I hope that this book reflects, at least in some small way, the breadth and depth of the education that I have been fortunate enough to receive from these and other teachers over the years.

Friends and colleagues near and far also made important contributions to what turned out to be a much larger project than I had anticipated. The University of North Texas and its Department of History have been supportive, particularly in granting me a semester of paid leave during which I wrote a large portion of the manuscript. I thank Johan Elverskog for his insights on religion, the Mongols, and Central Asia, and Margherita Zanasi for her comments on a number of chapters. Special thanks are due to Sarah Schneewind. Her encouragement of this project, close reading, and frank comments on many chapters were particularly helpful and well beyond the call of duty. I have also benefited tremendously from the comments of the external reviewers for this book: Joanna Waley-Cohen, Ruth Dunnell, Paul Fischer, Charles W. Hayford, Roland Higgins, Michael Loewe, Peter Perdue, Caroline Reeves, and Roger Thompson. I am grateful to my editor, Deborah Wilkes, for recruiting such notable scholars and for performing all the other tasks required to turn my ideas into a manuscript, and the manuscript into a book. Tracy Ellen Smith of Creative Design Resources has done a remarkable job of transforming my often unrealistic ideas into maps. While expressing my thanks to all those who have assisted in making this book possible, I reserve to myself the responsibility for any remaining errors or infelicities of style.

Finally, but most importantly, I offer my deepest thanks to my wife, Yiyun, and our children, Sophia and William. For years, and with good grace, they have made the sacrifices that seem to go along with research and writing, allowing me to work on too many evenings, too many weekends, and too many otherwise perfectly beautiful summer days, and putting up with my trips to archives and conferences. This book is for them, with my love and affection.

A Note on Transliterations

Chinese names in this text have been written using the Hanyu pinyin system of Romanization. Most words are pronounced roughly the way an English-speaker would guess. There are a few important exceptions to this rule: "c" is pronounced as "ts," "q" as "ch," and "x" more or less like "s." I have used non-pinyin spellings for a few individuals and entities whose names have become universally recognized under those earlier spellings in English-language literature. Thus, Sun Yat-sen (known in Chinese as Sun Wen or Sun Yixian), Chiang Kai-shek (pinyin Jiang Jieshi), the Kwantung Army (pinyin Guandong Army), and "Manchukuo."

Mongolian names have been rendered in line with the system used in Christopher P. Atwood, *Encyclopedia of Mongolian and the Mongol Empire* (New York: Facts on File, 2004), ix. For Tibetan names, I have followed the system used by the International Association of Tibetan Studies (online at http://thdl.org).

About the Chinese Characters

Chinese characters from the Zhou Dynasty divination text, the *Book of Changes* (*Yi jing*), have been used as symbols for the Introduction and for each of the two parts of this book. The *Book of Changes* uses sixty-four hexagrams (combinations of broken and unbroken lines) to represent the stages of change in a cyclically changing universe. The hexagrams used in this text, their names, and their meanings are as follows:

Introduction: 乾 (*qian*) "The Creative." The first hexagram of the *Book of Changes, qian* symbolizes beginnings, justice, the way of the superior man, and the primal creative force of the universe.

Part I: 豐 (*feng*) "Abundance." The fifty-fifth hexagram conveys the meaning of having surmounted challenges in order to achieve a glorious abundance, like the sun standing high in the sky at midday.

Part II: 革 (*ge*) "Change." *Ge,* the forty-ninth hexagram, suggests change, or even removal, as fire and water subdue each other, or as the new replaces the old. In modern Chinese, the character *ge* forms the first half of the two-syllable word *geming*—revolution.

List of Maps

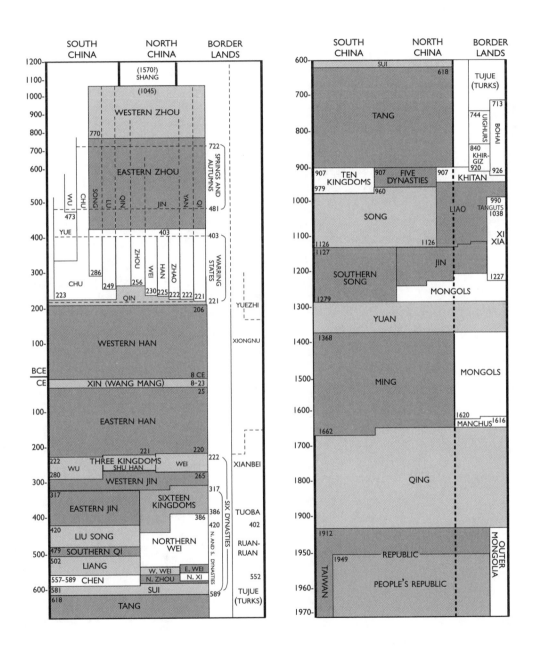

China

A HISTORY

乾

At 8:08 p.m. on the eighth of August, the eighth month of 2008, China re-introduced itself to the world with the grand opening ceremony of the Beijing Summer Olympics. China's Communist Party leaders had chosen the date and time in accord with popular superstition: the Chinese words for "eight" and "to get rich" are homophones, which makes eight a very auspicious number. The theatrical opening ceremony, the ultramodern Olympic venues, extensive investment in urban infrastructure (including a new international terminal at Beijing's airport) and the Chinese athletes' record haul of fifty-one gold medals (more than any other country) all stood as testimony to China's wealth and power.

An event like the Beijing Olympics is often portrayed as a symbolic moment in the history of a nation. But symbolic of what? That all depends on the way you write the history of the decades, centuries, or millennia that preceded the time of the event itself. As they watched and discussed the Beijing Olympics, Chinese and American audiences attached different symbolic meanings to the same event because they approached it with different histories of China in mind.

For Chinese audiences, the opening ceremony and the games themselves symbolized a recovery of lost glory. Until the early 19th century, China had been one of the largest and most productive economies on earth and the dominant military and cultural power in East and Central Asia. Then, in the

The People's Republic of China and neighboring areas.

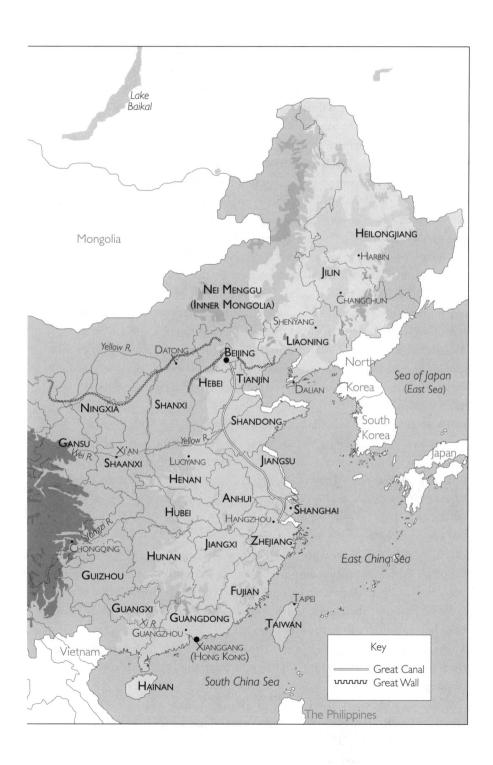

mid-19th century came what Chinese history textbooks and politicians often refer to as "national humiliation." The industrialized nations of the West and Japan invaded China, took its resources, dominated its markets, stunted its economic growth, and mistreated its people. Now, after more than a century of poverty, war, and revolution in which it had been dismissed as the "sick man of Asia," China was back on the road to wealth and ready to join the ranks of the developed industrialized nations as an equal.

Most American spectators approached the Beijing Olympics with a very different idea of China's history. The American media consistently portrayed the games as China's "coming-out party." The picture created for the American public was one of a country emerging from centuries of isolation and/or a country "opening" to the capitalist, democratic West after decades of control by an anti-Western Communist leadership. American journalists and spectators tended to interpret much of what they noticed in Beijing—Starbucks coffee, rock and roll, and Chinese fans' enthusiasm for American basketball stars like Kobe Bryant, for example—as encouraging signs of "opening." Americans were also quick to point to evidence that China's Communist leadership had not completely signed on to the spirit of "openness." Much was made, for example, of continued government blocking of politically sensitive Web sites.

These two simple versions of Chinese history—one Chinese, the other American—are mutually contradictory. On the one hand, we have invasion; on the other, self-imposed isolation. Both stories are fundamentally wrong. China's history is not a drama of strength and glory, downfall at the hands of Western imperialists, and redemption through rapid economic growth, nor is it an object lesson in the dangers of isolation and the value of open doors and open markets.

The goal of this book is to tell the story of China in a way that goes beyond the simple but misleading narratives of glory to downfall to redemption or of isolation to opening. Volume One traced the development of China's dynastic regimes, their economies, people, cultures, and interactions with neighboring peoples from the Neolithic age through the Qianlong era (1736–1796) of the Qing Empire (1644–1912). This volume will take the story from the founding of the Qing dynasty through the first decade of the 21st century.

The major theme of this history of modern China will be the fall of the Qing—a multi-ethnic empire with a premodern agricultural economy—and the attempts by Chinese leaders to transform the Qing Empire into a modern, industrial nation-state. Reformers in the late Qing, including the firebrand Confucian scholar Kang Youwei (1858–1927) and the famous Empress Dowager Cixi (1835–1908), tried to preserve both the empire and the position of the ruling house by seeking modernization and a constitutional monarchy. Revolutionaries including Dr. Sun Yat-sen (1866–1925), the inveterate plotter and theoretician of the Chinese nationalist revolution against the Manchus, argued that only a republican form of government would be able to achieve the modernization, economic growth, strength, and unity that the Qing imperial government had failed to deliver.

When revolutionaries did overthrow the Qing dynasty in 1911, there followed nearly a century of internal political turmoil and brutal foreign invasion in which a variety of leaders—President Yuan Shikai (1859–1916), Chiang Kai-shek (1887–1975) and his Guomindang (Nationalist Party), Mao Zedong (1893–1976) and the Chinese Communist Party, as well as a variety of warlords, rival factions within both the Nationalist and Communist parties, and intellectuals ranging from anarchists to traditionalist Confucianists—all suggested and, to the best of their abilities, attempted to put into practice their own visions of how to build a strong, wealthy, unified Chinese nation-state. In the late 20th and early 21st centuries, it appeared that the second-generation Chinese Communist Party leader Deng Xiaoping (1904–97) and his successors had hit upon the formula for sustained economic growth and military development. Still, China's identity as a unified nation-state remained subject to question, with underlying ethnic tensions bursting into violence in both Xinjiang and Tibet, two of the most important non-Chinese areas that had been conquered by the Qing Empire in the 18th century and subsequently became part of the modern Chinese state.

As we review the story of the collapse of the Qing Empire and the struggle to build a modern China, we will see how that political story intertwines and interacts with changes in the arts, literature, and music, in the economy, and in the everyday lives of the generations of elite and ordinary men and women who were witnesses to, participants in, and often victims of, the ideologies, the plots, the strategies, and policies of political and military leaders. We will begin, however, with an overview of China's geography.

The Lay of the Land

The territory that we now refer to as China is vast: over 3,705,386 square miles (9,596,960 sq km), extending from over 50 degrees latitude in the north to below 20 degrees latitude in the south, from the alluvial plains and

乾

river valleys of the east to the forbidding mountains, high plateaus, and deserts of Tibet and Xinjiang in the west. This territory has been home to a variety of ethnic groups. Kingdoms and empires have risen and fallen on this huge landmass: in many cases, what we now refer to as "China" has been home to two or more different kingdoms or empires at the same time. In the 20th century, we observe the emergence of a unified, modern nation-state, the Republic of China, and then the People's Republic of China, dominated by a single large ethnic group—the Han, whom we generally call "Chinese." In addition to the Han (who comprise 91.5 percent of China's population), China has fifty-five other officially recognized ethnic groups, or "minority nationalities" as they are called in China.

The unification of all the territory and peoples now falling within the borders of the People's Republic of China is the relatively recent product of a very long historical process. The origins of that territorial unity lie in the empire-building of the Han and later dynastic regimes and in waves of migration in which Han people, their agricultural civilization, and the power of their dynastic governments spread across the land, as described in Volume One (and briefly summarized in "Neolithic Cultures to the Great Qing Empire: An Overview" in this volume). The process of migration and government action and the ethnic, economic, and cultural transformations that come along with them continue to this day.

The homeland of the Han people is that area which geographers refer to as "China Proper." The territory includes the drainage areas of three major river systems and their tributaries: the Yellow River in the north, the Yangzi River in the center, and the Xi (West) River in the south. The area includes the Central Plains, the Yangzi Valley, the Guangdong (Canton) Basin, and the Sichuan Basin—the latter relatively isolated behind mountain ranges and (until recently) the forbidding Three Gorges of the Yangzi River. China Proper is well suited to settled agriculture and is the area in which the Han Chinese came to be the dominant ethnic group by the tenth century.

China Proper itself may be divided into two parts, north and south. The line of division is created roughly by the Qin (or Qinling) Mountains, running along the Han River until the river turns south, and then cutting across to the Huai River and following its path to the Yellow Sea. North China is relatively dry and cool. The soil and climate are suitable for the cultivation of millet, barley, wheat, and soybeans. South China is a place of heavier rainfall and is blessed with an abundance of rivers and lakes. The soil and climate are suitable for irrigated rice agriculture. As we shall see, south China was originally home to many ethnic groups other than the Han. Some remain today as ethnic minorities; others were gradually absorbed or displaced as Han Chinese migration, supported by military force, changed the ethnic composition and the economy of this fertile area.

Standing in contrast to China Proper is a vast area that we will refer to as China's Inner Asian periphery. The Inner Asian periphery includes Tibet, Xinjiang, Ningxia, Inner Mongolia, and Manchuria.[1] These areas have historically been the homelands of people other than the Han ethnic group. Relations between the predominantly Han people of China Proper and the various peoples of China's Inner Asian periphery have been characterized at times by trade, and at other times by warfare. Government based in China Proper sometimes conquered and administered parts of the Inner Asian periphery. At other times, nomadic confederations, kingdoms, or imperial states ruled over parts of the Inner Asian periphery, asserting their identity against and variously trading and/or fighting with the states of China Proper. Occasionally Inner Asian peoples subjugated and ruled northern portions of China Proper or even, in the cases of the Mongols and the Manchus, brought all of China Proper under their control. Also peripheral to China Proper was the island of Taiwan, lying 150 miles (240 km) off the southeast Chinese coast. Only in modern times, under the Qing dynasty (1644–1911), did a government based in China Proper build an empire that included the entire Inner Asian periphery and the island of Taiwan.

People and Provinces

It would be historically inaccurate to assign any single ethnic identity to any one of the regions of the Inner Asian periphery or Taiwan and to assume that it has always been the homeland of that particular ethnic group. Many peoples have come and gone, fought, intermarried, and melded with one another, not just in these outlying areas, but even in China Proper itself. Nonetheless, it is useful to make some general statements about the major ethnic groups of Taiwan and the Inner Asian periphery.

Taiwan was originally inhabited by aboriginal people whose native languages are related to the Polynesian languages of the Pacific islands. Migration of Han Chinese from the mainland, gradual and small in numbers at first, increased markedly in the 17th century. Han Chinese migrants clashed with the aboriginal people, pushing them up into the mountains. In 1684, the Qing government incorporated the island as a prefecture of Fujian province, thus marking the beginning of Taiwan's administration from the mainland.[2]

Before the third century CE, the southwestern areas of Yunnan, Guizhou, and Annam (now northern Vietnam) were also parts of the periphery of China Proper. The numerous ethnic groups of these areas, including Hmong (whom the Chinese refer to as Miao), Dai, and Annamese, interacted with Chinese migrants and with the imperial states which absorbed what became China's southwestern provinces and, at times, Annam as well.

To the west of China Proper, at elevations of 6,500 feet (2,000 m) and more above sea level, lies the area inhabited by Tibetan people. This includes the contemporary Xizang Autonomous Region (Tibet), Qinghai province, some of the western fringes of Sichuan and Gansu Provinces, and parts of northern Yunnan province. The Tibetan region consists largely of sparsely inhabited plateaus on which nomadic herders of sheep and yak eke out a living. In river valley areas, sedentary farmers cultivate barley, potatoes, and other crops. Over a period of time, but particularly in the eighth century, the Tibetans converted from their animistic religion, Bon, to Buddhism—although retaining many of the elements of Bon, so that the resulting variety of Buddhism has distinct Tibetan characteristics.

To the northwest lies the Xinjiang Uighur Autonomous Region. This area has been home to various people, including Buddhist kingdoms (during the Tang period) and, more recently, to the Uighur and other Turkic peoples whose religion is Islam and who sometimes refer to the area as "East Turkestan." The center of Xinjiang is dominated by the forbidding Taklamakan Desert and Tarim Basin. At the outer edges of this desert area are rich oases fed by run-off from the snow-covered Tian and Kunlun Mountains. In the northern corner of Xinjiang the Zunghar Basin (Zungharia) is defined and watered by the Altai and other mountain chains. Together, these various mountain chains define Xinjiang, dividing it from the other Central Asian Turkic lands, while the trade routes across the desert and down through the Gansu Corridor (that finger of Inner Chinese cultivated land lying between the Gobi Desert and the Tibetan Plateau) bring the area into commercial and cultural contact with China Proper. Thus the people of Xinjiang have functioned as middlemen, agents of trade and cultural exchange between Turkic Central Asia and Han China Proper, developing their own mixed cultural identity in the process. The independence of the Central Asian states after the fall of the Soviet Union reinvigorated the old trade routes: Xinjiang once again functions as a route of contact between China Proper and Central Asia.

To the north of China Proper is Mongolia—an area that, for our purposes, is comprised of both the contemporary Inner Mongolian Autonomous Region and the republic of Mongolia. Mongolia includes the Gobi Desert, mountains in the northwest, and, in between, vast grasslands that have supported nomadic pastoral peoples, most recently the Mongols, but in previous centuries others, including the Uighurs (during the Tang dynasty) and the Xiongnu (during the Qin and Han periods). The nomadic economy relied on a triumvirate of animals: sheep for wool and food, horses for warfare and communications, and camels for transport. The tribal peoples of the grasslands would sometimes form larger federations, the largest and most significant being that formed by the Mongol leader Chinggis Khan. The relations of the nomads of the steppe with the settled agricultural people of China Proper have varied from trade to raiding to conquest. To the east of Mongolia lies Manchuria. In premodern times, this area was populated by tribal peoples who practiced a combination of farming, animal husbandry, hunting, and trading.

As we move on through the histories of the peoples and kingdoms, the wars, the cultures, and the remarkable individuals who came and went on this vast stage that we call China, we will be harking back to these basic geographical areas and features, adding refinements here and there and taking note of change over time. We will also be referring to China's provinces.

From the Qin dynasty (221–206 BCE) through the present time, Chinese governments have divided their territories into larger administrative units that we generally call "provinces." In some periods, two or more provinces and their governors would be grouped together under a governor-general. Each province was subdivided into a number of counties. At times there would be an administrative layer consisting of a number of counties between county and province. Provincial and county boundaries and even names changed over the years. Nonetheless, there is enough stability in enough of the provincial names that it is useful to become familiar with them as they appear on a contemporary map of the People's Republic of China. The names and boundaries of China's provinces reflect the country's multi-ethnic character and the way in which China Proper became the economic, political, military, and cultural center of a country that includes the Inner Asian periphery.

China Proper consists of nineteen provincial-level units. In the north are Shandong, Hebei, and Shanxi, with Shaanxi and Gansu in the northwest. Gansu is the province whose "corridor" reaches up toward the oases of Xinjiang and thus carried trade over the famous "Silk Road" to and from the Central Asian kingdoms and beyond. Straddling the border of north and south China are Jiangsu, Anhui, Henan, and Hubei provinces. The Yangzi River flows through all four, bringing with it the blessings of irrigation and transport and the curse of periodic floods. Firmly in the south we have Zhejiang,

Jiangxi, Hunan, Fujian, Guangdong, and Hainan. In the mountainous south-west lie the provinces of Yunnan, Guizhou, and Sichuan.

Also in the southwest is the Guangxi Zhuang Autonomous Region, a mountainous region with a sizeable population of non-Han peoples collectively referred to as "Zhuang." China's "Autonomous Regions" (there are five of them) are provincial-level units whose populations have a majority or a very sizeable minority of non-Han people. The logic behind the autonomous regions is to provide a degree of self-rule to the non-Han people who have been the majority population in these peripheral areas. In the same way, historically ethnic minority areas within some provinces have been designated as autonomous counties or autonomous prefectures. In practice, the "autonomy" has been largely ceremonial, as Han Chinese Communist Party bureaucrats hold real power.

China's Inner Asian periphery includes both provinces and autonomous regions. The Tibetan ethnic area is divided among the Tibet (Xizang) Autonomous Region, the province of Qinghai, and a number of autonomous counties and prefectures in Yunnan, Sichuan, and Gansu provinces. In the extreme northwest, the Uighurs and other Turkic Muslim groups make up a slim majority of the population of the Xinjiang Uighur Autonomous Region. The Ningxia Hui Autonomous Region, bordering on Gansu and Shaanxi, is home to a large population of Hui people—Chinese Muslims who trace their descent from Arab and Central Asian Muslim traders who came to China centuries ago. The Hui are a minority even within Ningxia. Mongols likewise are a minority in the Inner Mongolia (Nei Menggu) Autonomous Region. Manchuria, where the overwhelming majority of the people are Han Chinese, is divided into China's three northeastern provinces: Heilongjiang, Jilin, and Liaoning. A few rural areas that have Manchu communities have been designated as autonomous counties or prefectures.

Villages, Towns, and Cities

For all of Chinese history, the vast majority—eighty percent or more—of the Han people of China Proper were farmers. Their world was the world of the village—but not merely of the village itself, but of the standard marketing area within which the males of the family, in particular, were accustomed to doing business with men from other villages and even from one of the larger cities that served as the intermediate markets to which the standard market towns were oriented.

Certainly, farmers spent most of their time in their home villages and found their identity in "family, fields, and ancestors."[3] For most of Chinese history the best arrangement, from the point of view of both government and the farmers, was a system of independent landholding by small family farmers. Family identity and solidarity was very strong—the ideal living arrangement was "three generations under one roof." In practice, this was rarely achieved for long, as families went through natural cycles of growth and contraction. But even while most families were nuclear families most of the time, they were knit together into clans. Clan organizations were stronger in the south than in the north. Throughout China, however, clan identity was symbolized and maintained through ancestral temples and sometimes through clan leadership, commonly held land, and other clan-run institutions.

For all their deep local roots, Chinese farmers were not self-sufficient peasants, living their lives in the narrow confines of their fields and villages. Instead, they were actively involved in a wider community—the standard marketing area—in which they shared not only goods, but culture. These marketing areas ranged from 5 or fewer square miles (approx. 15 sq km) in flat, fertile areas to over 60 square miles (150 sq km) in sparsely populated mountainous and infertile border areas. Market systems and market towns grew in numbers over time, so that by the Qing period, virtually every farming household lived in an area that was accessible to a market town.[4] These market towns were not grand places. Typically, they would have one real street, some permanent shops, and various discrete market areas, each dedicated to a particular product or craft. Marketing would be on a regular schedule, generally once every three or five days, for a few hours on each designated market day.

Each of these standard market towns would be linked to two or three larger "intermediate" market towns, which occupied a position between the central and the standard markets. It was in the intermediate market towns that one would expect to see members of the landholding local elite—those families who had accumulated larger amounts of agricultural land, which they rented out to farmers who had little or no land of their own. There, these elite families would have access to books and writing implements, fine fabrics, and other luxury goods that would not be found in a humbler standard market town.

Above the intermediate market town one would find the central market towns and, above them, local and regional cities. These larger and more sophisticated central market towns, local cities, and regional capitals would typically be located at important transportation junctions and would be the sites of warehousing and wholesaling. The higher one went in this hierarchy of central places, the more likely it would be that one would find fully walled cities that not only had marketing functions, but also served as administrative centers. These were Chinese cities in the real sense—urban settlements with walls and a government office. It is to the cities that we shall now turn our attention.

The productivity of Chinese farmers supported one of the most sophisticated and, in terms of sheer numbers, one of the largest urban civilizations in world history. China's cities were the natural environment of the elite, the centers of trade, administration, and higher culture. Towns and cities and town and city people thus take up a disproportionate amount of the attention of the student of Chinese history.

China's towns and cities are as varied as its landscape—from the flat, dry, and dusty cities of the north, laid out in squares, to Sichuan's Chongqing in the southwest, where the streets writhe up and around (and, in the future, will punch through) the hills, to canal-laced southern cities like Suzhou and Ningbo. Some towns had exclusively commercial functions, while other towns, and virtually all cities, were both administrative and commercial centers.

There was an ideal model, informed by cosmological principles, according to which a city should be constructed.[5] This model called for walled and moated rectangular cities laid out on a north-south axis, horizontal and vertical streets, palaces in the center of the city facing south, and markets in the shady position to the north. When it came to real-life urban construction, Chinese rulers were practical, not slaves to tradition or to one ideal model. Some capital cities more or less approximated the ideals expressed in the classical model; others followed quite different plans.[6] Some cities, for example, had designated marketplaces (but generally not in the north), while in others (such as the Northern Song capital of Kaifeng), business took place everywhere. City walls often departed from the ideal square model to accommodate natural features: rivers or hills. Tang Chang'an had the imperial palace on the northern edge of the city, facing south. The Mongol Yuan capital of Dadu placed the imperial palace in the center, according to the classical model. So too did Ming-Qing Beijing, which was built on the site of Dadu. Smaller cities were often walled (some were not), and could be roughly square, rectangular, or even round.

The variety of Chinese city plans, the many ways in which they did not conform to classical ideals, and both their elements of continuity and their change over time remind us that modern China's territory, from the Inner Asian periphery to China Proper to Taiwan, contained (and still contains) a variety of languages, dialects, cultures, and peoples which have changed over the course of history. Even within the China Proper of the Han people, strong elements of continuity as well as the development and popularization of a unifying elite culture were accompanied by a range of local variations, inter-action with other cultures, and significant changes over time, even before the onset of developments spurred by new relationships with the industrialized nation-states of the West and Japan. Therefore, an understanding of mod-ern China must begin with at least a brief look at the earlier eras of China's history.

Notes

1. It is necessary from the outset to admit that labeling this entire territory as "China's Inner Asian periphery" is to take a China-centered view of history. Since the purpose of this volume is to relate the history of regimes centered in China Proper, for which Inner Asia really did lie on the periphery, perhaps this act of Sinocentrism can be forgiven. A history placing Inner Asia or some part of Inner Asia (Mongolia, for exam-ple) at the center and relegating China Proper to the role of periphery would be different, but just as valid as the Sino-centric perspective adopted here.

2. Denny Roy, *Taiwan: A Political History* (Ithaca: Cornell University Press, 2003).

3. The phrase is taken from Lloyd East-man, *Family, Fields, and Ancestors: Con-stancy and Change in China's Social and Economic History, 1550–1949* (New York: Oxford University Press, 1988).

4. G. William Skinner, *Marketing and Social Structure in Rural China* (Ann Arbor: Association for Asian Studies, 1964, 1965), 6.

5. This and the following paragraph draw on Arthur F. Wright, "The Cosmology of the Chinese City," in G. William Skin-ner, ed., *The City in Late Imperial China* (Stanford: Stanford University Press, 1977), 33–73.

6. Nancy Shatzman Steinhardt, "Why Were Chang'an and Beijing So Different?" *The Journal of the Society of Architectural His-torians* 45.4 (Dec. 1986): 339–57.

乾

FROM NEOLITHIC CULTURES
TO THE GREAT QING EMPIRE

An Overview

Chinese written history goes back to around 1200 BCE. Traditional myths that push the history of the Chinese people back to 2852 BCE or earlier still inform popular views, so that one typical overview, published in 1999, begins: "Our great China, treading a difficult path of five thousand years, has a long history, created a brilliant ancient culture, and is one of the world's famous civilized ancient countries."[1]

While no one would deny the brilliant and fascinating achievements of millennia of artists and intellectuals, artisan, inventors, and merchants in what is now the territory of the People's Republic of China, any straightforward narrative of a single great country over five thousand years simplifies the past to the point of untruth. More accurate, richer, and more interesting is the story of how a number of distinctive Neolithic cultures and their descendents interacted, eventually creating a Han Chinese centralized bureaucratic imperial state based in China Proper but continually interacting with other peoples and states, particularly those across Asia as far as India but including the Middle East and Europe. We know that cultural and political debate and national identity in the English-speaking world draw selectively on national histories and cultural references ranging from the contemporary

For more illustrative material, please see the title support page for *China: A History* at www.hackettpublishing.com.

16

to the biblical. In the same way, discussion, debate, and construction of culture, politics, economics, and national identity in China draw on the rich past as it survives in texts, practices, and objects. To understand the history of modern China and the present of the People's Republic requires some basic historical background, beginning with the Neolithic age.

From Neolithic Cultures to a Centralized Imperial State 5000 BCE–220 CE

Modern humans—*homo sapiens*—evolved in East Africa around two hundred thousand years ago and migrated to China (and elsewhere around the globe) around one hundred thousand years ago. Around ten thousand years ago, human communities, including those in China, made the leap from hunting and gathering economies to economies based on agriculture. Between 8000 and 3000 BCE, in a relatively warm climate, a number of different agricultural cultures emerged in northern and southern China Proper, Manchuria, Mongolia, and Qinghai. Over time, some of the cultures of northern China's Central Plains area, particularly the Longshan culture (c. 3000–c. 2000 BCE), developed a set of characteristics that, taken together, mark the beginnings of Chinese civilization: a complex agricultural economy, clan organization, reverence for ancestors, a high degree of social stratification, distinctive pottery styles, the beginnings of bronze technology, drinking and feasting rituals associated with social solidarity and social hierarchy, relations ranging from trade to warfare with neighboring peoples, rammed-earth construction of walls and foundations, and square-shaped symbols that may be an early form of the written Chinese language.

According to traditional Chinese histories, a state known as the Xia (which historians in China now date at c. 2070–c. 1600 BCE) united some of the Longshan communities of the Central Plains into a kingdom; but many archeologists and historians still debate whether a Xia kingdom really existed. What is certain is that another Bronze Age kingdom, the Shang (c. 1570–1045 BCE), did emerge in the Central Plains somewhere around 1570 BCE.

The Shang dynasty is particularly known for its visually stunning and technologically sophisticated bronze ritual vessels and weapons. Supported by agricultural laborers working large tracts of land, the Shang elite were loosely ruled by kings, who practiced divination using tortoise shells and cattle scapulae, on which they would sometimes inscribe the questions asked of their ancestors, the answer divined, and occasionally even the actual outcome

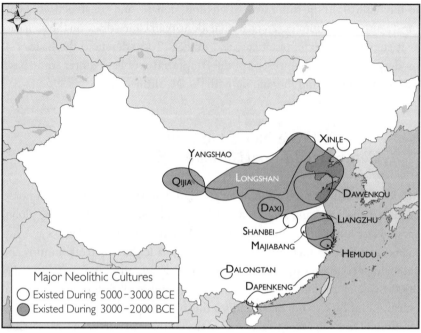

Major Neolithic cultures, 5000–3000 BCE.

of events. These "oracle bones," dated to around 1200 BCE, are the earliest written records of East Asian civilization and offer valuable insights into Shang religion, politics, family life, and warfare.

The Shang were often at war, for they shared China Proper with a number of other peoples. Some, like the distinctive cultures of Jiangxi to the south of the Yangzi River or of Sichuan in the southwest, were powerful bronze-working states whose levels of technology, agriculture, and political organization were similar to those of the Shang. Others were stateless peoples, including pastoral nomads in the north and practitioners of slash-and-burn agriculture in the south. Still others, like the Zhou people located in the west near modern Xi'an, were loosely affiliated with the Shang but harbored their own ambitions. It was a Zhou leader known as King Wu who defeated the Shang in 1045 BCE, marking the establishment of the Zhou dynasty (1045–221 BCE).

The Zhou explained that the last rulers of the Xia and then of the Shang had fallen because they had become cruel, arrogant, and immoral. Heaven had bestowed a mandate upon the Zhou rulers—a mandate that justified their position, but one that their heirs could only maintain if they held fast to moral virtue generation after generation. If the rulers should depart from the way of virtue, Heaven might show its displeasure through natural disasters, or even bestow its mandate upon a rival.

The Western Zhou (1046–771 BCE) with its capital near Xi'an was a patchwork of over seventy feudal states whose hereditary lords were theoretically (and sometimes actually) both related to and subordinate to the Zhou kings. Although little is known directly about the Western Zhou, idealized accounts of its feudal system, its egalitarian land tenure system, its family and political rituals, and its poetry and music remained touchstones of Chinese culture to which intellectuals would refer back (often very selectively) for the next two thousand years.

In 771 BCE pastoral tribes from the north drove the Zhou kings from their capital. Re-established in a new capital city to the east, near the modern city of Luoyang, the kings of the Eastern Zhou (770–221 BCE) were unable to maintain their authority over the feudal lords. With no one powerful enough to maintain peace between them, the various feudal states competed with each other, forming and breaking alliances and fighting wars, the larger states absorbing the smaller ones throughout the Eastern Zhou's Springs and Autumns period (770–475 BCE) until ten major states faced off against each other in the Warring States period (475–221 BCE).

Although chaotic, the Eastern Zhou is notable for new developments in political and moral philosophy, literature, technology, and warfare. The three schools of thought known as Confucianism, Daoism, and Legalism all have their origins in the Eastern Zhou. Confucius and his followers Mencius and Xunzi argued that order could be restored if the elite would simply return to the correct practice of ritual behavior in their family and public lives and that the essence of successful rulership was for a feudal lord or king to practice morality so that his exemplary behavior and his care for his subjects would transform all around him. The Daoists Laozi, putative author of the *Dao de jing,* and Zhuangzi suggested that the secret of good rulership or of survival in chaotic times was to understand and follow the "dao" or "Way" of the universe—which involved, above all, simplicity. Legalists countered that peace would only be restored to the world if a strong ruler at the head of a rationally organized, efficient bureaucracy used written laws, rewards, and punishments to manage his officials and to encourage his people to devote themselves to the two activities most essential to a state's success: agriculture and war.

All of the feudal states followed the advice of the Legalists. Improved technology, including the use of iron, contributed to more productive agriculture and to more brutal wars. Ultimately one state, the kingdom of Qin,

乾

defeated all the others, including the powerless royal house of Zhou, establishing the Qin dynasty (221–206 BCE).

Together, the Qin and the Han dynasty (202 BCE–220 CE) established a basic institutional framework of centralized government, a political philosophy synthesizing Confucian, Legalist, and Daoist ideas, and a difficult strategic relationship with the pastoral peoples of the Mongolian steppes that would continue to be of relevance through to the end of the Qing dynasty and, in some ways, to the present day. This early imperial period also saw important developments in the arts, literature, and the writing of history.

In politics, Qin Shi Huangdi, the founding emperor of Qin, eliminated the feudal system and introduced a new, centralized system in which Qin territory was divided into provinces and counties, with the emperor and his central government responsible for the recruitment, appointment, evaluation, transfer, promotion, and dismissal of local and provincial officials. Written laws, enforced by harsh punishments, were used to discipline officials and commoners.

After Qin Shi Huangdi's death in 210 BCE, the government of Qin collapsed under the multiple pressures of economic strain, domestic rebellions, and court factionalism. Liu Bang, a low-ranking local official under Qin, arose to found a new dynasty, the Han (202 BCE–220 CE). Building on the Qin model of centralized government and written laws, the Han dynasty re-established order in China Proper. During the centuries of Han rule, scholars like Dong Zhongshu developed a new synthesis of Confucian, Legalist, and Daoist thought which contributed significantly to the foundations of the art of government. Sima Qian, Ban Gu, and his sister Ban Zhao wrote histories covering events from the Xia dynasty through their own times, thus laying the foundations of the standard Chinese approach to history until about 1900.

As the rulers of a wealthy agricultural society, both the Qin and Han emperors faced a strategic challenge from the pastoral Xiongnu tribes to their north. Qin Shi Huangdi's territorial expansion to the north eliminated the buffer zone that had existed between the pastoralists of Mongolia and the settled peoples of the Central Plains. Qin Shi Huangdi's solution had been to link together various older defensive works into a "Long Wall," the precursor of the "Great Wall" constructed during the Ming dynasty (1368–1644) for similar purposes. The Han dynasty tried various ways of dealing with the Xiongnu: wall-building, trade, alliances that pitted one group of nomads against another, and aggressive territorial expansion into the northwest (the region of modern Xinjiang). Each of these methods met with some success, but none brought long-lasting peace on the frontiers. The Han dynasty's search for allies and its expansion into the northwest helped to stimulate long distance trade over the Silk Road, which brought Han products—most notably fine silks—to the Middle East and the Mediterranean world in exchange for goods ranging from glass to silver vessels to fine horses.

Cultural Interaction and Transformation, 220 CE–1368

In 220 CE popular rebellions fueled by decades of floods, droughts, and epidemics ended the Han dynasty. After a period in which China Proper was divided among three competing kingdoms, a wave of migration brought pastoral peoples into the northern part of China Proper. Many Chinese elite families and households associated with them fled as refugees to the Yangzi valley, which in the Han period was still a lightly populated, relatively undeveloped frontier area. From 317 to 589 China Proper was divided. In the north, the Central Plains—the traditional heartland of the Xia, Shang, Zhou, Qin, and Han—came under the control of a series of short-lived dynasties, most established by Turkic and Tibetan elite families. The south, with its center of gravity in the lower Yangzi region, saw the rise and fall of five dynasties, all supported by elite families who regarded themselves as the legitimate heirs of the culture of the Han dynasty.

Culturally speaking, the period of division was the beginning of a long era of intensive cultural interaction between China Proper (particularly the Central Plains area, whose elite families were now of pastoral background), the lands of China's Inner Asian periphery, and places beyond, most notably India. Buddhism and related elements of South and Central Asian culture (styles of art and music, food and medicine, fashion and architecture) had already begun to enter China Proper via the Silk Road from India and Central Asia and the maritime trade from Southeast Asia to the port of Guangzhou (Canton). During the period of division the transference of Buddhism and other aspects of South and Central Asian culture increased, contributing to a fundamental transformation of Chinese culture.

As Buddhism entered the Chinese religious and cultural world, it combined with Confucian moral philosophy, Daoist philosophy, and Daoist popular religion so that most people regarded these "Three Teachings" as being mutually compatible. Artists drew on Daoist and Buddhist aesthetics in creating a tradition of scholar-amateur painting and in making calligraphy into an art form, most famously exemplified by the scholar Wang Xizhi's (303–361) famous "Preface to the Poems Composed at the Orchid Pavilion." In the north, a warrior aristocracy of mixed Han Chinese and Turkic background patronized art, literature, and religious institutions as well as dominated military and political life.

The powerful general who founded the Sui dynasty (581–618), himself a member of that warrior aristocracy, finally reunified north and south, synthesizing northern and southern cultural styles, but the dynasty quickly collapsed under the stress of the flooding of the Yellow River and four expensive and unsuccessful attacks on the Korean kingdom of Koguryo. Nonetheless, intensive interaction with Central Asia and India continued in the Sui and its successor, the Tang dynasty (618–907).

The Tang is often regarded as the most glorious period of the Chinese past, famous for its poets, artists, and calligraphers. A confident Tang government staffed by highly-educated aristocratic men harnessed the productive agriculture of the Central Plains and, increasingly, the rice-producing Yangzi valley, built one of the most powerful armies of its time, and expanded the empire into northern Vietnam, parts of the Korean peninsula, and deep into Central Asia. The Tang capital of Chang'an (near modern Xi'an) was a cosmopolitan city of Chinese bureaucrats and businessmen, Sogdian merchants, Uighur and Turkic horse-traders, Nestorian Christians, Muslims, Manicheans, Zoroastrians, and, of course, Buddhists and Daoists. Tang aristocratic women were active in public life and business, and owned property. In one notable instance of women playing important roles in politics, Wu Zhao (623?–705), an imperial concubine and then an empress and empress dowager, took over from her son and ruled in her own right from 690 to 705 as China's only female emperor. To employ talented men who would not despise her background as a commoner, she relied heavily on a system of civil service examinations that was already in place.

The rebellion of General An Lushan (703?–757), lasting from 755 until 763, and the concessions the dynasty had to make to its loyal generals, severely weakened the Tang from within. The rebellion also contributed to the Tang's loss of control over the "Western Regions" of Qinghai and Xinjiang, with their trade routes and horses. Nonetheless, Tang emperors continued to rule over a still-impressive territory in China Proper until 907, when internal rebellions and pressure from nomadic peoples to the north and northwest finally destroyed the dynasty.

The end of the Tang did not mean the end of Chinese interaction with other peoples; but during the Song (960–1276) and Yuan (1271–1368) periods, the governments and the people of China Proper interacted more passively with the hunting and pastoral peoples of the Inner Asian periphery. In the Han and Tang dynasties, armies, diplomats, and merchants had pushed aggressively out to the north and northwest, asserting Chinese power and influence, particularly in the area of modern Xinjiang. The Song dynasty, by contrast, was forced to deal in the Northern Song period (960–1127) on equal terms with the neighboring Khitan Liao and Tangut Xi Xia empires to the north and northwest. In 1127, the Song lost China Proper north of the Huai River to the Jurchen Jin Empire (which had also defeated the Liao). The Southern Song (1128–1276) never recovered the lost territory.

Although a "lesser empire," the Song was a wealthy and sophisticated society. Significant advances in agricultural production and technology, a rapidly growing market economy, mass production of commodities like porcelain, high rates of urbanization, and the invention of gunpowder, the compass, and printing, and the further development of a sophisticated civil service examination system lead historians to view the Song period as a time of revolutionary change. In the intellectual realm, members of the literati elite, most notably Zhu Xi (1130–1200), drew on Buddhist ideas to redefine and reinvigorate the "Learning of the Way" associated with Confucius. From 1313 until 1904, Song Neo-Confucianism, as it is known in the West, was the orthodox philosophy of government and the basis of the curriculum for the civil service examinations.

The Song's neighboring states, the Xi Xia (1038–1227), the Liao (907–1125), and the Jin (1115–1234), consisted of pastoral/hunting dynastic regimes (Tangut, Khitan, and Jurchen respectively) ruling over mixed populations of nomads, hunters, and agriculturalists. All three combined their own and Chinese cultures and styles of rulership, generally administering their pastoral and their agricultural subjects each according to their own traditions.

Yet further north, a number of competing pastoral peoples inhabited the forbidding grasslands of Mongolia, wresting a hard living from herding, supplemented by hunting, fishing, raiding, and trade. In 1205 the Mongol leader Temüjin, better known as Chinggis (or Genghis) Khan (c. 1165?–1227), united the tribes of Mongolia into a single confederacy. Chinggis, his followers, and his sons built a world empire centered on Mongolia and, ultimately, extending into the Middle East, Eastern Europe, Korea, and northern China.

Chinggis' grandson Qubilai (or Khubilai) (1215–1294) established his own Chinese-style dynastic government, the Yuan (1271–1368), in northern China. He conquered the southern Song in 1276, thus reunifying northern and southern China. Internal struggles among the heirs of Chinggis Khan meant that Qubilai's Yuan dynasty did not control Outer Mongolia or Xinjiang, much less Central Asia. However, the Yuan did establish indirect rule over Tibet and launched unsuccessful invasions of Japan, Burma, Champa, Annam, and Java.

Mongols and Central Asians dominated top government positions during the Yuan dynasty, but China's elite culture, now shared by literati and merchants, flourished nonetheless, enriched by the musical traditions of Muslim Central Asia and by Tibetan art. Unfortunately, the Yuan was a period marked by environmental crises: harsh winters, declining agricultural productivity, floods, droughts, and epidemics (possibly the bubonic plague). The Yuan's weak and inefficient government, unable to address multiple challenges, fell in the midst of a wave of popular rebellions in 1368.

A New Confucian Empire: The Ming Dynasty, 1368–1644

Of the many rebel leaders of the late Yuan period, one, Zhu Yuanzhang (1328–1398) would become an emperor. Zhu was an unlikely ruler: a man of very poor background, he was orphaned at the age of sixteen, entered a Buddhist monastery, which turned him out to roam the countryside as a beggar-monk, and joined a millenarian rebellion, proving himself a military genius and a charismatic employer of men. In 1368, Zhu, already well on his way to defeating the Yuan and rival rebel groups, ascended the throne as Hongwu, the founding emperor of the Ming dynasty (1368–1644).

Together, Hongwu (r. 1368–1398) and his son, the Yongle emperor (r. 1402–1424), secured control over Ming territory and laid the foundations of a system of government and law—a bureaucracy—and a system of state-sanctioned orthodox thinking that would provide a model not only for the rest of the Ming, but also for its successor, the Qing dynasty. In terms of territory, Hongwu and Yongle established control over a realm that included China Proper and some agricultural areas in modern Liaoning Province in southern Manchuria. Like the Song dynasty, the Ming was not able to extend its power into the Inner Asian periphery and had no control over Tibet, Xinjiang, Mongolia, or much of Manchuria. Taiwan, too, lay outside the scope of Ming power. Annam (northern Vietnam), though invaded in 1407 and occupied for a time, successfully threw off Ming control in 1427. The Yongle emperor's interest in Southeast Asia and points beyond also led him to order

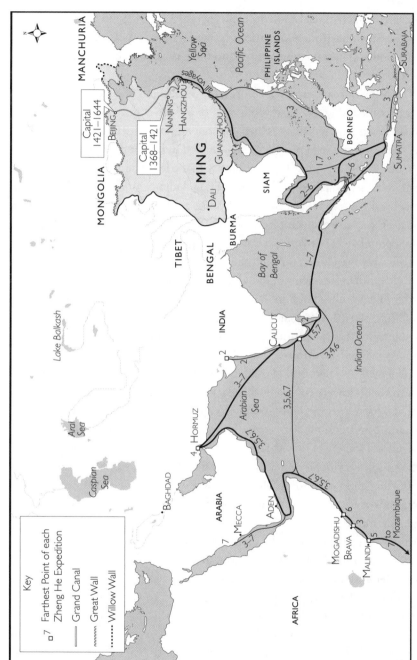

The Ming Empire and the Zheng He voyages.

a Muslim eunuch official named Zheng He (c. 1371–1435) to organize a series of seven huge maritime expeditions to modern Malaysia and Indonesia, Sri Lanka, India, the Arabian peninsula and the East African coast between 1405 and 1433.

The Ming bureaucracy, which drew on the models and experience of past dynasties including the Yuan, consisted of a central government of a court and six functional ministries (Rites, Personnel, Revenue, Punishment, Works, and War), and thirteen provinces, subdivided into a total of 159 prefectures, 240 sub-prefectures, and 1,144 counties. In the late Ming, about twenty-four thousand officials staffed the bureaucracy, including around fifteen hundred in the central government in Beijing. This was a rather small number of men to manage the affairs of an empire of 1,500,000 square miles (3,900,000 sq km) with a population of over two hundred million in 1600.

Officials were chosen through an extremely rigorous civil service examination system. The curriculum on which candidates were examined was based on the Zhu Xi school of Song Neo-Confucianism, chosen because it emphasized filial piety, loyalty, and the use of authoritative texts (rather than personal intuition) as the ultimate sources of moral standards. The culture of the landowning, examination-taking elite families placed tremendous emphasis on filial piety (respect and obedience to one's parents), female chastity (that is, a woman's loyalty to one husband), and the restriction of women's roles.

The system that the Hongwu and Yongle emperors put in place was highly autocratic and designed to serve the founding emperor's vision of a stable agricultural society of honest farmers, hereditary soldiers, and obedient, honest, and self-sacrificing officials. Zhu Yuanzhang often suspected his officials of plotting and corruption. He responded with massive purges and tens of thousands of executions. One of the purges eliminated both Hongwu's prime minister and the post of prime minister itself. As a result, Ming emperors (or their surrogates, such as favorites or eunuchs) exercised direct autocratic power over officials at court—power that they used to have officials criticized, demoted, brutally flogged, or executed.

Although the early Ming emperors intended to construct a system that would guarantee social, economic, and political stability, nearly three hundred years of Ming rule provided the framework within which tremendous changes took place. A growing population (eighty-five million in 1380, rising to two hundred sixty million in 1600), an expansion of the area of cultivated land and more intensive agriculture generated sixty percent more crops per *mou* (one sixth of an English acre or approx. 7,000 square feet [650 sq m]) of land than in the Song dynasty. The growth in agricultural production spurred significant growth in textiles, consumer items, luxury goods, and, consequently, in both domestic and maritime trade.

Economic growth made the Ming a very wealthy society. Scholars, merchants, and a growing population of functionally literate common people made a profitable market not only for classical texts, but also for primers, encyclopedias, almanacs, stories, novels, and manuals of Confucian family ritual. The paintings and calligraphy of scholar-amateur and professional artists alike were bought and sold by dealers and collectors, as were antique furniture, ancient bronzes, and other art objects and luxury goods.

The wealth of the Ming did more than stimulate commerce within the empire. The governments and merchants of neighboring states like Korea and Japan came to China Proper to do business, as they had been since the Tang. So too did Europeans. Portuguese merchants, later joined by the Spanish, Dutch, British, and others, brought loads of silver to Guangzhou and other ports, exchanging it for silk, tea, porcelain, and other goods. Since the Ming used silver ingots as an important medium of exchange, and since China produces little silver of its own, the Ming appeared to have an inexhaustible demand for the precious metal, which was worth more in the Ming lands than anywhere else on the globe. Along with silver, the European traders brought Catholic missionaries (most notably Jesuit priests) who played important roles in facilitating technology exchange between China and Europe. Knowledge of China's culture, philosophy, and politics and Chinese technology such as standardized machine parts, porcelain, and suspension bridges were brought to Europe. Catholic priests working in the Ming brought Western astronomy and mathematics (which supplemented, but did not by any means replace, Chinese knowledge of those fields), as well as guns and cannon.

For all its successes, the Ming did have a number of problems. Like any premodern agricultural economy, the Ming was highly vulnerable to natural disaster—such as a series of uncommonly frequent floods and droughts in the first decades of the 1600s. The Ming bureaucracy was burdened by incompetent emperors, endemic corruption, and by invidious and often deadly factional struggles. In one famous incident, an official named Hai Rui (1513–1587) accused his emperor (Jiajing, r. 1521–1566) of being a failure as a man and a ruler. Demoted and imprisoned, Hai Rui survived only because Jiajing died, thus clearing the way for Hai Rui's pardon and release. But no matter who was emperor, the factional struggles continued to roil the court while emperors devoted themselves to the Daoist pursuit of immortality or to carpentry, or, as with the Wanli emperor (r. 1572–1620), simply refused to meet their officials for decades at a time.

The Ming also faced serious challenges from the Mongols on its northern frontiers. The Yongle emperor had moved the Ming capital from Nanjing, in the Yangzi Valley, to Beijing in order to be closer to the troublesome northern frontier. Yongle's strategy involved a series of fortifications far north of the present-day Great Wall and several aggressive expeditions in which his forces pursued the nomads deep into Mongolia. However, the expenses of frontier security finally led, in the mid-16th century, to a policy of constructing a system of static defenses which, in time, were connected to form what we know as the Great Wall: a system of walls, towers, and forts extending from Jiayuguan in the northwestern province of Gansu to the sea at Shanhaiguan, the primary invasion route from Manchuria to northern China.

In dealing with the people beyond the Great Wall, the Ming granted status and limited trade privileges to selected tribal leaders in an attempt to "use barbarians to control barbarians." Among these, as we will see in the next chapter, were the Jurchen tribes of the northeast (Manchuria) and one particular Jurchen leader, Nurhaci (1558–1626). But while the Mongols and the Jurchens remained serious threats, it was domestic rebellion that finally overthrew the Ming in 1644.

The rebellions began in the arid and unproductive northwestern provinces of Shaanxi and Shanxi.[2] Drought and famine hit this area hard in the late 1620s and 1630s. Starving people sold their children and were reduced to eating bark or earth. Some turned to cannibalism. In 1627, rebellions broke out in communities across the northwest. Some were uprisings against local officials who insisted on collecting tax grain from their starving people. But the major source of rebel strength came from military garrisons whose soldiers were angry because the government consistently failed to send them pay and supplies. In one incident, troops from Gansu, Shaanxi, and Shanxi ordered to fight the Manchu invasion of 1629 joined the rebels when the government failed to deliver their pay and rations. In 1630, when the Ming government tried to save money by cutting the postal system by thirty percent, laid-off postal couriers joined the rebels. In the 1630s more and more men joined rebel bands, which merged to become huge armies, tens of thousands strong, which swept across Shanxi, Shaanxi, and neighboring provinces to the south. Of the several major rebel leaders who emerged, the most important was Li Zicheng (1606–1644)

Like many rebels, Li Zicheng had been a soldier in the Ming army before joining a rebel group in 1629. His fortunes rose and fell over the next decade, but in 1640–1641, he led his army from Shaanxi into Henan province. Here, in the heart of the Central Plains, drought and famine had devastated towns, villages, and cities. Desperate men flocked to Li's armies, which grew first to five hundred thousand then a million men. Some Confucian scholars, who saw Li as a man who might become emperor, also joined him. With their advice and assistance, he began to build a reputation as a man who cared for the people by remitting taxes and distributing wealth seized from corrupt Ming princes. Li Zicheng and his advisors also set up a shadow imperial government. In 1642, Li Zicheng announced the establishment of the Shun dynasty—but carefully did not yet claim to be emperor.

With the area of modern Henan and Hubei provinces under his control in 1643, Li Zicheng faced a strategic choice: turn south to conquer Jiangnan and the Ming southern capital of Nanjing? Or go north to Beijing? The southern option would cut the Grand Canal and leave the Ming court to face a two-front war against the Manchu and Li Zicheng's Shun without the tax revenue of Jiangnan. An advance to the north would bring a swift end to the Ming dynasty, but it would leave Li Zicheng to face the Manchu army.

Li Zicheng chose to strike north toward Beijing. Ming forces crumbled before the power of the armies of the Great Shun. The Ming Chongzhen emperor's advisors, torn between competing factions, offered conflicting advice: stay in Beijing and defend the capital, or flee to Nanjing and resist the Shun "bandits" from there? Paralyzed by indecision, the Chongzhen emperor did nothing until it was too late. Then, on the morning of 25 April 1644, abandoned by his officials, and after having murdered his female relatives, the last Ming emperor climbed partway up the hill behind the Forbidden City and hanged himself.[3]

With the Chongzhen emperor dead, it might seem that Li Zicheng's Shun dynasty had triumphantly taken the "Mandate of Heaven." But the situation in the spring of 1644 was anything but clear. Li Zicheng, it is true, had captured Beijing. But other rebel groups continued to roam across the territory north of the Yangzi. In the south, officials in Jiangnan were choosing a Ming prince to serve as their emperor and lead them in a re-conquest of the north. To the northeast, a powerful Ming army under commander Wu Sangui (1612–1678) guarded the strategic pass of Shanhaiguan against the Manchus—who had been observing the misfortunes of the Ming with keen interest. Would Wu Sangui accept Li Zicheng as his emperor or remain loyal to the Ming? Or could he be convinced to defect to the Manchus?

乾

Notes

1. Hu Feng, ed. *Xin bian shang xia wuqian nian* (The new chronicle of five thousand years) (Hohhot: Nei Menggu renmin chubanshe, 1999), 1.

2. This account draws on Frederic Wakeman, Jr., *The Great Enterprise: The Manchu Reconstruction of Imperial Order in Seventeenth Century China* (Berkeley: University of California Press, 1985), vol. 1, 225–318; Albert Chan, *The Glory and Fall of the Ming Dynasty* (Norman: Oklahoma University Press, 1982), 333–44; and William Atwell, "The T'ai-ch'ang, T'ien-ch'i, and Ch'ung-chen Reigns, 1620–1644," in Twitchett and Mote, eds., *The Cambridge History of China, Volume 8*, 615–16, 621–3, 634–7.

3. Wakeman, *The Great Enterprise,* 265–6.

Part I

A MULTI-ETHNIC EMPIRE, 1644–1911

Chapter 1   A MANCHU EMPIRE

The Qing Dynasty to 1799

While the Ming descended into famine and rebellion, a local strongman named Nurhaci (1558–1626) and his son Huang Taiji (1592–1643) were building a new kingdom in the Northeast. In 1636 Huang Taiji gave his people, a combination of Jurchen tribes, a new name, "Manchu," and established a new dynasty: Qing (meaning "pure"). In 1644, when the Chinese rebel and would-be emperor Li Zicheng overthrew the Ming, the Manchu warriors came through the Great Wall, absorbed some of the remaining Ming armies and claimed the Mandate of Heaven for their Qing dynasty, which ruled in Beijing until February 1912.

In many respects, life in China went on much as it had before the Manchu conquest. The Manchu conquerors ruled as Chinese emperors, adapting the institutions, techniques, and laws of Ming government to their own purposes. Economic, cultural, and intellectual trends present in the late Ming continued on into the Qing period. These elements of continuity draw our attention once again to the fallacy of dividing historical eras rigidly according to the rise and fall of dynastic governments. Some historians even prefer to talk about a "Ming-Qing" period or a "late imperial period" that includes both Ming and Qing.

Nonetheless, the Qing dynasty was in some ways very different from the Ming. From 1644 to 1799 the first four Manchu emperors consolidated control over China Proper and drew on its resources to build an empire larger than those of any of the earlier dynastic states of China, stretching from Siberia to the Burmese border, from the oases of Central Asia to the island of Taiwan. The Qing's large territory, diverse population, huge economic power, and sophisticated culture made it one of the most powerful empires of the 18th century. But by 1799, signs of the weaknesses that would bring the dynasty to its knees in the 19th century were already lurking below the surface of Manchu imperial grandeur.

The Origins and Rise of the Qing Dynasty

In the 16th century, the Ming considered Manchuria to be a part of their territory. Farmers cultivated the land lying west and east of the Liao River in modern Liaoning province, guarded by Ming military colonies. Identity was fluid in this frontier area. Some Ming farmers and hereditary military families picked up the language and culture of the Jurchen people of Manchuria, and even acquired Jurchen names.[1] Some Jurchens practiced settled agriculture, interacted with Ming officials, and learned the Chinese language. The Jurchens, after all, had a long history of interaction with China: in the 12th century one branch of the Jurchens had established the Jin dynasty and ruled northern China until they, in turn, were conquered by the Mongols in 1234.

Manchuria beyond the Liao Valley was still a land of Jurchen tribes whose interaction with China and Chinese culture was relatively limited. The Jurchens lived in permanent villages, but some raised livestock, which they moved from one pasture to another in a seminomadic lifestyle. Hunting, fishing, and trade in ginseng, furs, and other mountain products were very important, particularly in the areas farthest from Chinese influence. The Jurchen tribes were grouped into unstable, shifting confederations. The Ming tried to control the Jurchen through a "divide and rule" strategy in which the court "appointed" (in effect, recognized) a number of different Jurchen chieftains. Those men who gained Ming appointment received seals of office and were allowed to come to Beijing to "offer tribute." They also had access to frontier markets where they exchanged horses, furs, and ginseng for Chinese textiles, salt, grain, iron goods, and oxen.

Ming forces occasionally intervened in disputes among the Jurchens. In one such operation in 1583, Ming troops killed—perhaps by mistake—the father and grandfather of the Aisin Gioro lineage of the Jianzhou Jurchens. They swiftly moved to make amends by confirming the grandson, Nurhaci, as successor to his father's position as clan leader. Nurhaci played along, but he evidently felt that he was owed a blood debt. First, he moved against his Jurchen rivals, forcing enemy tribes to submit to him. The Ming, who still regarded him as their client, awarded him the title "Dragon-Tiger General" in 1595.[2]

As the Dragon-Tiger General became stronger, Ming officials began to see him as a threat, closed down the border markets in order to deprive him of income, and lent military support to his enemies. In response, Nurhaci raided Ming territory repeatedly between 1616 and 1626. The immediate cause of the attacks was the need for food. The Jurchens were hungry.[3] They were also very effective warriors. Some Ming forces were defeated. Others surrendered, the officers and men joining the Jurchens rather than lay down their lives for the Ming. To protect his eastern flank, Nurhaci had built an alliance with some of the Mongol tribes, who saw cooperation with the Jurchen khan as a way of restoring unity and stability to the fractured and warring tribal society of Inner Mongolia.[4]

While fighting the Ming and gaining the adherence of the Mongols, Nurhaci began to use Mongolian and Chinese techniques to build a stronger state and military. He declared himself khan, a Mongol title, of the "Later Jin dynasty" and established a capital, the captured Chinese city of Shenyang (called Mukden in Jurchen). His scholars devised a writing system for the Jurchen language, using the Mongolian alphabet as their model. Along with his newly conquered territories east and west of the Liao River (modern Liaoning province), he acquired a population of Chinese farmers and land on which to settle Jurchens as farmers or as landlords collecting rent from Chinese tenants. Nurhaci was creating a new style of governing, one which combined Chinese bureaucratic practices with the collegial, consultative decision-making typical of the Jurchens.[5]

Military reorganization accompanied political innovation. Nurhaci drew on Mongol precedent to reorganize the Jurchen tribes into companies and Banners. A company consisted of three hundred soldiers plus each soldier's household. Thus a company included not just fighting men, but the entire familial support system for each warrior.[6] About fifty companies formed one regiment.[7] Regiments were combined in groups of five to form larger units, each symbolized by a banner: four of solid colors, yellow, white, red, and blue, and four more of the same colors, but each with a red border (except the red banner with white border). By 1642, Nurhaci's successor Huang Taiji had added a further Eight Mongol Banners and Eight Chinese Banners. The Banner system weakened tribal and clan structure, focused loyalty on Nurhaci and gave him a strong, disciplined, self-supporting military. Over two hundred years later, it remained one of the fundamental institutions of the Qing dynasty.

When Nurhaci died in 1626, the Jin khanate was already a power to be reckoned with. His son and successor, Huang Taiji, built on this foundation. Huang Taiji forced more Mongol tribes to submit, took the rest of the territory west of the Liao River from the Ming, and launched raids across the Great Wall, deep into Ming territory, in order to support his growing army. Huang Taiji also moved farther away from the collegial Jurchen style of leadership and toward a more centralized, Chinese-style bureaucratic system. Huang Taiji ordered that key Chinese texts, including the *Analects* and histories of the Warring States and Three Kingdoms periods, be translated into Manchu so that he could read them. He used Chinese advisors in his government and Chinese officers and men, including men who could make and use cannon, in his armies.

As he built a more centralized government, Huang Taiji gave the Jurchen tribes a new name and identity: Manchu. In order to make his intention of conquering Ming territory perfectly clear, he also changed the name of the dynasty. On 14 May 1636, Huang Taiji, the khan of the Jurchen "Later Jin" dynasty, became Taizong, emperor of the Qing dynasty.[8] When Huang Taiji died in September 1643, he left the throne to his son, the Shunzhi emperor (1638–1661), age five. Huang Taiji's brother, Prince Dorgon, acted as regent. All this happened just as Ming armies were collapsing under the onslaught of the rebel forces of Li Zicheng, the "Dashing Prince" who would shortly enter Beijing.

The Qing Conquest

The Manchu conquest of China began 190 miles (300 km) east of Beijing, at Shanhaiguan—the mountain pass from the North China Plain to Manchuria where the eastern end of the Ming Great Wall meets the sea. In 1644 these fortifications were the key to defending Beijing from the Manchus. Even as Beijing fell to Li Zicheng, Ming commander Wu Sangui (1612–78) guarded Shanhaiguan with a formidable army of forty thousand. General Wu's immediate family was in Beijing, captured by Li Zicheng's rebels. An uncle and cousins were on the other side of the pass, serving the Manchu Qing dynasty.[9] Would Wu join Li Zicheng? Or would he defend the Ming imperial house against the rebels?

As the general was weighing his options, word came that Li Zicheng had executed Wu Sangui's father. It was a fatal mistake on Li's part. General Wu asked Dorgon to bring the Banner forces through Shanhaiguan to assist in suppressing Li Zicheng's "bandits." In return, the Manchus would reap the rewards of plunder—and return to Manchuria. Dorgon and his Chinese advisers welcomed the opportunity, but had something else in mind: they would enter the pass, liberate Beijing, and go on to conquer "all under Heaven." General Wu agreed. The Manchus came through the pass, incorporated Wu Sangui and his army under their command, defeated Li Zicheng, and proceeded to Beijing. There Dorgon famously announced to the Ming people and former Ming officials:

> The empire is not an individual's private enterprise. Whosoever possesses virtue holds it. The army and people are not an individual's private army and people. Whosoever possesses virtue commands them. We now hold it. We took revenge upon the enemy of your ruler-father in place of your dynasty. We burned our bridges behind us, and we have pledged not to return until every bandit is destroyed. In the counties, districts, and locales that we pass through, all those who shave their heads and surrender, opening their gates to welcome us, will be given rank and reward, retaining their wealth and nobility for generations. But if there are those who resist us disobediently, then when our Grand Army arrives, the stones themselves will be set ablaze and everyone will be massacred.[10]

The conquest of Ming territory went much as Dorgon had announced. Qing forces, greatly strengthened by the addition of Wu Sangui and other Ming turncoat generals and their armies, restored order to northern China and then marched south. Ming resistance was poorly organized. Some Ming loyalists organized their own armies to fight the Manchus. For example, Liu Shuying, the daughter of a Ming official, used her fortune to build an army of a thousand, which she herself trained and led into battle.[11] In the Yangzi Valley, Ming officials organized a "Southern Ming" court, placing first one, then another Ming prince on the throne, but they had few men and fewer resources. In a particularly famous case, a Southern Ming general stubbornly tried to defend the wealthy Jiangnan commercial city of Yangzhou. When he took the city, the Manchu commander chose to make Yangzhou an example to all others who might think of resistance: he turned his normally well-disciplined troops loose for five days of looting, killing, and rape.[12]

Most Ming officials were in no position to offer any serious military resistance. Rather than fight, they surrendered. Some chose the route of passive resistance. Many women and men of the Ming elite, sometimes entire families, committed suicide rather than live under the Qing. The mother of Gu Yanwu (1613–1682), a noted scholar, starved herself to death, exhorting her famous son never to serve the "barbarians." Others, like Gu himself, while unwilling to commit suicide, refused to serve the new dynasty. Such exemplars of loyalty were a minority whose spirit, though respected (even by the Qing rulers), faded with time. Together, the Manchus and their subjects transformed the Ming into a part of the Manchu Qing Empire, and the Manchu aristocracy into minority rulers of a realm that had its economic, political, geographical, and cultural center of gravity in China Proper.

The articulation of this new relationship between Manchu rulers and Chinese subjects can be seen in concrete terms in the changing cultural geography of China's major cities, starting with the capital city of Beijing. The Ming capital consisted of two parts. In the north was the original walled city with the imperial palace, government offices, and the residences of princes and officials. In the south, outside the original city walls, was the commercial section, which had been walled afterwards to defend it from Mongol invasions.[13] When they took over Beijing, the Manchus cleared the north city of Han Chinese inhabitants to make way for the Banner forces and Manchu aristocrats. Banner forces were also garrisoned in other major cities, where they lived in segregated walled areas from which they could not stray far without permission.

The physical segregation of the Banner forces was meant to underline and preserve the distinct identity of the Manchu conquerors. The Manchus were a very small minority in their own empire. Even in the Banners, families of Jurchen ethnic background were only sixteen percent in 1644. In 1723, after Han Chinese Banner families had been urged to become ordinary citizens, the ethnic composition of the Banners was roughly sixty-eight percent Han, eight percent Mongol, and twenty-three percent Manchu.[14] Banner people did not intermarry with the commoner population, and were not subject to control or punishment by the civilian government. Bannermen were barred from trade or other professions: they were to be a hereditary military elite.[15] Physical and legal separation ensured that Banner people retained a separate identity, but it did not prevent their identity from changing over time. Within a few generations, ethnic Jurchen Banner people had largely lost the ability to speak, read, or write Manchu. They had also acquired many aspects of Chinese culture: they ate Chinese food, wrote Chinese poetry, and served in a bureaucracy inherited from the Ming.

While Manchus adopted the culture of the Chinese elite, Chinese literati became loyal servants of the Manchu emperors. As a symbol of their submission, Chinese men were forced to adopt the Manchu male hairstyle—shaving the forehead and braiding the rest of the hair into a long queue. Scholars serving the Manchu court had to give up the long, loose robes of a Ming official and don the trousers, tight-sleeved coats, and boots, whose origins lay with the Manchu traditions of horsemanship and archery. More than one Chinese man lost his head for refusal to wear the queue or for suggesting that the world would be more peaceful if Qing officials were required to wear Ming-style court dress.[16] But in the long run, the Ming people and their descendants adapted to Manchu rule.

Qing Empire-Building

The Qing Empire of the 18th century could not have been built without China and the Chinese. In retrospect, Nurhaci and Huang Taiji's unification of Manchus and Mongols and Prince Dorgon's conquest of China Proper appear

as the first two stages of the construction of what became the Qing Empire of the 18th century. But neither the early Manchu leaders nor Dorgon could have predicted the way events unfolded in the generations that came after them. Dorgon's conquest of China took place during the reign of his nephew, the Shunzhi emperor (r. 1644–1661). Shunzhi died of smallpox in 1661. His successors, the Kangxi emperor (r. 1661–1722), the Yongzheng emperor (r. 1722–1735), and the Qianlong emperor (r. 1735–1796), used the immense economic and manpower resources of the Chinese agricultural economy to push their imperial domain outward into Inner Asia and over the sea to Taiwan.

Official court portrait of the Kangxi emperor in informal dress, holding a brush. Hanging scroll, ink and paint on silk.

Kangxi was a model emperor: intelligent, curious, hardworking, an avid hunter, a dedicated reader of philosophy and history, and the father of over fifty-six children.[17] He came to the throne in 1661, at the age of eight. The early years of his reign were dominated by a regent, Oboi (?–1669— discussed further below), but Kangxi began to emerge from Oboi's shadow in the late 1660s. As an adult, he was deeply involved in the day-to-day management of affairs of state: reading memorials, writing responses (rescripts), meeting regularly with his officials, inspecting troops, and leading armies in the field.

Kangxi's first major challenge was the revolt of the "Three Feudatories"— three former Ming generals, including Wu Sangui, who had played a key role in the Qing conquest of the south, and had earned large fiefs as their reward. Wu Sangui controlled the southwestern provinces of Yunnan and Guizhou. Two other Ming turncoats had been awarded Guangdong and Fujian. Concerned about the military and economic power of these virtually independent Three Feudatories (who also received generous subsidies amounting to nearly half the imperial government revenue in the 1670s), the young Kangxi emperor, against the advice of his ministers, tried to maneuver them into retirement.[18] This prompted Wu Sangui to rise up in arms against the Qing in 1673. The Chinese generals of Guangdong and Fujian joined him. In 1681, after eight years of devastating civil war, Qing armies finally defeated the revolt of the Three Feudatories and established direct imperial rule over the south.

Operations against the Three Feudatories led to further moves to consolidate and expand the Qing Empire and to secure its frontiers. Off the coast of Fujian, a Ming loyalist merchant-pirate named Zheng Chenggong (known to Europeans as Coxinga—1624–62) had captured the island of Taiwan from the Dutch East India Company traders who had been based there. Zheng and his heirs ruled the island as their personal kingdom and used it as a base for trade and piracy. An early Qing ban on maritime trade, intended to starve the Zheng forces of income, failed, partly because the Three Feudatories ignored it. In 1683, Qing naval forces defeated the Zheng fleets. For the first time in its history, Taiwan was brought under the direct administration of a government based on the mainland of China.

Even during the war against the Three Feudatories, problems in Inner Asia also intruded on the Kangxi emperor's attention. Wu Sangui had won the tacit support of the Mongol-supported Dalai Lama in Lhasa and had entered into the tea-horse trade with Tibet—a serious matter, as horses were a strategic asset to whoever controlled them.[19] Mongolia, too, was a threat. Manchu influence over the Mongols was loose—more a matter of alliances with numerous Mongol tribes than of control. And in the far west of Mongolia and the northern part of modern Xinjiang, the Zunghar Mongol khan, Galdan, was forging his own state, establishing close relations with the Dalai Lama, competing with the Qing for the loyalty of the Mongolian tribes, and seeking support from the Russian Empire.

The Kangxi emperor regarded the Zunghars as his most dangerous enemy. But before he could deal with the Zunghars, he needed to negotiate a peace deal with the Russians. As Russia expanded eastward in search of furs from the late 1500s to mid-1600s, they had begun to encroach on the Amur River Valley, which the Qing considered part of its own territory. After three years of careful preparations—building ships, preparing cannons and guns, gathering intelligence—some thirty-four hundred Qing troops attacked the Russian fort of Albazin on the Amur River in 1685, and again in 1686.

Aware that the Qing was militarily powerful, and more concerned about selling furs on the Chinese market than about territory, Russia agreed to negotiate. In the Treaty of Nerchinsk (1689), Russia and the Great Qing Empire agreed to a boundary along the Argun River and along the crest of the Outer Khingan (Stanavoi) mountain range. The treaty was negotiated according to European custom, with two of the Kangxi emperor's Jesuit priests serving as go-betweens and interpreters. Manchu, Latin, and Russian copies of the treaty were exchanged and solemnized by Christian oaths.[20]

In signing the Treaty of Nerchinsk, the Russians gained access to the Chinese market. The Kangxi emperor gained a free hand in dealing with Galdan and his Zunghars, who now were unable to win Russian support. Kangxi carried out four grueling campaigns against Galdan, one in 1690 and three in 1696–97. The emperor himself took to the field to lead his troops in these operations, which he seems to have enjoyed:

> While on the move, I'd live roughly and without formality—those passing in front of me didn't have to dismount, and as on hunts we would cook fish or food we caught in a simple way, and sit sometimes in the herders' tents and eat, and drink kumiss as we talked.[21]

Driving deep into Mongolia in pursuit of the Zunghar leader, stretching their fragile supply lines to the limits, Qing forces inflicted some serious defeats on the enemy, but failed to capture or kill Galdan, who could always flee beyond the reach of the Qing armies. In 1697 Galdan, on the run and with his forces decimated and divided, died suddenly—probably poisoned by one of his followers—just as the Kangxi emperor was carrying out logistical operations for his fourth campaign. The emperor adjusted the date of Galdan's death and announced it as a suicide in order to make it appear to be the result of his expensive military operation.[22] Galdan was dead, but the Zunghar Empire remained in place, still a threat to the Qing, and still working to build relations with the Russians and the Tibetans. One of the Kangxi emperor's last actions was to send his armies into Tibet in 1720, in order to deprive the Zunghars of Tibetan support.

Kangxi's heir, the Yongzheng emperor, took a defensive attitude toward the Zunghars and Tibetans, though he did conquer the Tibetan/Mongol area currently known as Qinghai Province, which he incorporated into the Qing Empire in 1723. He also negotiated a second treaty, the Treaty of Khiatka (1727), with the Russians. Yongzheng is best known for having built a more strongly centralized government and a more efficient tax system, which left his heir, the Qianlong emperor, with a generous surplus in the imperial treasury. Qianlong used his power—and his treasure—in a series of campaigns which more than doubled the size of the empire.

First, Qianlong finally succeeded in thoroughly defeating the Zunghars. This required two campaigns. First, in 1755, Qianlong's armies helped to install Amursana (1722–1757) as khan of the Zunghars. Qianlong expected Amursana to be grateful and obedient. When Amursana rebelled, Qianlong responded with a second, larger expedition in 1756–57. The Zunghar campaigns "included three main armies, totaling fifty thousand men each, who stayed on each campaign for one to two years."[23] In the second campaign, Qianlong, angered at Zunghar resistance, ordered a massacre. Deliberate killing of hundreds of thousands, combined with a smallpox epidemic, battlefield deaths, starvation, and enslavement completely destroyed the million or so Zunghars as a people.[24]

Following up on his victory over the Zunghars, the Qianlong emperor moved to gain control of Altishahr and the Turfan Basin, both territories lying in Xinjiang, south of the Tianshan Mountains. The Turkic-speaking Muslim inhabitants of these regions lived in the oases that had been key links in the Silk Road trade since the time of the Han dynasty. The Qianlong emperor's forces allied with Muslim elite families in the Turfan region, closer to China, in order to wage a war of conquest against the oasis towns of Altishahr in 1758–59. Altishahr, subdued in 1760, was combined with Turfan and Zungharia to form a new administrative region: Xinjiang (which means "new frontier").

The Qing dynasty's wars against the Three Feudatories, the Zunghar Mongols, and the Muslims of Altishahr drove home the strategic importance of

Qianlong emperor in ceremonial armor.

Tibet. Tibetan religious figures, particularly the Dalai Lamas, had exercised tremendous political influence over the Mongols ever since their mass conversion to Tibetan Buddhism during the Ming. Mongol leaders, in turn, often played key roles in Tibetan politics, including in the selection and manipulation of Dalai Lamas. The Kangxi emperor's invasion in 1720 had broken Zunghar influence and marked the beginning of a Qing protectorate over Tibet. Subsequent expeditions and political deals during the Yongzheng and especially the Qianlong reigns shaped Tibet's place within the Qing Empire.

The conquests of Zungharia and Altishahr and the incorporation of Tibet mark the height of Qing imperial expansion. A Qing invasion of Burma (1765–1768), prompted by violent border incidents, proved to be a disaster. Manchu cavalrymen floundered in the jungle and were hit hard by disease and by enemy action. The Qianlong emperor's reaction to initial setbacks was fury: "How could we stop abruptly in midcourse? . . . Moreover, our dynasty is right at its ascendancy. The Zunghars and the Muslims have all been suppressed. How can this trifling Burma not be exterminated?"[25] Further efforts led only to further defeats. In the end, the emperor was forced to conclude: "This is the gods' manifestation that it is no use for us to penetrate deeply into Burma. Moreover, the soldiers are all unable to withstand malaria. They are our servants and slaves; our heart cannot bear it. In addition, sustaining many casualties at the hands of the Burmese bandits is not worth it."[26]

Like so many leaders, before and since, Qianlong declared victory and withdrew. An attempt to intervene in a dispute over the Annamese (northern Vietnamese) throne in 1788–1789 also went poorly. This time, apparently having learned his lesson, the emperor agreed to a quick end to hostilities and again proclaimed a fictional "victory." In 1788, and again in 1791, the Qing waged war against the Nepalese Gurkha kingdom, which had trade disputes and territorial ambitions in Tibet. The second Qing-Gurkha war brought Qing troops across the Himalayas to the outskirts of Kathmandu, where they were defeated but, as in Burma and in Annam, declared victory.[27]

The Qianlong emperor's fictitious "victories" in Burma, Annam, and Nepal were possible because the rulers of all three states agreed to enter into tributary relations with the Qing. In this way, they joined the outer defense perimeter of the Qing Empire. Tribute-paying states like Nepal, Burma, Annam, and Korea sent "tribute missions" to the Qing court according to a regular schedule. Their emissaries were received with pomp and ceremony, kowtowed before the Qing emperor, offered valuable goods as "tribute," and received gifts, which were often of greater value than what they gave. The tribute system offered the Qing a series of friendly buffer states on its borders. Foreign rulers, even those whose armies had defeated Qing forces, entered this relationship because it brought lucrative opportunities for trade, because Qing troops could be expected to help defend them from external and internal enemies, and because tributary status did not compromise their sovereignty within their own kingdoms.

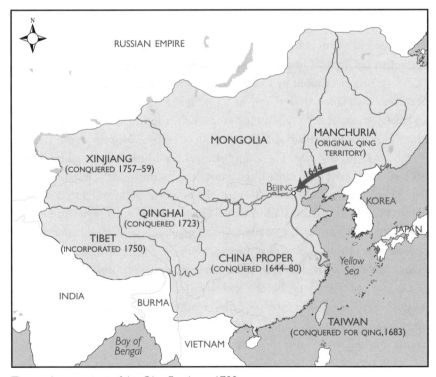

The maximum extent of the Qing Empire, c. 1780.

The Kangxi, Yongzheng, and Qianlong emperors had conquered such far-flung areas as Xinjiang, Mongolia, Tibet, and Taiwan. The results of their conquests are still apparent in the shape of the map of China. The Qing had become a vast, sprawling, multi-ethnic empire, ruled from Beijing by Manchu emperors, but incorporating Han Chinese, Mongols, Tibetans, Muslims, and a variety of ethnic groups along the southwestern frontiers and on Taiwan. Ruling this vast empire and winning and maintaining the loyalty or at least the acquiescence of its people was a daunting task.

Governing the Empire

The first four Qing emperors and the regents who occasionally exercised power on their behalf each had their own particular style of rulership. Prince Dorgon, regent for the Shunzhi emperor, and Prince Oboi, regent for the young Kangxi emperor, both placed their trust in Manchu aristocrats. Shunzhi, and then Kangxi, fighting to free themselves from the influence of these powerful regents, used Chinese officials in their power struggles against the Manchu aristocracy. Shunzhi died of smallpox at the age of twenty-three, before he could develop fully as a leader. Yongzheng, Kangxi, Qianlong, and their key officials built the institutions and styles of imperial rule that would define the Qing and, to a great extent, its successor states, the Republic of China and the People's Republic of China.

Qing emperors presented different faces to different subject peoples. To the Mongols and Tibetans, Qing emperors were successors of the Mongol khans, and they were also Cakravartin kings and patrons of Tibetan Buddhism. To the Manchu, the Qing emperor was the personification and preserver of Manchu ethnic identity. To the vast majority of his subjects, the Chinese, a Qing emperor presented himself as the holder of the Mandate of Heaven and patron and practitioner of the civilized arts of painting, prose, and poetry. These different faces of the emperors were expressed in court art. Yongzheng was painted in various guises expressing Manchu and Chinese roles. The Qianlong emperor was portrayed as a warrior in ceremonial armor, as a hunter facing down deer and tiger, as a bodhisattva in a Tibetan mandala, as a filial son revering his mother, and as a Confucian scholar. Both Kangxi and Qianlong underlined their identity with their Chinese subjects by taking grand tours of the Yangzi Valley, stopping to worship at Mount Tai in Shandong and to inspect hydraulic engineering projects on the Grand Canal and Yellow River, and visiting the great cities and temples of the wealthy Yangzi Valley itself.[28]

The many different imperial images were accompanied by different techniques of administration. In the non-Chinese frontier areas of the southwest, west, and northwest, the Qing often chose to rule indirectly by appointing or recognizing local leaders, many of whom manipulated the Qing in order to enhance their own wealth and power. In the Muslim areas of Xinjiang, the Qing ruled through the *begs,* hereditary local leaders.[29] In Tibet, the emperors stationed a small garrison and one or two personal representatives called *amban* in Lhasa. The *amban* exercised loose supervision over a Tibetan government run by the hereditary nobility. The Qing court patronized the Dalai Lama, the Panchen Lama, and the Tibetan aristocracy in order to prevent any one of them from becoming too powerful. Qing authority was also expressed in the ceremonies surrounding the recognition of each new incarnation of the Dalai Lama. Tibetan monks would choose the next incarnation from among several candidates. Their choice was then validated by drawing lots from a golden urn presented to the Tibetans by the Qianlong emperor in 1793.

Administration of China Proper followed the Ming example. In Beijing, the emperors and their personal staff oversaw the work of the Six Ministries: Rites, Personnel, Revenue, Works, Punishments, and War. The Censorate exercised oversight and filed regular reports on current problems and cases of bureaucratic malfeasance and corruption. The territory of China Proper was divided into 18 provinces, the provinces were divided into 177 prefectures, and the prefectures in turn divided into 1,528 counties.[30]

As hands-on administrators, the Qing emperors, like their Ming predecessors, concentrated power within their own hands and could exercise fearsome discipline against recalcitrant officials. But as minority rulers, they needed to balance power between the Manchu aristocracy and their far more numerous Chinese subjects. They did this by balancing Manchu, Mongol, and Han Chinese officials against each other when staffing the upper levels of government. For instance, by making dual appointments to positions such as minister and vice minister in each of the Six Ministries. The intent was to preserve Manchu ethnic sovereignty while preventing Manchu aristocrats from becoming a threat to the throne.

The Qing emperors also invented new ways to increase their personal control over the government. The Kangxi emperor established a secret "palace memorial" system through which high-ranking officials could submit memorials directly to the emperor, bypassing the multiple levels of bureaucracy that filtered normal communications before they reached the emperor's desk. This system gave the emperors an alternative source of information and allowed them to deal with problems in a more innovative way than was possible when acting through normal bureaucratic channels.

The Yongzheng and Qianlong emperors further developed and used this "palace memorial" system. The Yongzheng emperor also relied on small ad hoc committees of personal staff members. Because he personally controlled and worked with these committees, the emperor could increase the degree to which he was actually in control of the administration of the empire.[31] The Qianlong emperor went a step further: rather than use ad hoc committees, he created a permanent "Grand Council," a special committee standing outside and above the regular bureaucracy which assisted him in handling day-to-day business. The effect was to put the Qing emperors in even closer personal control of their government and their officials than the Ming rulers had been.

No matter how closely they gathered power into their own hands at the center, the emperors needed a large field bureaucracy to manage the business of the empire. Manchu and Mongol officials could be appointed on the basis of their aristocratic heredity, but the vast majority of the Qing officials (even some Manchu aristocrats) earned the right to be appointed to their posts by passing the civil service examinations.

The Qing examination system, like the government administration itself, was inherited from the Ming. There were four levels of examination. Candidates first took a qualifying examination and then, if they passed, the triennial county-level examination, which bestowed the status of licentiate (*shengyuan*). Licentiates enjoyed privileged status before the law (exemption from corporal punishment), and were officially registered as students in the county school—a formality, since the county schools held no classes. Next were the triennial provincial examinations for the status of "recommended man" (*juren*), and then it was on to Beijing for the triennial Metropolitan Examination. Candidates who passed the Metropolitan Examination received the *gongshi* (tribute literatus) degree. Those who placed in the top three ranks of Metropolitan Examination passers could go on to take the Palace Examination where, if successful, they would be recognized as *jinshi* (presented literatus).[32]

Preparation for the examinations required years of intensive, and expensive, education. Boys would begin memorizing the Four Books, the Five Classics, the dynastic histories, and classical poetry from around the age of seven.[33] A boy's first teacher might well be his mother. More formal education

Rows of twelve thousand cells in the civil service examination compound in Guangzhou, photographed in 1900.

was the task of hired tutors or of clan- or community-supported schools. Here students memorized texts and learned how to write poetry and how to turn out polished essays on the classics, on moral philosophy, and on issues of state policy, all in the very formulaic "eight-legged" style, and written in classical Chinese.

The examinations were highly competitive, multi-day affairs, held in sealed, guarded examination compounds. Of the two million men who might compete for the *shengyuan* degree in a given year, perhaps thirty thousand would succeed; of those, fifteen hundred might achieve the status of *juren,* and three hundred would make it to *jinshi.*[34] Organizing the examinations was a gargantuan task. The sheer volume of work (several thousand candidates generating over fifty thousand essays on some twelve thousand rolls of answers in a provincial examination, for example) introduced a degree of

arbitrariness into the grading and ranking of candidates.[35] This, and the preva-
lence of cheating, encouraged a popular culture which regarded success in
the examinations as something of an obscure combination of talent, hard
work, fate, and the intervention of supernatural forces. Theoretically, the
examinations were open to all, but practically speaking, only well-to-do landholding elites, merchants, and officials had the means to educate their sons
and send them to sit for the examinations.

Those who passed the examinations at any level were eligible for official
appointment, but with over one million examination passers competing for
around twenty thousand civil service appointments, one practically needed
to be a *jinshi* to be sure of official employment.[36] The highest-ranking *jinshi*
might be directly appointed to jobs in the capital. Most degreeholders,
however, would begin and end their careers in lower-level posts across the
empire.

Grassroots Government: The County Magistrate

China's 1,528 counties were the basic building blocks of the Qing administration. The population of a county ranged from tens of thousands to several
hundred thousand people, with the average around two hundred thousand
by 1800.[37] Each county had one official in charge: the county magistrate,
sometimes called the "father-mother official." He was responsible for all aspects of government: collecting taxes, investigating and trying criminal cases,
adjudicating civil cases, managing public works projects, maintaining public
order, dealing with natural disasters, administering the county-level civil service examinations, and generally setting a good moral example. He typically
served a single term of four years before being rotated out, and, by law, could
not serve in his home province.

A magistrate was essentially the representative of the emperor. As the low-
est-ranking official in a complex and closely supervised bureaucracy, he
could not act in an arbitrary manner. His duties were clearly prescribed and
his handling of administrative, civil, and criminal matters had to follow imperial orders and a written law, the Great Qing Code. The Qing Code dealt
with administrative, civil, and criminal matters. Much of what we think of as
family and property law (marriage, adoption, disputes concerning the ownership of fields and houses) fell under the category of "revenue," as such things
bore directly on tax liability and collection. There were five sanctioned punishments, each further subdivided into different levels of severity: beating with

the light bamboo, beating with the heavy bamboo, penal servitude, exile, and execution.

County magistrates were routinely faced with the need to deal with disputes over property, which they could handle either by mediating between the parties involved or by applying the law. They were also responsible for criminal matters—many of which (particularly violent crimes) arose from property disputes.[38] The law contained detailed descriptions of offenses and the appropriate punishments. For example: "Whenever a horse, bovine animal, or dog rams, butts, kicks, or bites people and (*the owner*) has not marked or tied it in the right way, or if there is a mad dog and he does not kill it, he will receive forty strokes of the light bamboo."[39] If a socially undesirable act did not correspond exactly to one of the Qing Code's precisely-defined offenses, a magistrate could punish it by analogy to an existing offense or under the rule which stated "Everyone who does that which ought not to be done will receive forty strokes of the light bamboo. If the matter is adjudged to be more serious, he will be punished by eighty strokes with the heavy bamboo."[40]

Qing officials took great care in the investigation of criminal cases and in the assessment and imposition of punishment. Serious offenses were understood to have thrown the moral universe out of balance. The purpose of punishment was to restore that balance. Punishment had to be carefully calibrated to the seriousness of the offense and to the relationship between the offender and the victim. Patriarchal family ideology viewed an offense by a junior member of an extended family against a senior member of the family as more serious than vice versa. Inappropriate administration of punishment could have negative cosmic effects. It could also lead to social unrest. As a consequence, the Qing legal system provided multiple levels of appeal.[41] County magistrates could order beatings to be administered, but more serious cases had to be remanded to the provincial or even imperial government for sentencing and punishment.

With so many responsibilities, a county magistrate needed a sizeable staff. The magistrate's office and living quarters, and the offices of his assistants, were located in a walled compound called a yamen. Here, the magistrate carried out the business of government, assisted by his own personal secretaries (whom he paid from his own pocket) and a staff of yamen clerks and runners. Each yamen had a small budget which allowed for a small number of clerks and runners—perhaps around ten to twenty clerks to perform clerical work in the yamen, and as few as twenty-five to thirty runners, who were responsible for collecting taxes, apprehending criminal offenders, summoning witnesses, and so on. In practice, a magistrate might need around one to three hundred clerks and five to eight hundred runners in order to do the business of government.[42]

Since there was no budget to pay so many clerks and runners, they were allowed to collect fees from the public. Both the extra-statutory clerks and runners and their fees existed in direct violation of the law, but without them, the Qing government simply would not have been able to function. Because they and their fees were illegal, there was considerable latitude for abuse and corruption; but in general, clerks and runners, with the magistrates' knowledge and approval, set standard and fairly stable levels for the fees that they collected from taxpayers and from people involved in criminal or civil disputes.[43] Qing ideology frowned upon litigious behavior. Nonetheless, many Qing subjects did go to court, particularly to resolve property and inheritance disputes. When they did so, they might present their case themselves, or hire a professional scrivener to write their case materials up for them.[44]

Most commoners had no contact at all with a magistrate, and encountered yamen personnel only if there was some problem with their taxes, if they were involved in a criminal dispute, or if they chose to bring a civil suit before the magistrate. The magistrate and his small staff could not possibly manage day-to-day life in China's villages. Local elite families ran China's village society. These included gentry, that is, families whose male household heads or sons had passed at least the lowest level of the civil service examination, and also well-to-do local landholders whose men did not necessarily hold an examination degree.

It was these local families, and especially the gentry, who advised the magistrates about local conditions, mediated local disputes, organized local granaries and famine relief, built and maintained irrigation and flood control systems, opened schools, and led local militia. Their leading roles in local society were prescribed and justified by the Neo-Confucian philosophy of Zhu Xi. Their role in maintaining social and political order reminds us that the Qing's Manchu rulers did not simply impose their will on a subject population: they patronized and supported the social and moral norms that the Chinese elite subscribed to.

Neither emperors nor high-ranking officials nor local elites completely lived up to those social and moral norms. Emperors and officials could be brutal and corrupt; local elites could take advantage of their positions to evade taxes, exploit commoners, and even intimidate the magistrates.[45] But rulers, officials, and local elites were all constrained by influential ideas about the responsibilities of the ruler and the "superior man" to take care of the masses. Those ideals were both expressed and violated in the lives of ordinary and elite families alike.

Family Life

From the palaces of the Forbidden City to the mansions of great merchants to the humble dwellings of farmers, the boundaries between the exemplary, the acceptable, and the reprehensible were drawn and redrawn in the everyday life of families. The family—the *jia*—was the basic social, legal, and economic unit. Few families realized the ideal of "five generations under one roof," but most experienced long periods of two and three generations living, working, and holding property as a unit. Individual families were understood to be parts of a lineage (a group of families tracing direct lines of descent to a common ancestor) or a clan (a group of families sharing a surname and tracing descent through multiple lines to a real or fictive ancestor). In the north, lineage and clan were relatively weak. In some areas, particularly in the south, they were powerful corporate entities that owned land or commercial property that generated income that they used to support schools, temples, and rituals, and even to give lineage or clan members stipends.

It was in the family that gender roles were defined, and sometimes violated. The ideal model was one of separate "inner" and "outer" spheres.[46] Men acted in the "outer" sphere of work, socialization, and service to the state and community beyond the walls of the family compound. Women were to be of the "inner quarters," devoting themselves to the business of procreation, child rearing, household management, and certain types of productive labor, stereotypically weaving and embroidery, all carried on within the four walls of the family compound. Men held most property, but women could inherit land (if there were no male heir) and retained rights to their dowries, which could include land, commercial property, or cash, which could be invested.

As in the Ming, the state-supported cult of female chastity flourished, complete with memorial arches and publicly celebrated widow suicides. Footbinding also continued to be standard among elite Han women (Manchu women did not bind their feet), and was increasingly popular among urban and rural common folk of all levels. Bound feet were essential if a family wanted to marry its daughters well, and a beautiful daughter, if married to a family of higher social or political standing, could help to elevate her own family's status—daughters could be a form of social capital.

The ideal of separate spheres for males and females was conveyed throughout society in popular culture, literature, ritual, religion, and in the law, which upheld the gender hierarchy. It was difficult, though, for ordinary people to completely conform. Women in farming communities worked in the family fields and entered the labor force as artisans, tea pickers, servants, and prostitutes. Widows remarried more often than not, went to market, and did business on their own account. Some even brought complaints before the magistrate. Elite women were often educated, might manage large and complex households, and were more likely to live long and leisurely lives and to have influence on the worlds of politics, arts, and culture than common men. Nonetheless, the ideal, and to a great extent the reality, was that the places of men and women were defined in terms of a patriarchal hierarchy in which women were expected to be subordinate to their fathers and husbands, and everyone, male and female, was subordinate to their elders.

The vast majority of Qing families—perhaps ninety percent—were independent farmers, and a small percentage were artisans or workers in enterprises like porcelain kilns, mines, or salt works. But neither occupation nor social status was fixed by heredity. In theory, all but a few legally proscribed categories of people could at least hope to increase their wealth, purchase more land, educate their sons or grandsons, and rise into the ranks of the elite. In practice, it was more common for families to lose status than to enter the ranks of the examination-passing scholar-officials, but there was certainly some degree of movement into, as well as out of, the ranks of the local village, provincial, and even national elite.

The Qing elite, broadly defined, were a disparate group.[47] Local village leaders might be families who owned a bit more land than everyone else. Any family that had enough land or other resources to educate their sons could be considered elite, as could anyone who identified themselves as a "student." Merchants, although not students or holders of examination degrees, were members of the elite by virtue of their wealth. They shared the culture of the scholars, might educate one or more sons for the examinations, and could even gain the social and legal status of a scholar by purchasing a lower-level examination degree (which the state sold in order to generate revenue). In the narrowest sense, the scholar-official elite (sometimes referred to as the "gentry") included only examination-passers and their families, who amounted to perhaps five percent of the total population.

Politics, Money, and Culture

Art, literature, and philosophy had always been profoundly political. In the Ming, they had also become increasingly commercialized. The commercialization of art and even of philosophy continued during the reigns of the first four Qing emperors, as did the perpetual struggle between state-sanctioned orthodoxy and various unorthodox ways of thinking, writing, and behaving. The commercialization of culture could both strengthen and undermine orthodoxy. State orthodoxy itself could also offer opportunities for entrepreneurs. The imperial court, through the civil service exams, helped to define and inculcate orthodox thought and behavior as articulated through the texts of the Zhu Xi school of Neo-Confucianism. This meant that publishers could make great profits selling classical texts or, better yet, collections of sample examination essays, which were better sellers than the classics and the dynastic histories.[48]

The presence, the power, and the profitability of orthodoxy did not make the Qing Empire intellectually sterile or conformist. A number of Qing scholars and officials took very creative approaches to understanding their political and social worlds. In the early Qing, literati who had witnessed the fall of the Ming asked why their dynasty had collapsed. The explanation favored by straitlaced Confucian scholars was that the Wang Yangming school of Neo-Confucianism, with its Chan Buddhist–like subjectivism and relativism, had corrupted public morals. Huang Zongxi (1610–1695), himself a follower of the Wang Yangming school, placed the blame elsewhere. He argued that rulers had become selfish masters of all under Heaven instead of humble servants of the common good. Emperors, he said, needed to have their power checked by strong prime ministers and conscientious scholars and officials. These dangerous ideas received little circulation until the final years of the Qing dynasty.[49]

Huang Zongxi's contemporary and fellow Ming loyalist Gu Yanwu (1613–1682) was far more influential in the 17th and 18th centuries. Gu turned away from the metaphysics of both the Wang Yangming and Zhu Xi schools. He preferred empirical studies of phonology, geography, history, and classical texts. Gu analyzed the earliest possible primary sources—often stone inscriptions and bronzes—in order to verify historical events and to correct the errors or revisions that Song, Yuan, and Ming scholars had made when they transcribed, annotated, and interpreted ancient texts.[50]

Gu's work inspired 18th-century literati known as practitioners of "evidentiary scholarship." The practitioners of evidentiary scholarship believed that Song scholars, including Zhu Xi, had muddled the true meaning of the classics by mixing them up with Buddhist and Daoist influences. Following Gu's lead, they looked directly to the historical and philosophical texts of the Han dynasty, analyzing grammar and content in order to detect forgeries, hoping that they would thus gain access to the true principles of Confucian morality. The more idealistic of the evidentiary scholars believed that the ancient texts, purged of later distortions, would reveal timeless policies that, if put into practice, would restore order to the world.[51]

Though some may have pushed the idea of finding the key to good governance in restored Han texts to romantic extremes, the pragmatic, empirical strands of evidentiary scholarship had a significant influence on the theoreticians and practitioners of "statecraft" (*jingshi,* literally, "ordering the world").[52] Practitioners of statecraft did believe that the practice of ritual would contribute to the achievement of a moral society. However, they also believed that to build and maintain a morally satisfying society, the emperor's officials would need to find and implement practical solutions to economic, legal, administrative, military, infrastructural, and social problems.

Evidentiary scholarship also played a major role in the Qing state's attempts to define literary orthodoxy, and to root out literary heresy. It was the business of the imperial government to reaffirm and uphold Confucian morality in literature—and to reaffirm the legitimacy of dynastic rule by doing so. As a part of his own "ordering of the world," the Qianlong emperor initiated a major bibliographical project: the compilation of all the worthwhile literature of China into one massive collection, the *Complete Library of the Four Treasuries.*

Hundreds of scholars and editors worked from 1773 to 1782 to compile a list of 10,680 titles of extant works and copy 3,595 works in their entirety, each of which was placed in one of four categories: classics, history, philosophy, and *belles lettres.*[53] The Chinese scholars who carried out the bulk of the work were devotees of "evidentiary learning." As a result, their "Han Learning" approach to the Confucian classics had a strong influence on the choice of works included in the *Four Treasuries.*[54] They and the many local scholars who helped to gather material for the project also had a great deal of influence over what did not get included. One of their charges from Qianlong was to censor texts that made uncomplimentary references to Manchus, Jurchens, and other non-Han northern peoples, such as Mongols and Khitans. The search for such "seditious" material resulted in many legal cases and the destruction of around 2,400 undesirable works.[55]

While all educated men studied the same philosophical and historical texts, the fact was that only a small minority would ever pass the higher level of examinations and serve as officials. Fortunately, other careers were open to elite men. Employment as a professional secretary in county, provincial, or imperial government was one option. A life of leisure, supported by investments in land, commercial real estate, or business was another. And although it was the exception, some made their living as professional writers or artists. Manchu and Chinese alike saw appreciation of literature, and at least a moderate ability to produce essays, poetry, calligraphy, and painting as essential parts of elite identity. The empire's vibrant 18th-century commercial economy, growing urban population, and relatively high rates of literacy (two to ten percent for women, thirty to forty-five percent for men)[56] also created a strong market for popular literature.

Some of the most successful writers of popular literature were men who had failed the civil service exams or given up their official careers. Their novels and stories give us vivid and entertaining insights into the lives and beliefs of the educated elite and of ordinary people. Pu Songling (1640–1715), who earned only the lowest (*xiucai*) degree in the examination system and eked out a marginal living as a writer, teacher, and private secretary, collected tales of ghosts, fox spirits, demons, and uncanny phenomena of all sorts, which became one of the most popular books of the late 18th and 19th centuries when it was finally published as *Strange Tales from Liao Studio* in 1766.[57] Wu Jingzi (1701–1754), another *xiucai,* dissipated his family fortune living the high life in Nanjing. Rather than be an official, he wrote a novel, *The Scholars,* in which he satirized the hypocrisy, venality, and mediocrity of the literati.[58] Cao Xueqin (1716?–1763), the son of a clan of Han Chinese bond servants to the Manchu imperial house, described life in a wealthy but declining extended family in his novel *Story of the Stone* (also translated under the title *Dream of the Red Chamber*).

Their novels, even if published posthumously, made Pu Songling, Wu Jingzi, and Cao Xueqin famous to later generations of Chinese and foreign readers. Poetry and *belles lettres* could make a man famous and wealthy in his own time. There were many Qing poets—good, bad, and indifferent. One of the most famous was Yuan Mei (1716–1797). Precociously brilliant as a boy and serving as a magistrate in Nanjing at the age twenty-nine, Yuan abandoned his official career in 1748 and made his living as an essayist, poet, and teacher. Yuan Mei's fame became such that he could command as much as 1,000 ounces of silver for writing an epitaph. He was also known for his support of women poets (whose work he arranged to be published), his dalliances with prostitutes, and his close relationships with young male actors. When a Buddhist friend tried to convince Yuan Mei to curb his appetites in order to break the cycle of birth, death, and rebirth, Yuan Mei replied: "What makes a live man different from a dead one is precisely that he is capable of enjoying such pleasures. What you are asking me to do, is to behave as though I were dead, when in fact I am not dead. Can there be any sense in this?"[59]

Yuan Mei and other professional writers were able to take the attributes of a civilized gentleman—poetry and prose—and turn them into commodities. Many artists did the same with painting and calligraphy. The most famous painters of the early Qing were men who considered themselves "leftover subjects" of the former Ming. These included artists like Zhu Da (1626–c. 1705, also known as Bada Shanren) and Zhu Ruoji (1641–c. 1710, also known as Shitao), both Buddhist monks and descendants of the Ming imperial house. Bada Shanren's ruffled, grumpy-

looking birds, Shitao's landscapes, and other work by the leftover subjects expressed their mourning for the Ming dynasty, their resentment of the Manchus. Some, such as Shitao's self-portrait of himself overseeing the planting of pine trees on a barren mountain slope, even seem to express dreams of a Ming restoration.[60]

Bada Shanren, Shitao, and other notable painters of the early Qing were noted for their individualism and originality. As Shitao once put it, "When asked if I paint in the manner of the Southern or Northern School, with a hearty laugh I say I do not know whether I am of a school or a school is I; I paint in my own style."[61] Both he and Bada Shanren eventually broke their monastic vows and pursued careers as professional painters, Bada Shanren in Jiangxi province's Nanchang city, Shitao in Yangzhou, a wealthy town at the confluence of the Grand Canal and the Yangzi River.[62]

Bada Shanren's "Mynah Bird on an Old Tree." Hanging scroll, ink on paper, 1703.

Bada Shanren and Shitao were not alone, either in their individualist style or in their descent into the artistic marketplace. Most of the great Qing dynasty masters of the scholar-amateur style were neither officials nor wealthy men of leisure: their art was their main source of income.[63] They lived on sales of their work and relied on the patronage of wealthy officials, landowners, and merchants.

Competition for attention in the art marketplace drove some painters, notably some of the "Eight Eccentrics of Yangzhou," to adopt a cultivated "eccentricity" in order to distinguish themselves from the many competent, but run-of-the-mill artists of the 18th century.[64] All this blurred the theoretical distinction between the "amateur" and the "professional," so forcefully articulated in the Ming by Dong Qichang and still given fervent lip service in the Qing. The meaninglessness of the distinction was further underlined when professional artists, sometimes employing assistants, churned out hundreds of "scholar-amateur"–style paintings a year to be sold for cash.[65] The market for cheap decorative art also supported a booming business in mass-produced color woodblock prints, which featured urban scenes, beautiful women, illustrations from drama and literature, and special prints for Chinese New Year.[66]

Ritual and Religion

In the face of a changing world, both the Qing court and ordinary people used ritual and religion to provide spiritual solace, preserve stability, and generally keep the universe on track. As historians have pointed out, "the Qing state was not a secular institution: rather, its legitimacy depended on assumptions about the ties between the Son of Heaven and the cosmos, and on his crucial role in creating harmony between human society and the supernatural world."[67] People defined, redefined, and enforced family and state orthodoxy through ritual and religion. Others used ritual and religion to change or challenge the status quo.

Like the Ming emperors, Qing rulers or their surrogates ritually worshipped Heaven and Earth and a variety of state-recognized deities and carried out rituals to express reverence for their ancestors.[68] Also following on Ming precedent, the imperial government required county magistrates to hold regular Village Lectures, at which they were to teach moral lessons to the masses. Magistrates were also to read and explain the Sacred Edict, a sixteen-point list of moral injunctions originally issued by the Kangxi emperor and revised by his son Yongzheng. These included such standard Confucian fare as "Esteem most highly filial piety and brotherly submission," "Behave with generosity toward your kindred," and also messages of more direct political import, like "Put a stop to false accusations," "Warn against sheltering deserters," "Promptly remit your taxes," and "Do away with errant teachings, in order to exalt the correct doctrine."[69]

Doing away with errant teachings was not always easy. State-sanctioned Confucian family rituals continued to become more standardized and widespread, thanks to the publication and wide circulation of simple handbooks, most based on Zhu Xi's *Family Rituals*. While local practices still varied and scholars debated the details of ritual, there was wide agreement on the fundamentals: offering food and drink to the ancestors, introducing a bride to her husband's ancestors, donning mourning clothes and wailing on the death of a close relative, and so on.[70] But there were many points at which popular practice departed from strict Confucian ritual norms.

Some of these heterodox beliefs and practices, though abhorrent to Confucian purists, did nothing to undermine social or political stability. Placing Buddhist statues in the ancestral temple, the incorporation of "delivery of dowry" (with all its un-Confucian implications of weddings as business transactions), and the incorporation of Buddhist and Daoist rites and lavish feasts into funeral ceremonies were all condemned by sticklers for proper ritual, but were standard practice nonetheless.[71]

What was far more threatening to local elites and to the imperial government itself was the spread of heterodox religions. The government patronized and controlled institutional Buddhism, Daoism, and a state-sanctioned pantheon of gods. But across the empire, some people continued to worship non-sanctioned local gods. Loosely organized religions with names like "White Cloud," "Yellow Heaven," and "Heaven's Principle" provided alternative communities for the alienated, for elderly folks without family to care for them, for single men on the rough, lawless peripheries of the world, for farmers living in hopeless poverty, and for uprooted people working along the canals or in the cities.

Though "heterodox" in the sense of not enjoying the sanction of the state, these sects shared fundamental assumptions with the state-sanctioned religions, such as the concepts of re-incarnation, concern with the preservation of health and longevity, and the belief that the cosmos and its natural phenomena are closely linked to the human world.[72] The heterodox religions even used Buddhist and Daoist scriptures, worshipped Buddhist and Daoist deities, and shared the basic moral assumptions that we associate with Confucian moral philosophy. However, they also generated their own scriptures and worshipped their own deities.

Some gathered in groups to chant religious texts or eat vegetarian feasts.[73] Others initiated followers into esoteric meditation techniques, breathing exercises, healing rituals, and martial arts exercises or spirit possession. Women often played leading roles in these sects. Most offered some form of healing ritual or medicine. Many also offered the promise of an easy journey through the underworld after death and a good re-incarnation—sometimes by selling paper or silk "passports" that guaranteed smooth passage through the underworld. Some taught that a new millennium was coming, and that it was their responsibility to prepare the way for a world savior, be it the Maitreya Buddha (the Buddha of the Future) or some other deity.

Generally, these popular religions posed little threat to the government, which tolerated them unless they showed signs of formal organization, such as building a temple or openly recruiting large numbers of followers. But under the right conditions, charismatic leaders could inspire large numbers of followers to take up arms against the government. Among them, the most notorious (from the government's point of view) were the followers of the White Lotus religion. White Lotus beliefs involved worship of the "Eternal Mother" and the idea that she, or her messenger, the Maitreya Buddha, would soon usher in a new millennium of peace and prosperity. White Lotus devotees were generally content to chant their religious texts and wait. But the right confluence of events—economic stress, natural disaster, and perhaps the emergence of a charismatic leader—could inspire White Lotus followers to rise up in rebellion against the government in order to prepare the way for the imminent arrival of the Buddha of the Future.

The Troubles of Empire

The late 18th century provided just the sort of context in which sectarian uprising was liable to break out. In 1796, the Qianlong emperor, unwilling to exceed his grandfather the Kangxi emperor's thirty years on the throne, formally abdicated in favor of his son the Jiaqing emperor (1760–1820). Qianlong had been increasingly distant from the day-to-day business of governing since around 1780. He had delegated much authority to his favorite, a young Manchu guardsman named Heshen (1750–1799), who used his power to place supporters in key positions and to accumulate a substantial fortune through corruption. Nonetheless, the empire appeared to be at the height of wealth and power. But the factors that would fatally undermine Manchu rule in the 19th century were already present. These included imperial overreach, environmental stress, social unrest, ethnic tensions, and the increasing interest and strength of Western merchants and of their home governments in Europe and North America.

The size of the empire itself was one source of vulnerability. The Manchus had more than doubled their territory when they acquired Xinjiang, Qinghai, Tibet, and Taiwan. Control of Xinjiang and Tibet was particularly challenging. Garrisons and administrators in northern Xinjiang (Zungharia) cost tens of thousands of taels of silver annually. Qing officials tried to generate revenue from within Xinjiang by running businesses and taxing merchants, but their efforts fell short of the mark. As a result, every year, silver collected in agricultural taxes from the wealthier provinces was sent to subsidize the imperial apparatus in Xinjiang. Indirect rule of the Muslim Uighur oases of southern Xinjiang (Altishahr) was cheaper than the extensive garrisons in Zungharia, but left the frontiers poorly defended and open to invasion from neighboring Central Asian khanates.[74] As for Tibet, maintenance of garrisons and an administration would have been too expensive. Instead, the Qing allowed Tibetan monasteries and aristocrats to run Tibet with little intervention from the *ambans* and the small, underpaid Qing garrison in Lhasa.

Administration of the Chinese areas of the empire brought its own challenges. The Qing emperors had inherited and strengthened Ming autocracy. But even Yongzheng, Kangxi, and Qianlong were hemmed in by law, procedure, precedent, and by the sheer volume of the paperwork, much of which they had to delegate to their advisors. In addition, both practical and ideological constraints prevented the Qing imperial government from achieving a high degree of control over China's people and economic resources. First, there was the practical impossibility of managing a large territory and population within the constraints of premodern communications and transportation technology. As population rose from one hundred million to over three hundred million during the 18th century, the county magistrate's office, the lowest level of the Qing bureaucracy, was responsible, on average, for a population of two hundred thousand.

Second, the Qianlong emperor committed the Qing to a policy of minimal taxation and minimal government intervention in China's society and economy. A quintessential "small government" man, Qianlong "was content to see government revenues progressively shrink as a percentage of total economic output and even . . . to let a growing percentage of the empire's wealth simply go unrecorded by the state."[75] In keeping government administration relatively small and taxation light, and avoiding active government involvement in the commercial economy, the Qianlong emperor was putting Neo-Confucian principles into practice.

The same principles, and practical necessity, called upon local elites and social organizations to perform many of the tasks that would be performed by government in a modern Western state. County magistrates relied on local elites to provide information, help collect taxes, lead local militia, mediate disputes, and repair and maintain dikes and irrigation works, city walls, public buildings, and schools. Clan and lineage organizations played a prominent role in their local communities, especially in southern China. Merchants from Shanxi, Shaanxi, Anhui, and other provinces built provincial guild-halls in major cities throughout the empire to provide their fellow provincials with lodging, financial services, and social and business connections. Boatmen manning the tribute grain barges on the Grand Canal organized for mutual economic support and religious salvation. In the south and southeast, young men formed gangs known as "Heaven-and-Earth Societies" or "Triads" (referring to the triad of Heaven-Earth-Man). As mentioned above, religious organizations like the White Lotus Society offered spiritual, social, and material aid to their members.

Weak government, low levels of taxation, and a reliance on local elites and social organizations to deliver goods and services are not necessarily bad things. But they did leave the Qing government underfunded and poorly prepared to deal with major internal challenges. And although 18th-century China was one of the wealthiest places in the world, the weaknesses that would grow to crisis proportions in the 19th century were already evident.

The growing pressure on China's natural environment was one of the fundamental sources of popular unrest and state weakness. Over a century of relative peace in China Proper, increased agricultural production (partly driven by the introduction of New World crops like maize, potatoes, and peanuts) and lower death rates had combined to push the empire's population from one hundred million to over three hundred million during the 18th century. Since the acreage of arable land only doubled, the amount of land per family declined.[76]

In highly productive areas like the Yangzi Valley, increased population density did not cause major social instability. But in drought-prone areas like Shandong province and the northwestern provinces of Shanxi and Shaanxi, less farmland per family and environmental degradation translated directly into grinding poverty, young men unable to afford marriage, and families living on the edge of disaster: prime conditions for banditry, the growth of

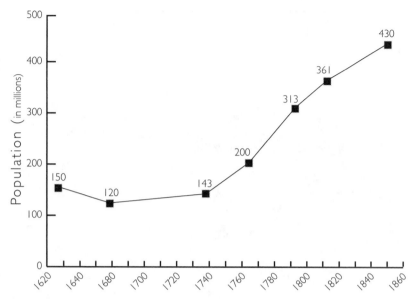

Population growth in the Qing period.

religious sects, and rebellion. Population pressure spurred migrations of Chinese farmers and merchants to the more sparsely populated border regions of western Sichuan, Yunnan, Guizhou, Guangxi, Hunan, Taiwan, and (although Han migration was illegal there) to Manchuria. A small number of migrants, particularly merchants, moved north and northwest, into Mongolia and Xinjiang.

If imperialism is the acquisition and control of territories and their peoples through military domination and if colonialism is the settling of people on the conquered territory at the expense of its native inhabitants, then Manchu empire-building had created the framework under which Han Chinese colonialism flourished.[77] As Chinese colonists moved into areas inhabited by other peoples, disputes broke out over access to land, water, and mineral resources. Chinese merchants, well-supplied with attractive goods and money to loan at interest, often clashed with native peoples over debts and land ownership. Han migrants opening new fields and felling timber for sale put added pressure on the delicate natural environment of mountain areas, causing soil depletion, erosion, and flooding.

The Qing government's attempts to deal with ethnic difference and ethnic tensions were met with limited success. Moves to extend formal administrative control to Tibetan communities in western Sichuan and to Hmong (Miao) and other native peoples of Guizhou led to large-scale rebellions.

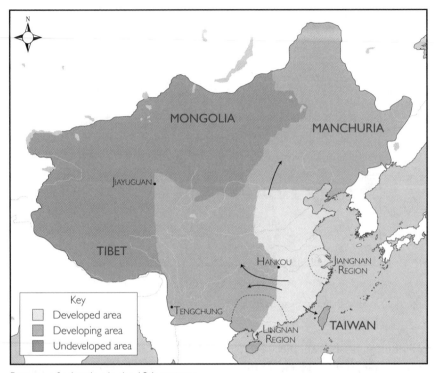

Patterns of migration in the 18th century.

Both were defeated, but at considerable expense. Attempts to prevent ethnic tensions by limiting migration into sensitive areas of Taiwan and the southwest and by keeping Han and non-Han communities separate failed because enforcement was impossible. As a result, Taiwan, Yunnan, Guizhou, and parts of western Sichuan developed into lawless frontier areas.

Ethnic tension, poverty, environmental pressure, religious sectarianism, and government ineptitude combined to create a major rebellion at the close of the 18th century. The mountainous Sichuan-Gansu-Shaanxi border region had seen an influx of tens of thousands of migrants, who barely eked out a living as they opened marginally productive mountain land for agriculture. In 1796, White Lotus sectarians engaged in multiple small-scale clashes with the Qing authorities. The government's heavy-handed attempts to suppress White Lotus sectarian activity led to even larger and more violent uprisings. The Qing court transferred troops from around the empire to suppress the rebels. Generals and high-ranking officials exaggerated the scope of the rebellion in order to keep resources flowing to the military which provided tremendous opportunities for embezzlement.[78] Such scheming and corruption made many men's fortunes. It also helped to stretch operations against the White Lotus rebels out for nine years and pushed expenses up to over 200,000,000 taels of silver.[79]

Although it was stretched thin, the Qianlong emperor's government was able to suppress uprisings like Sichuan's White Lotus rebellion and others, including a White Lotus rebellion in Shandong (1774) and a rebellion by the Heaven-and-Earth Society in Taiwan (1787). Qianlong also responded with decisive force against the more subtle internal threat of Han Chinese treason. The discovery in 1751 of multiple copies of a forged memorial (falsely attributed to a high-ranking official), which evidently contained personal attacks on the emperor and challenged the dynasty's legitimacy, led to thousands of arrests and the execution by slicing of the alleged perpetrator.[80] In 1768, the emperor received reports that itinerant Buddhist and Daoist monks and beggars were stealing the souls of men and boys by clipping off their queues—the symbol of Chinese male subordination to the Manchu. Convinced that there were serious political ramifications behind the reported incidents, he ordered officials across the empire to pursue such cases vigorously, only to conclude, after months of prosecution and torture of witnesses and accused, that the reports were the product of villagers' superstitions and their suspicions of the itinerant monks, beggars, and tradesmen who traveled through the countryside trying to eke out a living.[81]

Frontier violence, sectarian rebellions, and sorcery scares are all indicative of some of the problems lurking below the surface of wealth and power of the Great Qing. Economic growth had clearly not brought equal benefits to all parts of the empire and all of its subjects. But economic growth in the 17th and 18th centuries had made the Qing Empire, overall, one of the wealthiest and most productive places on the face of the earth. Western merchants recognized Qing wealth, and participated in its generation, by continuing to bring their ships to the ports of south and southeast China, particularly to the city of Guangzhou, also known as Canton.

The Qing rulers welcomed Western merchants, goods, and technology, but on their own terms. Jesuits had gained access to the Qing court with their command of mathematics, astronomy, metallurgy, mapmaking, and other useful arts. The Jesuits' open-minded attitude toward Chinese ritual helped them to make some converts and even to attract the curiosity of the Shunzhi emperor.[82] The Jesuits defined Chinese ritual as "civil" and therefore compatible with Catholic Christianity. When the far-away Catholic pope, acting on reports from the Jesuits' Franciscan and Dominican rivals, ruled that Chinese rites were paganism and thus taboo for Chinese Catholics, the Kangxi emperor responded that the pope had no business dictating to the subjects of the Great Qing and then ordered an end to Catholic missionary work.

This did not prevent Kangxi and his heirs from continuing to employ Jesuits in all manner of useful, nonreligious capacities. Jesuits instructed Kangxi's court eunuchs in the playing of Western music on the clavichord; designed Italianate buildings for the Qianlong emperor's great Summer Palace, the Yuanmingyuan; helped to make detailed maps of the Qing Empire; and cast cannon for use against the Tibetan rebels in western Sichuan. Jesuit painters, most famously Giuseppe Castiglione (1688–1766), painted for the Qing court and introduced European techniques of perspective and shading to their Chinese colleagues.

The maritime trade, too, continued to thrive under the Qing. Foreign merchants, particularly the English, having no products of their own that would be welcome in China, brought shiploads of silver to exchange for tea, porcelain, silk, and other goods. The trade centered on the southern port of Guangzhou, or Canton. Guangzhou was larger and better-equipped (in terms of merchants and warehousing) to accommodate Western traders than other ports on the southeastern coast. It was also close to the Portuguese enclave of Macao. When an English ship's captain petitioned (in Chinese) for more liberal trade policies in 1759, the Qianlong emperor responded with a decree that foreign ships would be allowed to trade only at the port of Guangzhou, and then only during the official trading season.

Each major nation trading at Guangzhou (Canton) maintained a "factory" —a complex of warehouses, offices, and accommodations—in a set area outside the city walls. Foreigners were confined to the factory quarter and were required to do business with one of thirteen licensed merchant houses, or "hongs," in the city. The "Canton trade," as it is called, generated its own cultural characteristics: Chinese artists painting portraits and landscapes in European oils for Western customers, the great porcelain works of Jingdezhen churning out dinner sets bearing European decorative themes and coats of arms, and Chinese merchants speaking a colorful and very serviceable pidgin English enriched by Portuguese and Cantonese vocabulary.

Foreign merchants chafed at the restrictions on their trade. They resented the need to pay various fees and bribes to port officials and to a man whom they called the Hoppo—actually a representative of the imperial household (*hubu*), whose job it was to supervise the trade and to collect taxes for the emperor. They resented, too, the fact that foreigners could be tried and punished under Qing law. When, for example, a salute fired from the ship *Lady Hughes* killed a Chinese bystander, Qing authorities, acting on the principle

The western factories at Guangzhou (Canton) as painted by the British artist George Chinnery in 1833.

of collective criminal responsibility, rejected the captain's argument that no one could be punished because it was impossible to say which gunner's cannon had inflicted the fatal injury. In the end, a gunner was handed over for execution.

Despite their complaints, foreign merchants kept coming to Guangzhou. For all the difficulties, the taxes, and the bribes, the trade was profitable. The English had developed a gargantuan appetite for tea, on which China still had a monopoly. Wealthy Europeans and Americans enjoyed Chinese porcelain and other items so much as to drive two periods of *chinoiserie*—Chinese styles of garden and interior design. Qing officials and the Qing emperor himself were so confident of their wealth, their power, and the innate value of their civilization that they could easily look upon the foreign trade as a matter of peripheral interest. In 1793, the British diplomat George Lord Macartney (1737–1806) came to Beijing to negotiate the opening of more ports, the establishment of a permanent British trading post on a convenient island off the coast of Guangdong, and diplomatic representation in Beijing. He brought many gifts, including astronomical instruments, scale models of British warships, and examples of British manufactures.[83]

The Qianlong emperor received Macartney and his gifts with great politeness, but little interest. He turned down all of Macartney's requests, saying: "I set no value on objects strange and ingenious, and have no use for your country's manufactures. . . . Our Celestial Empire possesses all things in prolific abundance and lacks no product within its borders."[84] The Qianlong emperor's rhetoric belies the fact that he employed Jesuit astronomers, architects, painters, mapmakers, and ballistics experts. With hindsight, we can see how environmental degradation, population pressure, social unrest, ethnic tensions, a weak, underfunded government, and the European indus-trial revolution—all phenomena whose roots we can discern in Qianlong's time—would combine to create an unprecedented crisis for his dynasty fewer than fifty years after he so confidently gave Lord Macartney the brush-off. But before we judge Qianlong too harshly, we might ask how well we can discern the trends of the future in our own world and predict their po-litical and economic consequences half a century out!

Notes

1. Frederick Wakeman, Jr., *The Great Enter-prise: The Manchu Reconstruction of Imperial Order in Seventeenth-Century China* (Berke-ley: University of California Press, 1985), 42–5.

2. Zhang Kaizhi, ed., *Zhongguo lishi: Yuan Ming Qing juan* (Chinese history: Yuan, Ming, and Qing volume) (Beijing: Gao-deng jiaoyu chubanshe, 2001), 185.

3. Thomas J. Barfield, *The Perilous Frontier: Nomadic Empires and China* (Cambridge, Mass.: Blackwell Publishers, 1989), 255.

4. Johan Elverskog, *Our Great Qing: The Mongols, Buddhism, and the State in Late Imperial China* (Honolulu: University of Hawaii Press, 2006), 14, 25–7.

5. Pamela Kyle Crossley, *A Translucent Mir-ror: History and Identity in Qing Imperial Ideology* (Berkeley: University of Cali-fornia Press, 1999), 157–8.

6. Mark C. Elliott, *The Manchu Way: The Eight Banners and Ethnic Identity in Late Imperial China* (Stanford: Stanford Uni-versity Press, 2001), 56–63.

7. Barfield, *The Perilous Frontier,* 253.

8. Wakeman, *The Great Enterprise,* 203–8.

9. Ibid., 296–7.

10. Quoted in ibid., 316–7.

11. Victoria Cass, *Dangerous Women: War-riors, Grannies and Geishas of the Ming*

(Lanham: Rowman & Littlefield, 1999), 122.

12. Lynn A. Struve, ed., *Voices from the Ming-Qing Cataclysm: China in Tigers' Jaws* (New Haven: Yale University Press, 1993), 28–9.

13. Susan Naquin, *Peking: Temples and City Life, 1400–1900* (Berkeley: University of California Press, 2000), 4.

14. Susan Naquin and Evelyn S. Rawski, *Chi-nese Society in the Eighteenth Century* (New Haven: Yale University Press, 1987), 141.

15. This and the following paragraph draw on Edward J. M. Rhoads, *Manchus and Han: Ethnic Relations and Political Power in Late Qing and Early Republican China, 1861–1928* (Seattle: University of Washington Press, 2000), 35–51.

16. Evelyn S. Rawski, *The Last Emperors: A Social History of Qing Imperial Institutions* (Berkeley: University of California Press, 1998), 39–43; Wakeman, *The Great En-terprise,* 975–83.

17. Jonathan D. Spence, *Emperor of China: Self-Portrait of K'ang-Hsi* (New York: Vin-tage Books, 1975), 122.

18. Paul Lococo Jr., "The Qing Empire," in David A. Graff and Robin Higham, eds., *A Military History of China* (Boulder: Westview Press, 2002), 118–21.

19. Pamela Kyle Crossley, *The Manchus* (Cambridge, Mass.: Blackwell Publishers, 1997), 118.

20. Peter C. Perdue, *China Marches West: The Qing Conquest of Central Eurasia* (Cambridge, Mass.: Harvard University Press, 2005), 161–73; Vincent Chen, *Sino-Russian Relations in the Seventeenth Century* (The Hague: Martinus Nijhoff, 1966), 98–105.

21. Spence, *Emperor of China,* 17.

22. Perdue, *China Marches West,* 203.

23. Peter C. Purdue, "Military Mobilization in Seventeenth and Eighteenth-Century China, Russia, and Mongolia," *Modern Asian Studies* 30.4 (Oct. 1996): 776.

24. Ibid., 759.

25. Richard J. K. Jung, "The Sino-Burmese War, 1766–1770: War and Peace Under the Tributary System," *Papers on China* 24 (1971): 87.

26. Quoted in ibid., 90; Yingcong Dai, "A Disguised Defeat: The Myanmar Campagin of the Qing Dynasty," *Modern Asian Studies* 38.1 (2004): 145–88.

27. Yingcong Dai, "Reaching the Empire's Limits: The Qing Invasion of Nepal in 1792," The Annual Conference of the Chinese Military History Society, Texas Christian University, Fort Worth, 3 May 2008.

28. Interactive online versions of some of the Kangxi and Qianlong emperors' Southern Tour scrolls can be found in Maxwell K. Hearn and Madeleine Zelin, consultants, *Recording the Grandeur of the Qing: The Southern Inspection Tour Scrolls of the Kangxi and Qianlong Empire* (New York: Metropolitan Museum of Art; Asia for Educators Program and Visual Media Center, Columbia University, 2005), http://www.learn.columbia.edu/nanxuntu/start.html.

29. L. J. Newby, "The Begs of Xinjiang: Between Two Worlds," *Bulletin of the School of Oriental and African Studies, University of London* 61.2 (1998): 278–97.

30. Djang Chu, "Translator's Introduction," in Huang Liu-Hung, *A Complete Book Concerning Happiness and Benevolence: A Manual for Local Magistrates in Seventeenth-Century China,* trans. and ed. Djang Chu (Tucson: The University of Arizona Press, 1984), 16–7. These numbers reflect the situation in the Kangxi reign. The precise number of provinces, prefectures, and counties varied somewhat over time. For simplicity, I have combined the two categories of "department" (*zhou*) and "county" (*xian*). These two were on the same administrative level, but departments were generally a bit larger than counties.

31. Beatrice S. Bartlett, *Monarchs and Ministers: The Grand Council in Mid-Ch'ing China, 1723–1820* (Berkeley: University of California Press, 1991), 17. Bartlett argues that the Yongzheng emperor's ad hoc committees were the origin of the Qianlong emperor's Grand Council.

32. Benjamin A. Elman, *A Cultural History of Civil Examinations in Late Imperial China* (Berkeley: University of California Press, 2000), 659.

33. Ichisada Miyazaki, *China's Examination Hell: The Civil Service Examinations of Imperial China* (New Haven: Yale University Press, 1981), 15–6.

34. Frederic Wakeman, Jr., *The Fall of Imperial China* (New York: The Free Press, 1975), 22.

35. Elman, *A Cultural History of Civil Service Examinations,* 424–5, 428–9.

36. Wakeman, *Fall of Imperial China,* 22.

37. T'ung-tsu Ch'ü, *Local Government in China Under the Ch'ing* (Cambridge, Mass.: Harvard University Council on East Asian Studies, 1988), 2; Wakeman, *Fall of Imperial China,* 29.

38. Thomas M. Buoye, *Manslaughter, Markets, and Moral Economy: Violent Disputes over Property Rights in Eighteenth-Century China* (Cambridge: Cambridge University Press, 2000).

39. *The Great Qing Code,* trans. William C. Jones (Oxford: Clarendon Press, 1994), Article 234, "Animals That Bite and Kick People," 222.

40. *Great Qing Code,* Article 386, "[Doing] That Which Ought Not to be Done," 359.

41. Jonathan K. Ocko, "I'll Take It All the Way to Beijing: Capital Appeals in the Qing," *The Journal of Asian Studies* 47.2 (May 1988): 291–315.

42. These numbers are rough estimates based on Bradley W. Reed, *Talons and Teeth: County Clerks and Runners in the Qing Dynasty* (Stanford: Stanford University Press, 2000), 44–51, 144–9.

43. See the discussion in Reed, op. cit.

44. Melissa Macauley, *Social Power and Legal Culture: Litigation Masters in Late Imperial China* (Stanford: Stanford University Press, 1998).

45. Ch'ü, *Local Government in China Under the Ch'ing,* 180–92.

46. The definition of "separate spheres" for males and females is not unique to China. Similar definitions of gender roles are found in most, perhaps all, premodern societies. The intent here is not to make an argument for Chinese exceptionalism, but simply to show how male and female roles were constructed in the Qing.

47. The following definitions of the "elite" follow Naquin and Rawski, *Chinese Society,* 115–6.

48. Elman, *A Cultural History of Civil Service Examinations,* 402.

49. William Theodore de Bary et al., eds., *Sources of Chinese Tradition, Vol. 2: From 1600 Through the Twentieth Century,* 2nd ed. (New York: Columbia University Press, 2000), 4–7. See also Huang Zongxi's own work, *Waiting for the Dawn: A Plan for the Prince: Huang Tsung-hs'i's Ming-i tai-fang lu,* trans. William Theodore de Bary (New York: Columbia University Press, 1993).

50. Willard J. Paterson, "The Life of Ku Yen-wu (1613–1682), Part II," *Harvard Journal of Asiatic Studies* 29 (1969): 211–2.

51. William T. Rowe, *Saving the World: Chen Hongmou and Elite Consciousness in Eighteenth-Century China* (Stanford: Stanford University Press, 2001), 87.

52. Rowe, *Saving the World,* 2–3.

53. R. Kent Guy, *The Emperor's Four Treasuries: Scholars and the State in the Late Ch'ien-lung Era* (Cambridge, Mass.: Council on East Asia Studies, Harvard University, 1987), 1. The following discussion follows Guy's analysis of the Four Treasuries project.

54. Ibid., 155–6.

55. Ibid., 1.

56. Evelyn Sakakida Rawski, *Education and Popular Literacy in Ch'ing China* (Ann Arbor: The University of Michigan Press, 1979), 23.

57. Allan H. Barr, "The Later Classical Tale," in Victor H. Mair, ed., *The Columbia History of Chinese Literature* (New York: Columbia University Press, 2001), 692.

58. Wai-Yee Li, "Full-Length Vernacular Fiction," in Mair, ed., *The Columbia History of Chinese Literature,* 644.

59. Arthur Waley, *Yuan Mei: Eighteenth Century Chinese Poet* (London: George Allen and Unwin, Ltd., 1956), 82.

60. Craig Clunas, *Art in China* (Oxford: Oxford University Press, 1997), 163.

61. Quoted in Laurence Sickman and Alexander Soper, *The Art and Architecture of China* (Harmondsworth: Penguin Books, Ltd., 1971), 358.

62. Clunas, *Art in China,* 164; Michael Sullivan, *The Arts of China,* 3rd ed. (Berkeley: University of California Press, 1984), 233.

63. Sullivan, *The Arts of China,* 239.

64. Ibid.

65. Clunas, *Art in China,* 193–4.

66. Ibid., 195–6.

67. Naquin and Rawski, *Chinese Society,* 88.

68. Illustrations and discussion of imperial religion and ritual in the Qing can be found online in Myron L. Cohen and Stephen F. Teiser, faculty consultants, *Living in the Chinese Cosmos: Understanding Religion in Late Imperial China (1644–1911)* (New York: Asia for Educators Online, Columbia University, 2007), http://afe.easia.columbia.edu/cosmos/.

69. de Bary et al., eds., *Sources of Chinese Tradition,Vol. 2,* 70–3.

70. Patricia Buckley Ebrey, *Confucianism and Family Rituals in Imperial China: A Social History of Writing about Rites* (Princeton: Princeton University Press, 1991), 200–1, 206–7.

71. Ebrey, *Confucianism and Family Rituals,* 211–5.

72. Daniel L. Overmyer, *Folk Buddhist Religion: Dissenting Sects in Late Traditional China* (Cambridge, Mass.: Harvard University Press, 1976), 162.

73. For this and the following, see Susan Naquin, "The Transmission of White Lotus Sectarianism in Late Imperial China," in David Johnson, Andrew J. Nathan, and Evelyn S. Rawski, eds., *Popular Culture in Late Imperial China* (Berkeley: University of California Press, 1985), 259–83.

74. Newby, "The Begs of Xinjiang," 295.

75. Rowe, *Saving theWorld,* 49.

76. Jonathan D. Spence, *The Search for Modern China,* 2nd ed. (New York: W.W. Norton, 1999), 79.

77. Margaret Kohn, "Colonialism," *Stanford Encyclopedia of Philosophy,* Fall 2008 ed., ed. Edward N. Zalta, online at http://plato.stanford.edu/archives/fall2008/entries/colonialism/, accessed 23 May 2008. The phenomenon described here is similar to the way in which Dutch control over Taiwan in the 17th century created the conditions for a growing Han Chinese colonial presence. See Tonio Andrade, *How Taiwan Became Chinese: Dutch, Spanish, and Han Colonization in the Seventeenth Century* (New York: Columbia University Press, 2008).

78. Yingcong Dai, "The White Lotus War: A War Fought on the Terms of the Qing Military," The Annual Conference of the Association for Asian Studies, Boston, 24 March 2007.

79. Zhang, ed., *Zhongguo lishi:Yuan Ming Qing juan,* 365–6.

80. The case is discussed in detail in Jonathan D. Spence, *Treason by the Book* (New York: Penguin Putnam Inc., 2001).

81. Philip A. Kuhn, *Soulstealers: The Chinese Sorcery Scare of 1768* (Cambridge, Mass.: Harvard University Press, 1990).

82. David Mungello, *The Great Encounter of China and the West, 1500–1800* (Lanham: Rowman & Littlefield, 1999).

83. Joanna Waley-Cohen, *The Sextants of Beijing: Global Currents in Chinese History* (New York: W.W. Norton, 1999), 102–3; Spence, *The Search for Modern China,* 122–3.

84. E. Backhouse and J. O. P. Bland, *Annals and Memoirs of the Court of Peking* (Boston: Houghton Mifflin, 1914), 322–31.

Chapter 2　　　　　　　　　　# THE QING DYNASTY'S
19TH-CENTURY CRISES

When the Qianlong emperor died in 1799, imperial armies were still struggling against the White Lotus rebels in Sichuan province. Soon, outraged officials mustered the courage to denounce Qianlong's favorite, Grand Councilor Heshen. The former Manchu guardsman was in charge of the floundering campaign to suppress the rebels and had built an immense fortune through corruption. Impeached and facing certain punishment, Heshen committed suicide. But despite rebellions and corruption, the foundations of the Qing Empire still seemed intact. No foreign power challenged the Qing's territorial integrity. Han Chinese scholars and officials did not seriously question the Manchu's right to rule. Still less did Chinese doubt the value and supremacy of their civilization.

A hundred years later, the Qing had lost a series of wars with European nations and Japan. It had ceded or leased parts of its territories to foreign powers and allowed foreign businesses, missionaries, diplomats, and naval forces unprecedented access to ports, Qing territory, and markets. A vociferous minority of Han Chinese intellectuals were calling for the overthrow and even extermination of the Manchu, questioning the authority of their own classical texts and cultural traditions, adapting Western learning, and agitating for an end to the monarchy. By 1901, even the Manchu court was convinced that only substantial reform drawing on Western and Japanese models could save the country and the dynasty.

What caused the 19th-century crises that led to such weakness and self-questioning? Part of the answer lies in the population growth, environmental pressure, and social tensions that had been building even in the 18th century. To these internal problems was added a new external challenge: Western powers whose technological, economic, and military strength enabled them to take an aggressive stance toward the Qing Empire.

The story of the Qing Empire's 19th-century decline, its struggles against Western and Japanese imperialism, and the increasing tendency of Han Chinese to question the Manchu right to rule and their own cultural heritage had a tremendous effect on 20th-century Chinese history and especially on the formation of Chinese national identity and nationalism. The narrative, as told and re-told by the Chinese state and by Chinese citizens, continues to play a powerful role in contemporary Chinese nationalist discourse. In the simple form most conducive to nationalist sentiment, it is a story of Manchu incompetence and Western and Japanese imperialist aggression, in which Han Chinese play the roles of victim and revolutionary. It is the goal of this chapter to offer an account of the Qing Empire's 19th-century crises in a way that will convey a more nuanced understanding while also showing why the events of this tumultuous period played and continue to play such a significant role in 20th- and 21st-century Chinese national identity.

Foreign Trade and the Opium War

The late Ming and early Qing governments had been able to trade with Europeans while keeping them at arm's length, confining trade to specified Inner Asian border towns (for the Russians) and to the port of Guangzhou (Canton) for the English and other maritime powers. Westerners, of whom the English were most important, were not satisfied with the restrictions on their trade, but the high market value of silver in China made it worth their while to bring shiploads of the precious metal to exchange for tea, porcelain, and silk.

This situation changed dramatically in the 19th century. The scientific revolution and the industrial revolution fueled by New World resources and easily accessible deposits of coal transformed England, then Western Europe and North America.[1] At the same time, the rationalist thought of the 18th-century European Enlightenment had, by the 19th century, led to new developments in Western government, law, economic policy, and society.

As the West became more powerful, Western impressions of China changed for the worse. The Jesuits' flattering descriptions of China, the French *philosophes'* portrayal of the Qing as an enlightened monarchy, and the European craze for *chinoiserie* were things of the past. By the early 19th century, Westerners had developed a strong sense of superiority toward China, which they now regarded as a backward, corrupt place that they must open, enlighten, civilize, and Christianize—by force, if necessary.[2] Merchants were as affected as anyone by this sense of superiority, and by the xenophobia and prejudice that went along with it. But merchants were also very much concerned about their profits. It was the search for profit, combined with (and sometimes legitimized by) the rhetoric of "spreading civilization," that led the English to the opium trade, and thence to a war over their right to deal in opium.

Since the Tang dynasty, Chinese had treated diarrhea and other diseases with medicine made by boiling the seedpods of the opium poppy. But smoking the addictive narcotic sap from the poppy was an innovation. Europeans introduced tobacco to China in the late Ming. Chinese and Manchus were soon enthusiastic smokers, and tobacco became a profitable cash crop for Chinese farmers, particularly in Fujian and Jiangnan.[3] In the meantime, in the Dutch East Indies, Chinese laborers and merchants smoked a combination of tobacco and opium known as *madak*. They brought *madak* to the Dutch colony on Taiwan around the 1630s. Smoking *madak*, and then just pure opium, spread to the mainland in the late 17th to mid-18th centuries.[4]

The developing Chinese market demand for opium presented the British East India Company with a great opportunity. The Company had been trading silver for tea and other products at Guangzhou. The profits helped pay for the conquest of India, and the tea tax was an important part of the British government's revenue. But by the late 18th to early 19th centuries, global silver production was in decline and the value of silver in the West had become greater than the value of silver in China: Westerners now found it unprofitable to exchange silver for tea.[5] They needed to find another commodity: one that was cheap for them, but in demand in China.

Opium was the ideal replacement for silver. In India, the East India Company had the land, climate, and cheap labor necessary to grow opium poppies, collect the sticky black sap from the seedpods, and process it into balls of opium for smoking. The Qing government had outlawed opium smoking in 1729, while still allowing medicinal use. Legal opium imports for "medicinal use" increased, as did smoking.

Repeated prohibitions on opium sales and opium smoking beginning in 1796 simply made the business more profitable. In order not to compromise its legal trade in Guangzhou, the Company held a monopoly on opium production and sales in India and had private merchants called "country traders" carry the opium to China on their ships. Since the traffic was illegal, British, American, and other foreign merchants anchored storeships ("hulks") in the Pearl River estuary, from which they sold their opium directly to Chinese smugglers, who brought it ashore in "fast crabs"—armed smuggling boats powered by twenty or more oarsmen to each side.[6] The trade flourished: 200 chests in 1729, 1,000 in 1767, around 4,500 chests per year in the first decade of the 19th century, an average of 7,979 chests from 1820–26, and as many as 40,200 in 1838–39.[7]

Qing officials regarded opium as both a social and economic problem. It is impossible to say what percentage of the Qing population smoked opium and how many of them were addicted to the drug.[8] Nevertheless, the court and leading scholars were concerned about the moral and social effects of opium, particularly among officials, students, and soldiers.

The economic impact of opium was part of a bigger problem. The Qing economy ran on copper cash, which ordinary people used for day-to-day transactions. But people paid their taxes in silver ingots assayed to a standard of purity and weight (1 tael, roughly 1.3 ounces or 37 g). The exchange rate of copper cash to silver changed dramatically in the late 18th to mid-19th centuries. From 1664 to 1760, the price of a tael of silver averaged around 780 cash. The same tael of silver cost around 1,650 cash in 1838.[9] For ordinary people, whose cash income was in copper, the higher price of silver was equivalent to a tax increase. Many farmers were pushed to the limits of their endurance. Tax evasion increased; government revenue declined.

We now know that many factors contributed to the scarcity of silver, and copper cash inflation, in the 19th century. The relatively higher value of silver outside China tended now to pull the metal toward the Western economies. The government spent tens of thousands of taels of silver suppressing rebels in frontier areas and to control and administer Xinjiang. Some of this silver was lost in transfrontier trade.[10] The opium trade at Guangzhou probably accounted for perhaps half of the outflow of silver, but this part of the outflow was the most obvious and the easiest to measure.[11] As Qing officials saw it, the opium trade was the single cause of the loss of silver. Repeated bans on opium smoking and the opium trade had failed. Corruption undermined every law. Something had to be done: But what?

In 1836, a group of officials, most with experience in Guangzhou, recommended that the government legalize the opium trade, tax it, and require that opium be paid for only with tea, silk, and other Chinese commodities— not with silver. Soon, another group of officials made strong arguments for opium suppression. The law, they said, must be enforced. Opium was a moral and financial issue on which there could be no compromise.

The Daoguang emperor was convinced. He ordered a crackdown, which began in October 1836.[12] In 1838, he appointed Lin Zexu (1785–1850) high commissioner to deal with the opium problem in Guangdong and Guangxi provinces, once and for all. Lin was already famous for his ability, his integrity, and his uncompromising stand against opium. He arrived in Guangzhou on 10 March 1839. By May, thousands of smokers had been arrested, tens of thousands of opium pipes destroyed, and thousands of catties of opium confiscated from Chinese dealers.

While working to eliminate demand, Lin also attacked the problem of supply. This obliged him to deal with the foreign merchant community, particularly the British and their chief superintendent of trade, Captain Charles Elliot (1801–75). At first, Commissioner Lin tried moral suasion and negotiation. He issued edicts to the foreign traders in Guangzhou, requiring them to surrender their opium and to give bonds promising not to deal in opium in the future. He also drafted, and later released, a now-famous letter addressed to Queen Victoria. In the letter, Commissioner Lin laid forth the moral arguments against the opium trade and asking her to cooperate with the Qing to bring "a perpetual end to this opium, so hurtful to mankind: we in this land forbidding the use of it, and you, in the nations of your dominion, forbidding its manufacture."[13]

On 24 March 1838, when the foreign traders had clearly refused to cooperate, the commissioner sent soldiers to seal off the Guangzhou factories, the 80,000-square-yard (67,000 sq m) complex of warehouses and offices where the foreign traders and the British superintendent of trade were required to live and carry out their business.[14] He also withdrew their Chinese servants. The foreigners did not suffer. They had plenty of food and water— but they had to cook and clean for themselves. They would not be allowed to leave, nor would any trade be permitted, until they had surrendered their opium.

So far, the anti-opium measures had been successful. Market demand for opium had collapsed, leaving foreign merchants holding more opium than they could sell at any price. This was a serious problem. Opium was not just any commodity: profits from the illegal trade in opium had been funding the legal trade in tea and silk, supporting the British conquest and administration of India, enabling merchants to remit profits back to England, and financing the purchase of American cotton for the mills of Lancashire—whose cotton textiles were, increasingly, being sold to consumers in India.[15] So when

The *Nemesis* fires on Chinese ships during the Opium War.

Captain Elliot told the British merchants that he would take their opium and turn it over to Commissioner Lin, and that the Crown would compensate them for their losses, the merchants were pleased. Lin received the opium, destroyed it, and lifted the cordon from the factories as promised.

The commissioner had won the battle, but he had given the British an excuse for war. Back in England, opium merchants and cotton textile barons lobbied the British government to take decisive action. Many in England (even some of the opium traders themselves) recognized the immoral nature of the trade. But no other product could generate the profits that opium did. In addition, British merchants and the British government firmly rejected the idea that British subjects should submit to Qing law when on Qing territory. Business interests and national pride alike seemed to require war.

The fighting began in earnest in 1840. British ships and soldiers were dispatched to the Chinese coast. Shallow-draft iron steamships like the *Nemesis,* designed for action in coastal waters and rivers, were particularly effective.[16] English accounts praised the strength and bravery of individual Qing soldiers, but as an organization, the Qing military was no match for the British, whose better weapons, ships, training, and organization guaranteed victory. Commissioner Lin, his reputation in tatters, was exiled to Ili, in far-off Xinjiang. Hard-nosed, but realistic Manchu princes negotiated an end to hostilities in the Treaty of Nanjing in 1842.

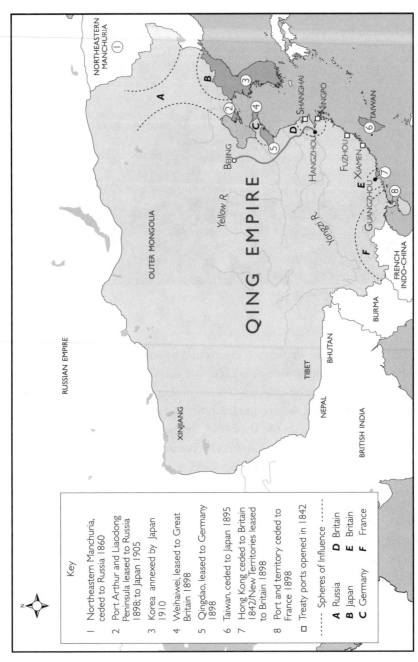

Key

1 Northeastern Manchuria, ceded to Russia 1860
2 Port Arthur and Liaodong Peninsula leased to Russia 1898; to Japan 1905
3 Korea annexed by Japan 1910
4 Weihaiwei, leased to Great Britain 1898
5 Qingdao, leased to Germany 1898
6 Taiwan, ceded to Japan 1895
7 Hong Kong ceded to Britain 1842/New Territories leased to Britain 1898
8 Port and territory ceded to France 1898

□ Treaty ports opened in 1842

------- Spheres of Influence -------

A Russia   D Britain
B Japan   E Britain
C Germany   F France

External challenges to the Qing, mid-19th to early 20th centuries.

The Treaty of Nanjing opened five ports (including Shanghai) to British trade, allowed a British consul in each port, gave Britain the island of Hong Kong "in perpetuity," required equal relations between Qing and British officials of the same rank, ended the monopoly of the licensed "hong" trading firms, set a low tariff on imports and exports, and obliged the Qing to pay Britain an indemnity of twenty-one million silver dollars. A supplementary treaty signed in 1843 provided British subjects with extraterritoriality (the right to have all criminal and civil disputes settled by British consular courts under British law), gave Britain the right to station gunboats in open ports, and granted Britain "most-favored-nation status" (which meant that Britain would automatically gain any privileges the Qing might grant to other foreign powers).

Later generations of Chinese would come to regard the Opium War as marking the inauspicious beginning of China's modern era: the beginning of a century of shame and humiliation. Because the Treaty of Nanjing imposed on the Qing Empire a relationship that was neither reciprocal nor equal, it and subsequent treaties between the Qing and the Western powers came to be known as the "unequal treaties."

But all this lay in the future. Neither the Daoguang emperor nor his officials saw the Opium War as the beginning of a new era. The Manchu negotiators had given the British privileges similar to those that they had earlier granted in far-off Xinjiang to merchants and consular officials from the Inner Asian kingdom of Kokand after suffering repeated invasions from the Kokandi army.[17] Lin Zexu and a few other officials talked of the need for better guns and ships, but there was no great effort to modernize the Qing military. Qing officials still knew almost nothing about the West, its languages, governments, technology, or culture. Westerners were simply another variety of uncivilized barbarian. As such, they were one of many problems. For the Qing soon faced serious challenges within its own borders: multiple rebellions, one of which nearly toppled the government and all that it stood for.

Mid-19th-Century Rebellions

From 1850 to 1878, the Qing struggled to suppress six major rebellions as well as numerous smaller incidents of rebellion and banditry. Two of the great mid-19th-century uprisings, the Taiping rebellion (1850–64) and the Nian rebellion (1851–68), occurred in the heartland of China Proper. The Panthay

Changes in Population/Arable Land Ratios in the Qing[18]

Year	Arable land (qing; 1 qing = 16.5 acres [6.6667 ha])	Population	mu/person (1 mu = .15 acres [.0667 ha])
1660	5,493,576	76,550,608	7.18
1684	6,078,430	81,366,952	7.47
1723	7,236,327	104,447,812	6.93
1752	7,352,218	183,678,259	4.00
1765	7,807,290	208,095,796	3.75
1783	7,605,694	286,331,307	2.66
1812	7,889,256	333,700,560	2.36
1821	7,562,102	372,457,539	2.03
1850	7,562,857	434,394,047	1.74
1901	9,248,812	426,447,325	2.17

rebellion (1853–73), the "Miao" rebellion (1855–72), the Tungan rebellion (1862–73), and Yakub Beg's Muslim kingdom in Xinjiang (1870–78) took place in the empire's always-unstable peripheral areas.

Population growth, environmental exhaustion, climate change, and migration were the fundamental causes underlying the 19th-century rebellions. In the 17th and 18th centuries, the Manchus had built an empire that encompassed China Proper, Taiwan, Mongolia, Xinjiang, and Tibet, as well as their own homeland of Manchuria. Peace, stability, and a period of warmer climate (in contrast to the cooler decades of the late Ming) all contributed to increasing agricultural production and a historically unprecedented population growth, from around two hundred million in 1700 to three hundred fifty million in 1800 and five hundred million by 1900.[19] The Qing also saw the continuation and intensification of the expansion of the urbanization and of the regional, interregional, and maritime commerce that had already so strikingly transformed life and economy in the Ming.

The opening of new fields and the cultivation of New World crops (sweet potatoes, maize, peanuts, and tobacco) were crucial in making continued population growth, urbanization, and commercialization possible.[20] Farmers who lived in areas with easy market access (particularly Jiangnan, Fujian, and the vicinity of Guangzhou) dedicated their fields almost entirely to commercial crops: mulberry trees (for silk production), tea, oil crops, cotton, sugar cane, and tobacco. Adjoining areas like Hunan and Guangxi developed as "rice bowls," exporting to the now grain-deficit areas that specialized in commercial crops.

Both the Qing government and ordinary people were conscious of the problem created by a rising population and too little land. One response was to bring more land under cultivation. The Qing government used a variety of tax incentives and state-sponsored transfer of new farming techniques to encourage the opening of new fields and the introduction of new food crops such as winter wheat in the south and fast-ripening rice in the north. Chinese farming families responded to the shortage of land by opening new fields on uncultivated mountainsides and by migrating into peripheral areas, including many areas already inhabited by non-Chinese peoples.

Migration patterns and the opening of new fields had both environmental and political consequences. In environmental terms, the burning and cutting of forests for timber and to bring land under cultivation caused loss of wildlife habitat, soil erosion, and flooding. By the late 18th century, China's agricultural economy had reached the limits of sustainability. In political terms, Han migration had the effect of knitting the non-Chinese peripheral areas of the Qing Empire more firmly to China Proper. But migration, combined with environmental exhaustion and the consequent competition for resources, created new tensions in many frontier areas and in parts of China Proper as well.

In Inner Mongolia, for example, Han migrants and Buddhist monasteries alike converted pastureland to agricultural uses. Mongol nomads found themselves struggling with decreasing resources and often in debt to Chinese merchants.[21] Han Chinese also migrated to Manchuria, ultimately becoming the majority in the Manchu homeland.[22] In Tibet, distance, altitude, and climate discouraged Chinese migration. The Qing supported the Dalai Lama and the Tibetan aristocracy, who managed Tibet's domestic and foreign affairs on their own. The Tibetan elite had little respect for the Qing but used Tibet's nominal status as a part of the Qing Empire as a diplomatic tool when dealing with aggressive neighbors like the Hindu kingdom of Nepal and British India.[23]

The Mongols did not have the organization or will to revolt, and the Tibetans had no reason to. But in the southwest and the northwest, the Hui (Chinese Muslim), Miao (known in the West as Hmong), and the Turkic Muslims of Xinjiang all found cause to rise up against Qing authority.

In both southwest and northwest China, Hui and non-Muslim Chinese clashed over scarce natural resources—land, water, and, in Yunnan, silver mines. When government response to lawsuits and to communal violence was clearly biased against Muslims, and when Muslims were subject to heavier taxes and criminal penalties than non-Muslims, communal violence became

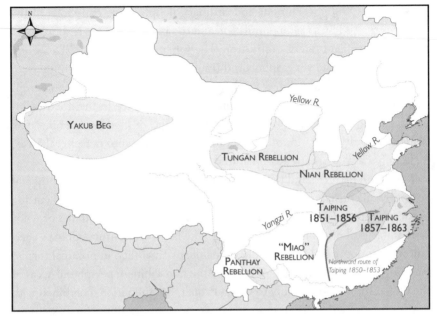

The mid-19th-century rebellions.

rebellion. From 1855 to 1873, Hui people in Yunnan province rose up in the Panthay rebellion. For a time, the rebels controlled all of western Yunnan province and approached France and Britain (unsuccessfully) for assistance.[24] Hui communities in northwest China (Shaanxi, Gansu, and parts of Qinghai, where Hui were also called "Tungan") fought Qing forces in the Tungan rebellion (1862–78).[25]

In the mountainous southwestern Guizhou-Hunan border region, the Qing (following Ming precedent) had repeatedly suppressed Miao communities, forcibly resettling the Miao on government land, where they were charged punitive rents and subjected to policies designed to eliminate their language, culture, and religion.[26] Miao, other non-Han peoples, Hui, and ordinary Han Chinese farmers were all subject to the same environmental pressures: a mountainous terrain, poor soil, endemic poverty, severe competition for resources, and unusually corrupt and abusive local and provincial government.[27] Miao, Han, Hui, and other ethnic groups responded with a series of rebellions (conventionally referred to as the "Miao" Rebellion) lasting from 1855 to 1872.

In Xinjiang, the Qing used military garrisons, military agricultural colonies, joint ventures with merchants, and encouragement of Chinese migrants to defend the frontiers and to generate grain and tax revenue to help pay the costs of administering the area. These techniques did not secure the frontiers, nor did they eliminate Xinjiang's chronic deficit, which still had to be made up with tax silver collected from the wealthy provinces of China Proper. The Qing government's use of local officials—*begs*—to exercise indirect rule over the Turkic Muslim majority of Kashgar, Turfan, and the other oases of southern Xinjiang could not erase underlying popular resentment at being ruled by non-Muslims.

The weakness of the Qing position in Xinjiang became more evident after 1850. The Qing garrison soldiers were underpaid, poorly-trained, and plagued with opium addiction and low morale. The imperial government, financially strapped by the expenses of foreign wars and the fighting against the Nian and Taiping rebellions, could no longer afford to underwrite military and administrative expenses in Xinjiang. *Begs* and Manchu officials attempted to generate more revenue (for themselves as well as to meet administrative expenses) by imposing punitive taxes and corvée labor requirements on the population.[28]

In 1864, rumors that the Qing emperor had ordered the extermination of Tungans (Chinese Muslims) in Xinjiang (and news of how Chinese militias in Shanxi and Gansu had actually conducted mass killings of Chinese Muslims) set off a massive revolt of Tungans, and then of Turkic Muslims. In 1865, a Tajik adventurer named Yakub Beg (c. 1820–77) took advantage of the chaos. With modest support from the British (who granted him a commercial treaty) and the Ottoman Empire (which sent weapons and military advisors), Yakub Beg controlled most of Xinjiang until his death, when Qing armies were already reconquering the territory. Russia helped the Qing to suppress Yakub Beg, but for a price. Russia occupied Xinjiang's strategically important Ili Valley and put itself in a position to dominate Xinjiang's economy through the mid-20th century.

The Muslim, "Miao," and Yakub Beg rebellions lasted as long as they did because two major rebellions in the heartland of China Proper had strained Qing resources to the breaking point: the Nian and Taiping rebellions.

The Nian rebellion resembled the many rebel movements of the Chinese past. In 1851, bandit groups (*nian*) in the drought- and flood-stricken Huai River Valley (the Anhui-Jiangsu-Henan-Shandong border area) coalesced into a loosely organized rebel movement under Zhang Luoxing, an illiterate landlord and salt smuggler who hoped to found his own dynasty. The Nian armies' earth-walled fortified villages and their crack cavalry put up strong resistance to the authorities until they were finally defeated in 1868.[29]

The Taiping rebellion was unlike any other popular rebellion in Chinese history: in addition to threatening the ruling dynasty, it also challenged the economic basis (private landholding) and important elements of the cultural identity of the literati elite. The roots of this massive rebellion, which laid waste to the productive Yangzi Valley, were in the poor remote mountain villages of Guangdong and Guangxi provinces, in the activities of Protestant Christian missionaries in the port city of Guangzhou, and in the experiences of a remarkable individual, Hong Xiuquan (1814–64).

Hong Xiuquan was the son of a farmer in Guangdong province. His family were Hakka—Chinese who had migrated from the north to Guangdong and Guangxi centuries earlier, but who had maintained their own dialect and customs, which kept their communities distinct from those of the majority *bendi* (local) people around them. A bright young man, Hong passed the county-level civil service examinations. In 1836 he went to the provincial capital, Guangzhou, to take the provincial-level examination. He failed, but while in Guangzhou, he was given a Christian tract entitled "Good Words to Admonish the Age," which contained translated passages from both the Old and New Testaments, as well as the Chinese translator's diatribes against Confucianism, Buddhism, and Daoism, and thunderous claims that Chinese civilization had fallen into corruption and immorality.[30]

In 1837, Hong took and failed the provincial examination for a second time. Afterwards, he fell ill. He spent days lost in delirium, in which he felt himself ascending to Heaven, where an old man and wife called him "son" and a younger man addressed him as "younger brother." The two men gave Hong weapons and taught him to kill "demon-devils." Hong recovered, continued to teach school and to try to pass the provincial examination. In 1843, after his fourth and final experience of examination failure in Guangzhou, he re-read "Good Words to Admonish the Age." Now he could interpret his earlier visions: the old man was the god Jehovah. The middle-aged man was Jesus. He, Hong Xiuquan, was God's second son, and he had a mission on earth. God and Jesus wanted him to return the Chinese to the true "Heavenly Teachings" and to kill the devil-demons who were leading them astray: namely, the Manchu and any Chinese who supported the Manchu regime. His victory would usher in a period of "Great Peace" (*Taiping*).

From 1843 to 1847, Hong Xiuquan tramped the countryside of Guangdong and Guangxi, dodging bandits, making converts, and further developing the tenets of his "God-Worshipping religion." Rural Guangdong and Guangxi were dangerous and unstable places. British anti-piracy campaigns had driven pirates upriver, where they preyed on shipping and raided towns and villages. Tensions between *bendi* and Hakka communities often led to violent clashes.

Hong and his earliest followers tapped into Hakka family and community networks to make new converts. They were especially successful in the poor rural Hakka villages in the mountains of Guangxi. Some of the converts experienced spirit possession. Yang Xiuqing, an illiterate Hakka charcoal-burner, began to speak with the voice of God the Father. Jesus spoke through Xiao Chaogui, a Hakka farmer. Others had visions of Hong's coming greatness.

As their numbers grew, the God-Worshippers offered their members a strong community and mutual protection, important benefits in the violent, militarized society of rural Guangxi. For the same reasons, local elites and local government began to view them as a dangerous cult. In 1850, a government attempt to suppress the God-Worshippers pushed them into rebellion. Pursued by Qing soldiers, the Taiping forces, men, women, and children, swept through the countryside, by land and by river, sometimes taking and holding towns for weeks or months, winning new converts and supporters, which more than made up for their losses.

Moving north from Guangxi, through Hunan province, they took the great city of Wuchang on the Yangzi River in January 1853, with its treasure, weapons, and people. From Wuchang, the Taiping moved downriver to occupy the city of Nanjing on 19 March. Here, Hong Xiuquan and his followers, a million strong, established the Heavenly Capital of the Kingdom of Heavenly Peace. A Taiping army struck out to the west to reconquer cities and territory along the Yangzi up to Wuchang. A second army was dispatched northward, to drive the Manchu out of their capital, which Hong had renamed "Demon's Den."[31]

Even while on the march, Hong and the other Taiping leaders continued to refine and write down their religious teachings and their political and social goals. The Taiping religion drew eclectically on the Christian Bible, the Confucian classics, and Chinese folk culture. The Manchu rulers, Confucian orthodoxy, Daoism, and Buddhism were to be destroyed, replaced by worship of the Christian God. Land would be taken from landlords and redistributed. Women and men would be strictly separated (other than for conjugal visits necessary for reproduction) and organized into teams and brigades, military style, for agricultural production and war. Both male and female units worked the fields and went into battle. Women (following Hakka tradition) would not bind their feet. Taxes and confiscated wealth would go into a common "Heavenly Treasury." Hong would rule benevolently over an egalitarian utopia.

The Taiping social program was scarcely put into practice. The Taiping armies did much damage to the areas that they passed through, but they never established effective county-level government. Landlordism remained intact in the countryside. In the cities, Taiping society was anything but egalitarian: distribution of goods varied according to rank. Hong and the other top leaders helped themselves to the "Heavenly Treasury" and enjoyed luxurious palaces well-stocked with food, drink, and concubines.

The leaders also fought among themselves. In 1856 the illiterate Yang Xiuqing, a brilliant general as well as the voice of God, moved to concentrate political and religious authority into his own hands. This sparked a series of bloody purges in which Yang, twenty thousand of his family and alleged supporters, and several other powerful Taiping leaders and their families were killed or driven away, leaving Hong Xiuquan in control.

Despite the killings, the Taiping were at the height of their power in 1856. They controlled important cities along the Yangzi from Nanjing to Wuchang and the rich agricultural land of Jiangxi.[32] With some of the most productive land (and its tax revenues) in the hands of the rebels or torn apart by fighting, and facing the Panthay, "Miao," Tungan, and Nian rebellions, the Qing government was in desperate straits.

At first, the Qing used its Banner forces and the Green Standard Army (a force composed of Han Chinese soldiers) against the Taiping and other rebels. These regular armies won some victories: cavalry under a Mongol general defeated the poorly planned Taiping northern advance. Local militias across the Yangzi Valley fought to defend their communities. None of these forces, however, were able to defeat the Taiping armies. The Green Standard and Banner forces lacked strength, discipline, and modern weapons. Local militia forces were too small and decentralized. The circumstances called for a new kind of army—and for new weapons.

Zeng Guofan (1811–72), a high-ranking Qing official, observed how local elites mobilized and coordinated militia to fight the Taiping in his home province of Hunan. He admired their spirit and initiative, but realized that they did not have the training, the weapons, the logistical capability, or the sheer numbers to defeat the Taiping. With the court's approval, Zeng built a new army. As a Hunan man, he drew on a network of family, friends, and former students to recruit officers. They in turn drew on their networks of friends and relations.[33] As a result, Zeng's army was closely identified with Hunan province and was known informally as the Hunan Army. Zeng also arranged funding for his army, negotiating with provincial governors for direct transfer of tax revenue to his coffers and getting an internal transit tax on goods in shipment—the *lijin* tax—similarly earmarked for his expenses. In 1856, Zeng had equipped his army with modern Western weapons and had put it into action.

By working with Zeng Guofan to create the Hunan Army and equip it with modern weapons, the Qing court was responding in new ways to the multiple crises that faced it in the summer of 1856. The learning curve was steep. It was about to get steeper.

Self-Strengthening and the 1898 Reform Movement

On 8 October 1856, a *lorcha* (a Chinese-built Western schooner with Chinese rigging) called the *Arrow* rode at anchor in Guangzhou harbor.[34] The Chinese merchant who owned the ship had obtained British registry and an Irish "captain of convenience" in Hong Kong. This was a common way in which Chinese took advantage of British extraterritoriality to put their ships beyond the reach of the Qing government. In this case, however, Qing forces had reliable reports that the *Arrow* was involved in piracy. Probably unaware of the *Arrow*'s British registry, Qing soldiers boarded the ship and took the crew into custody while the Irish captain was breakfasting with friends on a nearby vessel. Some witnesses later claimed that the Qing soldiers hauled down the *Arrow*'s British flag and flung it on the deck; other witnesses said that the flag had not been flying at all, and thus could not have been hauled down.

Whatever the truth of the matter, the British government had already been planning a second war in China. The alleged insult to the Union Jack, and the Chinese authorities' refusal to apologize, were sufficient cause for war. The British deemed it immaterial that the *Arrow*'s British registry had lapsed before the incident took place and that the ship therefore had no legal right to British protection. As with the Opium War, the real issue at stake in the *Arrow* War (1856–60) was the opium trade, which was still very important to both Britain and its colony in India. This time the British, joined by the French, invaded Beijing, looted the city, and burned the Yuanmingyuan Summer Palace with its ornate Italian-style buildings. In peace negotiations, the British, French, Russians, and Americans collectively demanded ambassadorial relations, more open ports, the right to run ships up the Yangzi River, lower tariffs, another indemnity, and that the Qing promise to protect the Christian religion.[35]

The Qing fought the *Arrow* War while still struggling with the Taiping and other mid-19th-century rebellions. Together, these wars sapped the Qing

government's strength and brought home the lesson that it had failed to take
to heart after the first Opium War: the need to modernize its military. From
around 1860 through 1894, the Qing government embarked upon a program
of "Self-Strengthening." The leaders of the Self-Strengthening movement were
the men who rose to prominence by creating the new armies that defeated
the Taiping rebellion.

Zeng Guofan's Hunan Army was the first of these provincial-based new
armies. Zeng urged his younger colleague, Li Hongzhang (1823–1901), an
Anhui man, to build another army—the Anhui Army. Zuo Zongtang (1812–
1885), another Zeng protégé, worked to modernize the regular Qing forces
that he commanded as governor-general of Fujian and Zhejiang provinces.
Zeng, Li, and Zuo used modern weapons and Western training methods to
build their armies and defeat the Taiping. By January 1864, the Qing forces
had isolated Taiping armies in the field and surrounded the "Heavenly Capital" (Nanjing). With the city under siege, Hong Xiuquan died, perhaps of
illness, in June. Zeng Guofan's troops captured the capital in mid-July, slaughtering over one hundred thousand Taiping rebels as they searched through
the city for resisters. The remaining Taiping armies and leaders were defeated, captured, and executed over the next few years, the last of them, who
had linked up with the Nian rebels, falling in 1868.[36]

With the Taiping finally defeated, the new armies went on to assist in the
suppression of the Nian, "Miao," Panthay, and Tungan rebellions. Zuo Zongtang crowned his career with the reconquest of Xinjiang—territory that
some Chinese advisors to the throne would have left to Yakub Beg or the Russians on the grounds that resources needed for maritime defense should not
be spent on recovering a desert.[37]

Zeng Guofan's Hunan army was disbanded after the victory over the Taiping, some of its units being assigned to other armies. But Zeng, until his death
in 1872, Li Hongzhang, Zuo Zongtang, and other Qing generals and officials
moved forward with Self-Strengthening. What, they asked, had made the foreigners so strong, while the Qing was so weak? "Strong ships and effective
guns," answered Feng Guifen (1809–74), another Self-Strengthening official.[38]

From 1865 through 1894, with Li Hongzhang playing a key leading role,
the Qing government invested heavily in modern military equipment, built
the new Tianjin, Nanjing, and Jiangnan arsenals, the Fuzhou shipyard, and
modern, Western-style naval and army units. Despite Feng Guifen's famous
"ships and guns" formula, Self-Strengthening went beyond the purely military: other projects included a steamship company, textile mills, mines, a
school of foreign languages, schools of science and technology in the Fuzhou

Empress Dowager Cixi.

shipyard and Jiangnan arsenal, and programs for sending Chinese students to America, England, and France. The government also acted to strengthen its administrative control over peripheral areas of the empire: Tibet, Xinjiang, Mongolia, and Taiwan. All were areas in which native non-Han people might collude with foreign powers—Britain, Russia, or Japan—to release themselves from Manchu control.

None of the Self-Strengtheners' projects would have been possible without the support, or at least the indulgence, of Manchu princes and the Empress Dowager Cixi (1835–1908). This powerful woman, the widow of the Xianfeng emperor (r. 1851–61), controlled the government after her husband's death, first placing her young son, the Tongzhi emperor (r. 1862–74), on the throne, and then, when he died of smallpox, enthroning her nephew, the Guangxu emperor (r. 1875–1907).

Cixi supported Li Hongzhang, who returned the favor, but the Self-Strengtheners were only one of several court factions which she needed to balance against one another. The strength of conservative factions limited the scope of Self-Strengthening. So too did the Qing government's financial weakness and the astronomical costs of Self-Strengthening projects, which relied on government funds and foreign loans. And like any government undertaking, Self-Strengthening enterprises were always subject to corruption.

Self-Strengthening built the beginnings of a modern military and a modern military-industrial complex. But it did not make the Qing powerful enough to defend its territory. Impressive victories in several battles during the Sino-French War (1884–85) were little compensation for the ultimate defeat, in which the French utterly destroyed a modern naval unit of eleven Chinese-built ships in Fuzhou in less than an hour. The French gained Qing acknowledgment of French control of Vietnam as well as access to trade in southwestern China.[39] Defeat at the hands of the French was bad enough, but an even more shocking setback was in store.

In 1852 the American commodore Matthew Perry forcibly opened Tokugawa Japan to relations with the West. In response to the Tokugawa shogunate's weakness, a group of samurai overthrew the shogun and set up a new government under the Japanese Meiji emperor (r. 1868–1912) and put Japan on the road to modernization. Seeking a colony of its own, Japan fought the Qing for control of Korea in the Sino-Japanese War of 1894–95. The Japanese defeated Qing forces at sea and on land.

In the Treaty of Shimonoseki (1895), the Qing ceded the island of Taiwan to Japan, paid an indemnity, and was forced to give Japan a ninety-nine-year lease on Manchuria's Liaodong Peninsula and its strategically important harbor of Lüshun (known in English as Port Arthur). A diplomatic "Triple Intervention" by Russia, France, and Germany forced Japan to back down from this last demand, but at a price—two years later, Russia demanded and received the same lease, thus fulfilling its dream of controlling an ice-free ocean port for its navy.

Defeat by Japan, a former tributary, was a shock after some thirty years of military modernization. For Qing officials and their increasingly concerned Chinese subjects, the question remained: Why are we so weak, and why are the Western powers—and now Japan—so strong? The Self-Strengtheners had focused heavily (though not exclusively) on technology. Their attitude had been to "take Chinese learning as the foundation, and Western learning for its applications." In other words, use Western techniques to defend the Qing dynasty and civilization. A new generation was now prepared to suggest new answers. Most prominent among them was a scholar from Guangzhou named Kang Youwei (1858–1927).

Kang was a voracious reader and observer of Western learning and society. In the 1890s, he shocked the scholarly world when he published a book arguing that Confucius had been a reformer and that all the standard "Old Text" versions of the Confucian classics (said to have been discovered in a wall of the home of Confucius' descendants during the Later Han dynasty), on which the civil service examinations were based, were forgeries. Instead, it was the "New Text" version of the classics (reproduced from memory in the Early Han and written in the "new script" of the period) that were authentic. This intellectual sleight of hand, which scholars now do not accept, allowed Kang to use key parts of the New Text classics to argue that human history is defined by progress and that government institutions need to be reformed to meet the needs of changing times.[40]

Confident that history had chosen him to save the Qing, Kang argued for reform in books and in memorials to the emperor. His reinterpretation of Confucianism made him too radical for many, but the young Guangxu emperor was impressed. On 16 June 1898, the emperor granted Kang, a relatively low-ranking official, an unprecedented two-and-a-half-hour audience during which he discussed reform proposals and asked Kang to continue to send him information and suggestions.[41] Kang urged Guangxu to imitate Peter the Great of Russia and Japan's Meiji emperor: rulers who had reformed and strengthened their governments and modernized their nations.

For about a hundred days during the summer of 1898, Guangxu issued a series of edicts inspired by Kang's advice. The examination system was to use "questions and themes" on contemporary issues instead of the formulaic old "eight-legged essays." There was to be compulsory education with a modern, Western curriculum for all children over six years of age. New naval academies and professional schools of mining, agriculture, manufacturing, business, and railroad technology were to be established. The government was to be reorganized.

At first, the Empress Dowager Cixi supported the reforms, or at least allowed them. But when the emperor tried to create a new Planning Board to coordinate reform policies and demanded that low-ranking officials be allowed to send memorials to the throne, he ran into serious trouble. Conservatives feared that this would sideline existing institutions and officials. In mid-September, they asked the empress dowager to intervene. At the same time, Kang Youwei and other reformers sought Anglo-American and Japanese support and tried to get General Yuan Shikai (1859–1916), commander of the powerful, modernized Northern Army, to participate in a coup against the empress dowager.

When Yuan chose to support his patron Cixi, the game was over. On 21 September, Cixi put the emperor under house arrest and resumed power. Kang Youwei and one of his young protégés, Liang Qichao (1873–1929), escaped to Japan, but many other officials associated with the "Hundred Days' Reform" were arrested and executed. Most of Guangxu's edicts had not even been carried out. Reform was over—for the moment. It would return again, in a most unexpected way. But when it did, the Qing would have to deal with far more than just its own weakness: changes in society and culture were eroding the foundations of the Qing system.

Imperialism, Nationalism, and Cultural Change

As the Western powers and Japan defeated the Qing in various wars, they acquired rights, privileges, indemnities, leases, and even a few pieces of Qing territory. The Sino-Japanese War (1894–95) intensified this "carving of the Chinese melon." Cautiously competing with one another, the major foreign powers defined parts of Qing territory as their "spheres of interest." The Russians regarded Xinjiang and Mongolia as parts of their sphere of interest, as well as Manchuria, where they had constructed the East China Railway and the South Manchurian Railway to link the naval base at Lüshun (Port Arthur), Vladivostok, and the Siberian Railway.

The Japanese challenged the Russians in Manchuria, owned Taiwan outright, and had their eyes on Fujian province, across the strait from Taiwan. Germany had a ninety-nine-year lease on the Shandong port city of Qingdao, and thus regarded Shandong as their sphere of interest. The British had Hong Kong and a lease on the adjacent "New Territories," and claimed the Yangzi Valley as their sphere. The French sphere of interest was in southwest provinces of Yunnan, Guangxi, and Guizhou, which bordered French Indochina. The Americans, not mighty enough to command a sphere of interest, announced in the "Open Door Policy" in 1899 that all powers must respect China's territorial sovereignty and (perhaps more to the point) allow merchants from other countries to trade without prejudice in their respective spheres of interest and leased "concession areas" in the treaty ports.

The concession areas in China's great port cities were permanent foreign communities, complete with governments, laws, police forces, newspapers, and places of entertainment. They were also home to many Chinese who worked with foreign businesses, missionary organizations, or who sought to use the foreigners' extraterritoriality to escape the control of the Qing government. In these foreign enclaves, especially in Shanghai, Chinese writers, publishers, and students interacted with Westerners and Japanese, many of whom were anxious to spread "civilization" and "progress" to China.[42]

Chinese in the concession areas were beyond the reach of Qing law. This was good not only for shady business deals, but also for writers, publishers, and leaders of anti-Manchu organizations. The treaty ports became centers of intellectual activity and publishing. Modern newspapers devoted to commercial news were published from the 1860s. After the Sino-Japanese War, concern about national and world affairs led to the development of an active political press operating from the safe havens of the treaty ports. Modern commercial publishing enabled reformist writers to reach a readership of perhaps three to four million in the first decade of the 20th century—that is, around one percent of the Chinese population.[43] This was a significant, but still small intellectual elite. Increasingly, this elite readership consisted of men and women who were interested in new ideas and educated in new schools that challenged the old civil service examination system's monopoly on learning.

The examination system had always been controversial. Song, Ming, and early Qing critics blasted the examinations for emphasizing rote memorization and failing to identify men with the knowledge and skills needed to solve practical problems. Late-19th-century reformers argued that "Western Learning" and contemporary political issues should be incorporated into the system. But the examinations were a bastion of entrenched interests. Conservatives deeply believed that the moral philosophy on which the examinations were based was essential to the survival of the government and of civilization. Practically speaking, many men's identities, lifestyles, careers, and salaries were bound up in the status quo. This made meaningful reform impossible.[44]

Since examination reform was impossible, new types of education and with them a new sort of educated man—and woman—developed outside the framework of the examination system. The new shipyards, naval units, military academies, private schools, missionary schools, women's schools, and study abroad produced a generation of intellectuals who owed nothing to the examination system or its curriculum.

The movement for women's education was one of the most revolutionary aspects of these changes. It also underlines the ways in which education was related to the larger project of "saving the nation."

Male reformers held that women's illiteracy was a cause of national weakness. Only when women were properly educated could they contribute to the economic life of the country and become better mothers in the bargain. (Male reformers tended to ignore the economically productive work that women had always performed as laborers and managers of households.) It was to bring women into the great task of strengthening the nation that Kang Youwei campaigned against foot-binding and a group of men including Liang Qichao laid plans for the first Chinese Girls' School in 1897.[45]

The Girls' School opened with sixteen students on 31 May 1898. Women like the reformer Xue Shaohui (1855–1911) were in charge of running the school and establishing its curriculum. For them, the goals of women's education went beyond strengthening the country. They wanted to prepare women to take part in public life on equal terms with men. As one of them put it in an editorial in the women-run *Women's Journal* in 1898:

> We have torn down the huge billboard that signals the difference
> between the public words [of men] and the inner words [of women],
> breaking down the barrier between the two.[46]

With the Girls' School, study groups, and the *Women's Journal,* women reformers began to redefine women's private and public roles, worked to raise female literacy rates, questioned the practice of concubinage (which male reformers generally did not), and challenged the cult of female chastity.

Feminism was only one of many new ideas which the Chinese adapted to their own purposes as they engaged more fully with the West. Translations of Western fiction and nonfiction revolutionized the way in which Chinese intellectuals thought about their own culture, the West, and their place in the world. Three men—Lin Shu (1852–1924), Yan Fu (1853–1921), and Liang Qichao—played major roles in translating Western ideas into Chinese.

Lin Shu, who did not read any foreign languages himself, had friends render oral translations of Western novels, which he then rewrote in elegant classical Chinese. His concern with China's weakness and the sources of Western power drove his choice of material: the works of H. Rider Haggard and other adventure novels illustrated the aggressive nature of Westerners; *Uncle Tom's Cabin* and Charles Dickens' novels revealed the racism and social injustice which lay at the very heart of Western "civilization."[47]

Yan Fu shared his friend Lin Shu's concerns, but his search for answers led him in other directions. In 1898, Yan Fu introduced the Chinese reading public to social Darwinism when he published *On Evolution,* a free translation, with commentary, of Thomas Huxley's lectures on "Evolution and Ethics."[48] In translations of Adam Smith's *Wealth of Nations,* John Stuart Mill's *On Liberty,* Baron de Montesquieu's *Spirit of the Laws,* and others, Yan Fu drove his message home. The Chinese nation was losing the struggle for the survival of the fittest. The key to winning was to learn what the Westerners and the Japanese had already discovered: when a state enables all the people to fulfill their potential, then their collective energy and achievements will produce tremendous national strength and unity of purpose.[49]

Like Yan Fu, whose work he read, Liang Qichao (in exile in Japan after 1898) feared that the "white race" was winning the evolutionary struggle and that a free, educated people were the key to national strength. Liang became an advocate of liberty and democracy, but he did not see these things as goals in and of themselves. Liberty would contribute to national wealth and power; democracy would provide a way for the people and the government to communicate effectively with one another and reach agreement on the best interests of the nation as a whole.[50]

Liang was convinced that democracy would bring national unity, but he was also convinced that the Chinese were not yet civilized and educated enough to participate rationally and effectively in democratic government. In order to spread his ideas and to contribute toward the enlightenment of the Chinese, Liang edited and published influential journals in which he and other reform-minded writers introduced a broad readership to new ideas. His publications, especially the *New Citizen,* published in Tokyo from 1903 to 1907 and smuggled into China, reached hundreds of thousands of readers.[51]

As they searched for the causes of Chinese weakness and the sources of Western wealth and power, some Chinese intellectuals began to question not just the efficiency of their government institutions, but the monarchy itself and the Manchus' right to rule. Self-Strengtheners like Li Hongzhang and reformers like Kang Youwei had tried to save their Great Qing. But more and more men and women were coming to the conclusion that the Manchus were part of the problem and that violent revolution was the solution. One of them was a young medical doctor named Sun Yat-sen (1866–1925).

Sun was the son of a poor farmer from a village near Macao. One of Sun's elder brothers had made his fortune running shops and managing sugarcane fields in Hawaii. Sun was educated (and converted to Christianity) in an Anglican mission school in Hawaii, and then at the College of Medicine for Chinese in Hong Kong. But Sun's real passion was not medicine: it was politics. After earning his medical degree, he tried to enter the service of Li Hongzhang. Li, who had no use or respect for a foreign-educated peasant, rejected him.[52] So in 1894, Sun created his own revolutionary organization, the Revive China Society, with branches in Hawaii and Hong Kong.[53]

At the time, Sun had no clear ideology or plans for China's future. He did have an immediate goal: overthrow the Manchus. Working in Hong Kong and

Guangzhou in 1895, Sun put together a shaky coalition of would-be rebels, Chinese Christians, Triad (criminal gang) members, and mercenaries. The plan was to attack and capture the walled city of Guangzhou, which would spark a general revolution. The plot fell apart. Sun fled to Japan, and then to England, a fugitive with a price on his head.

The Guangzhou plot was the first of Sun's eleven failed attempts to over-throw the Qing. It was also the beginning of his reputation as a world-famous revolutionary leader. In October 1896, men from the Chinese Legation in London captured Sun in order to send him back to Beijing for execution. Sun appealed to the Legation's English housekeeper and her husband as fellow Christians to deliver a note to his well-connected English friends, who alerted the British government. Diplomatic pressure soon gained Sun's re-lease. Now he was truly famous. He gave interviews, published an account of his imprisonment, and generally made himself into a celebrity.

When he returned to Tokyo in 1897, Sun was a leading (but not univer-sally loved) figure in the fractious community of Chinese students and polit-ical exiles. From exile, Sun observed the failure of Kang Youwei's 1898 reforms. He made friends with Japanese adventurers, Pan-Asianists, and gov-ernment officials. He raised money for the Revive China Society, directed another botched rebellion in 1900, and continued to think, write, and talk about overthrowing the Qing and driving the Westerners out of China. The Qing authorities were certainly aware of Sun's activities at the turn of the century, but they had many more immediate problems to deal with.

The Boxer Affair and the Empress Dowager's Reforms

The Qing government responded to Western aggression with diplomacy, war, and programs like Self-Strengthening. Intellectuals responded by using Chinese and Western ideas to identify the causes of Chinese weakness and the sources of Western power. Revolutionaries saw the Manchu as the problem. But when ordinary Chinese farmers believed that Western actions threatened their livelihood, they reacted with direct attacks on Westerners or manifes-tations of Western influence.

It was easy for common folk to identify Westerners and their Chinese Christian followers as "outsiders" and to blame them when things went wrong. Foreign goods and foreign technology threatened to put Chinese spinners, weavers, and boatmen out of business. Foreign houses, roads, and churches harmed the *feng shui* (the balance of geomantic forces). The practice of

Christianity offended the local gods. Attacks on Westerners and Chinese Christians occurred across the empire, but they were most common in places afflicted with flood, drought, scarcity, and high grain prices.[54]

The most famous instance of anti-foreign violence was the Boxer movement of 1899–1900. The Boxer movement began in the western hinterland of Shandong province. The area was poor to begin with. German Catholic missionaries brought instability and social tensions with their aggressive proselytizing, their churchbuilding, and their ability to intervene in lawsuits on behalf of Chinese Christian plaintiffs. Attacks on missionaries and Chinese Christians were common. The murder of two German missionaries in 1897, for example, gave Germany an excuse to demand a long-term lease on the Shandong port of Jiaozhou and its city of Qingdao, from which it proceeded to make Shandong its sphere of influence.[55]

In August 1898, the Yellow River flooded, destroying crops and homes in western Shandong. Drought followed across the North China Plain in 1898–1900. Rural men were left desperate and—since they had no crops to tend—unemployed. Many were attracted to the teachings of itinerant martial arts teachers and herbal medicine peddlers whose training included spirit possession and rituals that claimed to provide immunity to swords, spears, and bullets. In the spring of 1899, groups of these "Spirit Boxers" calling themselves the "Boxers United in Righteousness" launched large-scale attacks on Chinese Christians.

In the winter and spring of 1899–1900, the Boxer movement spread rapidly across the drought-stricken northern Chinese provinces of Zhili, Henan, and Shanxi. Boxers attacked Chinese Christians and Western missionaries, burned churches, clashed with Qing forces, and tore up railways and telegraph lines to hamper government communications and troop movements. When Boxers entered Beijing and Tianjin in the spring of 1900, foreigners feared for their lives and requested additional protection from their governments.

At first, the Qing court was ambivalent about the Boxers. Conservatives wanted to use the Boxers to fight the foreign powers. Reformers thought that the Boxers were rebellious commoners who should be repressed before their anti-foreign violence gave the European powers an excuse to demand further concessions or even start another war. The empress dowager resolved this ambivalence on 21 June, when she declared war against the eight foreign powers whose naval forces were gathering in Tianjin harbor: Britain, Japan, Germany, Italy, Russia, France, the United States, and Austria-Hungary. Imperial troops and Boxers had already put foreigners and Chinese Christians under siege in Beijing's Northern Cathedral and Legation Quarter. Boxers,

Men captured by the 6th U.S. Cavalry in Tianjin during the Boxer War.

sometimes with official support, were destroying property and killing Chinese Christians and Western missionaries in Henan, Shanxi, and Zhili provinces.

The empress dowager's Boxer War did not go well. Some modern Qing forces fought effectively against the Eight-Nation Army's invasion of Tianjin and its march on Beijing.[56] But General Yuan Shikai, now governor of Shandong, disobeyed orders to send his powerful Beiyang Army to defend the capital. Neither Yuan nor the governors of the southern provinces wanted to waste their armies in a hopeless war. Instead, they prevented any Boxer activity in their provinces. In return, the foreign armies left them alone. The allied powers took Tianjin on 14 July, and reached Beijing a month later, freeing their compatriots in the besieged Legation Quarter.

Defeated yet again, the empress dowager and her court withdrew to Xi'an. Her officials negotiated yet another set of treaties which required apologies to the governments whose nationals had been killed, punishment of officials who had supported the Boxers, and a total indemnity of 450,000,000 taels of silver (over 36,000,000 pounds or 16,000,000 kg), to be paid in installments (with four percent per annum interest) from 1901 to 1940.[57]

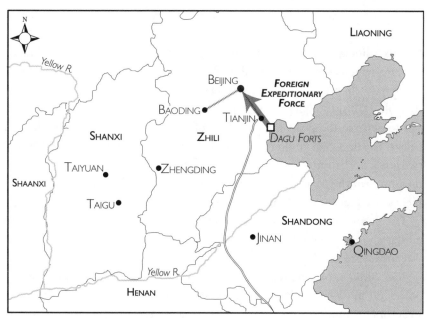

The area of the Boxer uprising, 1900.

The foreign troops inflicted their own, more direct punishment: wanton destruction of homes and buildings, pillage, looting, and rape in Tianjin and Beijing, systematic destruction of temples and walls, and executions (sometimes by crucifixion) of suspected Boxers in cities where foreign missionaries had been killed.[58] The foreigners had their revenge. The Qing court debated the reasons for its losses and began planning further reform and more military modernization.

No world leader would envy Empress Dowager Cixi's position in 1901. The Qing had just lost another war, the government was underfunded and deeply in debt, foreign powers continued to compromise the country's sovereignty, and tensions were building between the ruling Manchu elite and the Han Chinese who made up the vast majority of the population. Dire circumstances called for decisive action.

On 29 January 1901, Cixi asked high-ranking officials to "reflect carefully on the present sad state of affairs and to scrutinize Chinese and Western governmental systems, with regard to all dynastic regulations, national administration, official affairs, matters related to people's livelihood, modern schools, systems of examination, military organization, and financial administration. Duly weigh what should be kept and what abolished, what new methods should be adopted and what old ones retained."[59] Recommendations were expected within two months.[60]

This edict was the beginning of the "New Policies"—a series of major reforms which continued until the 1911 Revolution which led to the fall of the dynasty. In pursuing reform, Cixi hoped to strengthen the country in its struggle against foreign powers, to preserve the Manchu's position as rulers, and to reverse the growing alienation of Han Chinese from their Manchu rulers. The first goal could not be achieved in a short time, while the second two goals were mutually contradictory. Efforts to preserve and even enhance the power of the Manchu aristocracy further offended Han Chinese and fed their sense that the Manchu were simply a race of alien conquerors.

The empress dowager's New Policies began on the familiar ground of military modernization. Acquisition and domestic production of modern weapons were still high priorities, but so too were the education and training needed if modern weapons were to be used effectively. Yuan Shikai's powerful, modernized Beiyang Army served as a model and a source of instructors for modern New Army units, which were set up in the provinces. Japan, too, served as a model of military organization and drill and a source of instructors. Many young Chinese men attended Japanese military academies during this period, including future general and president of the Republic of China Chiang Kai-shek (1887–1975). Some efforts were made to modernize units from the old Banner and Green Standard armies, but for the most part, modernization bypassed these forces, which were becoming little more than financial burdens for the government.

The New Policies did not stop at military modernization. Imperial, provincial, and city officials built China's first modern police forces and prisons, drafted a new law code, and proposed changes in the educational system and in the structure of government. The changes resembled, but reached far deeper than, the changes which Kang Youwei had attempted to carry out (and which the empress dowager had rejected) in 1898. Reforms in education and proposals for constitutional government brought change to institutions that had existed in their present form since the early Ming. These reforms weakened the foundations of Qing rule and contributed to the dynasty's collapse in 1911.

The civil service examinations were the core of the Qing educational system. Reformers like Kang Youwei had criticized the examination system for producing men whose educational achievements were completely irrelevant to the business of government. But the examination system remained the only route to social status and a career in the civil service. The examination system also created a symbolic link between the Han scholar elite and their Manchu emperor, whose role as head of the examination system also made him, though a Manchu, the chief patron of Han Chinese civilization and its moral philosophy.

In 1905, Cixi, acting on the advice of Yuan Shikai and other Han reformist officials, issued an edict which ended the examination system as of 1906. Students who had been torn between the practical need for modern education and the career necessity of earning a traditional degree were relieved. The Ministry of Education planned and began to build a Japanese-style modern system of primary and secondary schools and universities, complete with state-mandated regulations, curriculum, and textbooks.[61] The reform was certainly necessary, even overdue. But with the abolition of the examinations, the Manchu throne was no longer the patron of Chinese learning or the sole source of professional accreditation that it had been.

Reform of the government, too, was inspired by the Japanese. From 1901 to 1905, government reform simply involved reorganization of the bureaucracy. The court jettisoned the old system of Six Ministries (Rites, War, Revenue, Personnel, Works, and Punishment) in favor of new ministries: Foreign Affairs, Commerce, Military Training, Police, Education, and so on.[62] But in 1904–1905, China witnessed yet another demonstration of Japanese strength when Japan fought, and won, the Russo-Japanese War on Chinese territory. Japan took Russia's leases and concessions in Manchuria, including Lüshun and the South Manchurian Railway. Japan was now the dominant foreign power in Korea and Manchuria. Japan's victory further compromised Qing sovereignty, but it was also an inspiration: an Asian nation had fought and defeated a European power.

What was the secret of Japan's success? Its program of military modernization, to be sure; but also its constitutional monarchy. It was this modern system of government, Manchu and Chinese observers concluded, that had built a strong nation and created identity and unity of purpose between the Meiji emperor and his subjects. Manchu reforms hoped that what a constitution could do for Japan and the Meiji emperor, it could do for the Manchu Qing emperor as well.

On 27 August 1908, the Qing court adopted its "Principles of the Constitution." This document, which Yuan Shikai had helped to draft, laid out a step-by-step plan for implementing constitutional government. As with Meiji Japan and Otto von Bismarck's Germany, the proposed system would be a constitutional monarchy with a strong throne. Elected provincial assemblies (to meet in 1909) and a National Assembly (to meet in 1910) would be advisory bodies. They would assist in the drafting of a constitution, which would be promulgated in 1916. A real elected parliament would follow in 1917.[63]

Whether they affected government, law, policing, prisons, or education, the New Policies were controversial. Even seemingly small matters could rouse storms of opposition. Manchu conservatives firmly rejected all suggestions that Chinese men be allowed to cut off the queues which symbolized Chinese subservience to the Manchu conquerors. Han Chinese pawnshop owners and clothing merchants lobbied intensively against proposals to Westernize court dress—proposals which would have left them holding worthless stocks of robes, caps, and shoes.[64] Major issues often required balancing of rival interests through compromise. A completely rewritten Qing law code which would not have been based on Confucian moral philosophy, filial piety, and family structure faced determined opposition from conservatives and had to be revised.[65] But the most dangerous thing about the reforms was they way in which they helped to widen the gap between the Manchu court and its Chinese subjects.

As she directed the design and implementation of the New Policies, Empress Dowager Cixi intended not just to strengthen the country, but also to strengthen the monarchy and the central government. She died on 15 November 1908. One of her last acts was to appoint Aisin Gioro Puyi (1906–67), then two and a half years old, as successor to her nephew the Guangxu emperor, who had passed away after a long illness on 14 November.[66] Puyi's father Zaifeng (1883–1951) ran the government as regent for his son, the emperor. He continued to implement the New Policies, but with even more emphasis on putting Manchu aristocrats in charge of the central government and the armed forces.

Cixi and Regent Zaifeng's policies of recentralization and re-Manchuization encountered resistance on many levels. Of course, it was relatively easy for Cixi and Zaifeng to stack central government offices with Manchu aristocrats and to transfer or fire governors and other high-ranking officials. For example, in 1908, Regent Zaifeng, who feared that General Yuan Shikai was too powerful, forced the reformer and creator of the Beiyang Army to retire, officially because of a "foot ailment." But the central government was never able to effectively centralize control over provincial finances or the provincially based New Army units which were paid for from provincial budgets. To do that would have required a major overhaul of the decentralized and chaotic tax system—a gargantuan task that the central government was simply not able to attempt.[67]

The Manchu court also had little control over developments in Chinese society during the years of the New Policies. China and overseas Chinese communities were seething with new ideas, new newspapers and magazines, political movements, movements for social reform, and movements for revolution. Kang Youwei and Liang Qichao continued to advocate reform from their base in Tokyo, but their voices were increasingly drowned out by the cries of more radical elements.

In China, an eighteen-year-old student named Zou Rong (1885–1905) published a pamphlet entitled "The Revolutionary Army" (1903), in which he cried: "Sweep away millennia of despotism in all its forms, throw off millennia of slavishness, annihilate the five million and more of the furry and horned Manchu race, cleanse ourselves of 260 years of harsh and unremitting pain, so that the soil of the Chinese subcontinent is made immaculate, and the descendants of the Yellow Emperor will all become Washingtons."[68] Qiu Jin, a young woman who had studied in Japan and liked to pose for photographs dressed in men's clothing and carrying an unsheathed knife, combined feminism with nationalism in her 1906 "Address to Two Hundred Million Fellow Countrywomen": "When a country is near destruction, women cannot rely on the men any more because they aren't even able to protect themselves."[69]

Zou Rong died in an English jail in Shanghai. Qiu Jin was executed for her part in a failed plot to assassinate a Manchu official. Young radicals like Zou Rong and Qiu Jin were not interested in reform: they wanted to see the Manchu government overthrown and the Manchu exterminated or at least driven back to Manchuria. Hatred of the Manchu, ideas of revolution, anarchism, and democracy, determination to resist foreign imperialism, and the beginnings of a rejection of China's patriarchal family ideology were everywhere, but these sentiments were not linked to any strong organization or clear goals for the future. The closest thing one could find to a recognized revolutionary leader was Sun Yat-sen—and even his status as a leader and organizer is questionable.

After the kidnapping in London, Sun spent time in Tokyo, traveled widely, refined his ideas, and built relationships with younger anti-Manchu students in Japan, the Americas, and Europe. Students often found him rough and uneducated. They were suspicious of his contacts with Triad criminal gangs. But in 1905, radical leaders in Tokyo including Huang Xing (1874–1916) and Song Jiaoren (1882–1913) joined Sun to create the Revolutionary Alliance, with Sun as president and Huang Xing as vice-president.[70]

By this time, Sun was an accomplished public speaker. He had also articulated the core of his ideological platform, the Three People's Principles:

Nationalism (by which he meant anti-Manchuism), Democracy, and "People's Livelihood" (a vaguely socialistic "equalize land rights" program that was never put into practice). But for all the hullabaloo of its founding, the Revolutionary Alliance was poorly funded and loosely organized. Cliques based on provincial loyalties clashed with each other. Huang Xing (supported by Song Jiaoren) feuded with Sun over the position of leadership. As for Sun, he spent most of his time traveling, building up his own network and sources of funds in overseas Chinese communities from Honolulu to San Francisco to New York to London.

Looking Toward Revolution

In the summer of 1911, the Qing dynasty stood on the verge of disaster. Over the course of the 19th century, the court had successfully suppressed Muslim and "Miao" uprisings, the Nian bandits and Hong Xiuquan's Taiping rebellion. They had done so in the context of a series of losing battles against foreign aggressors. The central and provincial governments had made efforts to modernize the Qing military and begun to build a military-industrial complex and, finally, had begun to carry out extensive reforms in education and government.

Despite its efforts, the Qing remained unable to defend its territory. Foreign powers had divided the empire into spheres of interest. Foreign governments leased substantial parts of China's main cities, notably Tianjin and Shanghai, as "concession areas." Taiwan and Hong Kong had been ceded to the Japanese and the British. The British clearly had designs on Tibet, the Russians on Xinjiang and Mongolia.

At home, the Manchu's inability to defend Chinese territory and Chinese civilization had caused their Chinese subjects to question Manchu rule and Chinese civilization itself. The influx of Western culture gave Chinese critics new concepts with which to launch their attacks and to suggest new ways forward: social Darwinism, nationalism, rights, democracy, anarchism, socialism, republicanism, and feminism. Anti-Manchu radicals had carried out numerous assassination attempts (some successful) on government officials. Revolutionary plots and uprisings had been suppressed, but revolutionary groups—the Revolutionary Alliance and others—were active throughout the country. They especially targeted the young officers in the provincial New Army units, some of whom had been exposed to revolutionary thought while studying abroad.

And in the midst of this building tension, Regent Zaifeng and the Manchu aristocrats were working to construct a strong, centralized constitutional monarchy. The provincial assemblies, already meeting in 1910, and the National Assembly, which would begin its deliberations in the summer of 1911, were to assist and support the Manchu court in its deliberations. That, at least, was the plan.

Notes

1. For discussion of the reasons behind the rise of the West and comparison with the sources of the Qing Empire's 19th-century crises, see Kenneth Pomeranz, *The Great Divergence: China, Europe, and the Making of the World Economy* (Princeton: Princeton University Press, 2000); and Robert B. Marks, *The Origins of the Modern World: A Global and Ecological Narrative from the Fifteenth to the Twenty-first Century* (2nd edition) (Lanham: Rowman & Littlefield, 2007).

2. David Mungello traces the transformation of European attitudes toward China in *The Great Encounter of China and the West, 1500–1800* (Lanham: Rowman & Littlefield, 2000).

3. Zheng Yangwen, *The Social Life of Opium in China* (Cambridge: Cambridge University Press, 2005), 25–35; Frank Dikötter, Lars Laamann, and Zhou Xun, *Narcotic Culture: A History of Drugs in China* (Chicago: The University of Chicago Press, 2004), 24–9.

4. Dikötter et al., *Narcotic Culture*, 32–6.

5. Richard von Glahn, *Fountain of Fortune: Money and Monetary Policy in China, 1000–1700* (Berkeley: University of California Press, 1996), 256.

6. Hsin-pao Chang, *Commissioner Lin and the Opium War* (Cambridge, Mass.: Harvard University Press, 1964), 32–3. Some opium also entered the Qing Empire via the old Silk Road trade routes, brought in by merchants from India and from the expansionist Muslim Central Asian kingdom of Kokand, which shared a border with Xinjiang. As demand grew along the coast, farmers and merchants in border provinces—Yunnan, Sichuan, and especially Xinjiang—planted opium. However, this small-scale production and shipment overland by camel caravan was minor in comparison to the tens of thousands of chests of opium that the British and other Western traders brought to Canton every year. See David Bello, "Opium in Xinjiang and Beyond," in Timothy Brook and Bob Tadashi Wakabayashi, eds., *Opium Regimes: China, Britain, and Japan, 1839–1952* (Berkeley: University of California Press, 2000), 127–51.

7. Chang, *Commissioner Lin*, 19, 223.

8. See the discussion in Dikötter et al., *Narcotic Culture*, 51–7.

9. Chang, *Commissioner Lin*, 39–40. Exchange rates for copper cash and silver fluctuated constantly, and varied from one place to another across the Qing Empire.

10. James A. Millward, *Beyond the Pass: Economy, Ethnicity, and Empire in Qing Central*

Asia, 1759–1864 (Stanford: Stanford University Press, 1998), 61–2.

11. Von Glahn, *Fountain of Fortune,* 256.

12. The following description and analysis of the Opium War draws on Chang, *Commissioner Lin,* and on J.Y. Wong, *Deadly Dreams: Opium, Imperialism, and the Arrow War (1856–1860) in China* (Cambridge: Cambridge University Press, 1998).

13. Quoted in Chang, *Commissioner Lin,* 135.

14. Ibid., 151.

15. Ibid., 192–3.

16. *The Nemesis in China: Comprising a History of the Late War in That Country; with an Account of the Colony of Hong Kong* (London: Henry Colburn, Publisher, 1847).

17. James A. Millward, *Eurasian Crossroads: A History of Xinjiang* (New York: Columbia University Press, 2007), 109–14; Hodong Kim, *Holy War in China: The Muslim Rebellion and State in Chinese Central Asia, 1864–1877* (Stanford: Stanford University Press, 2004), 28; Joseph J. Fletcher, Jr., "The Heyday of Ch'ing Order in Mongolia, Sinkiang, and Tibet," in John K. Fairbank, ed., *The Cambridge History of China, Vol. 10: Late Ch'ing, 1800–1911, Part 1* (Cambridge: Cambridge University Press, 1978), 375.

18. Lan Yong, ed., *Zhongguo lishi dilixue* [*Historical geography of China*] (Beijing: Gaodeng jiaoyu chubanshe, 2002), 76–7.

19. James Lee, Cameron Campbell, and Wang Feng, "Positive Check or Chinese Checks?" *Journal of Asian Studies* 61.2 (May 2002): 600.

20. The picture conveyed here and in the following paragraphs draws on Robert B. Marks, *Tigers, Rice, Silk and Silt: Environment and Economy in Late Imperial South China* (Cambridge: Cambridge University Press, 1998); and on Pomeranz, *The Great Divergence;* and Mark Elvin, *The Pattern of the Chinese Past* (Stanford: Stanford University Press, 1973).

21. Fletcher, "The Heyday of Ch'ing Order," 356–8.

22. See the description and analysis in James Reardon-Anderson, *Reluctant Pioneers: China's Expansion Northward, 1644–1937* (Stanford: Stanford University Press, 2005).

23. Fletcher, "The Heyday of the Ch'ing Order," 406–8.

24. Albert Feuerwerker, *Rebellion in Nineteenth-Century China* (Ann Arbor: Center for Chinese Studies, The University of Michigan, 1975), 43.

25. Dru C. Gladney, *Muslim Chinese: Ethnic Nationalism in the People's Republic* (Cambridge, Mass.: Council on East Asian Studies, Harvard University, 1991), 48–50.

26. Susan Mann Jones and Philip Kuhn, "Dynastic Decline and the Roots of Rebellion," in Fairbank, ed., *The Cambridge History of China, Vol. 10,* 133–4; Feuerwerker, *Rebellion in Nineteenth-Century China,* 42; Robert D. Jenks, *Insurgency and Social Disorder in Guizhou: The "Miao" Rebellion 1854–1873* (Honolulu: University of Hawaii Press, 1994), 20, 25, 50.

27. Jenks, *Insurgency and Social Disorder in Guizhou,* 5, 55–6.

28. Kim, *Holy War in China,* 1–36; Millward, *Eurasian Crossroads,* 116–23.

29. Jones and Kuhn, "Dynastic Decline," 314; Siang-tseh Chiang, *The Nien Rebellion* (Seattle: University of Washington Press, 1954).

30. This and the following description of Hong and the Taiping rebellion draw largely on Franz Michael, *The Taiping Rebellion: History and Documents, Vol. 1: History* (Seattle: University of Washington Press, 1966); Philip A. Kuhn, "The Taiping Rebellion," in Fairbank, ed., *The*

Cambridge History of China,Vol. 10, 264–317; and Jonathan D. Spence, *God's Chinese Son: The Taiping Heavenly Kingdom of Hong Xiuquan* (New York: W.W. Norton, 1996).

31. Spence, *God's Chinese Son,* 180–1.

32. Kuhn, "The Taiping Rebellion," 291.

33. Philip A. Kuhn, *Rebellion and Its Enemies in Late Imperial China: Militarization and Social Structure, 1796–1864* (Cambridge, Mass.: Harvard University Press, 1980), 145–8.

34. Wong, *Deadly Dreams* 3, 43. The following description and interpretation of the *Arrow* War draws on Wong.

35. Treaty of Tianjin. Text online in Joseph V. O'Brien, *Anglo-Chinese Relations (1858)* (New York: History Department, John Jay College of Criminal Justice, n.d.), http://web.jjay.cuny.edu/jobrien/reference/ob28.html, accessed 20 February 2007.

36. Michael, *The Taiping Rebellion: History and Documents,* 173–4, 182.

37. Millward, *Eurasian Crossroads,* 125–6.

38. Feng Guifen (Feng Kuei-fen), "On the Manufacture of Foreign Weapons," in William Theodore de Bary et al. eds., *Sources of Chinese Tradition, Volume 2* (New York: Columbia University Press, 1964), 46.

39. Kwang-Ching Liu, "The Military Challenge: The Northwest and the Coast," in John K. Fairbank and Kwang-Ching Liu, eds., *The Cambridge History of China, Vol. 11: Late Ch'ing, 1800–1911, Part 2* (Cambridge: Cambridge University Press, 1980), 251–2.

40. James Reeve Pusy, *China and Charles Darwin* (Cambridge: Council on East Asian Studies, Harvard University, 1983), 29–47; Hao Chang, *Chinese Intellectuals in Crisis: Search for Order and Meaning (1890–1911)* (Berkeley: University of California Press, 1987), 20, 53.

41. Young-tsu Wong, "Revisionism Reconsidered: Kang Youwei and the Reform Movement of 1898," *Journal of Asian Studies* 51.3 (Aug. 1992): 526. The following account and interpretation of Kang's role in the 1898 reform follows Wong.

42. Rhoads Murphy, "The Treaty Ports and China's Modernization," in Mark Elvin and G. William Skinner, eds., *The Chinese City Between Two Worlds* (Stanford: Stanford University Press, 1974), 17–22.

43. Leo Ou-fan Lee and Andrew J. Nathan, "The Beginnings of Mass Culture: Journalism and Fiction in the Late Ch'ing and Beyond," in David Johnson, Andrew J. Nathan, and Evelyn S. Rawski, eds., *Popular Culture in Late Imperial China* (Berkeley: University of California Press, 1985), 373.

44. On post-Taiping examination reform, see Benjamin A. Elman, *A Cultural History of Civil Examinations in Late Imperial China* (Berkeley: University of California Press, 2000), 578–84.

45. Nanxiu Qian, "Revitalizing the Xianyuan (Worthy Ladies) Tradition: Women in the 1898 Reforms," *Modern China* 29.4 (Oct. 2003): 407.

46. Ibid., 422.

47. Lydia H. Liu, "The Translator's Turn: The Birth of Modern Chinese Language and Fiction," in Victor H. Mair, ed., *The Columbia History of Chinese Literature* (New York: Columbia University Press, 2001), 1064–5.

48. Benjamin Schwartz, *In Search of Wealth and Power: Yen Fu and the West* (Cambridge, Mass.: Harvard University Press, 1964), 111.

49. Ibid., 239–41.

50. Andrew J. Nathan, *Chinese Democracy* (Berkeley: University of California Press, 1985), 57.

51. Ibid., 55.

52. Marie-Claire Bergère, *Sun Yat-sen* (Stanford: Stanford University Press, 1998), 36–41.

53. Bergère, *Sun Yat-sen,* 50–5. The following description of Sun's Guangzhou uprising and its aftermath follows Bergère, 55–68.

54. Judith Wyman, "The Ambiguities of Chinese Antiforeignism: Chongqing, 1870–1900," *Late Imperial China* 18.2 (1998): 103.

55. This and the following discussion of the Boxer uprising and war draw on Joseph Esherick, *The Origins of the Boxer Uprising* (Berkeley: University of California Press, 1987); Paul A. Cohen, *History in Three Keys: The Boxers as Event, Experience, and Myth* (New York: Columbia University Press, 1997); and Jane E. Elliott, *Some Did It for Civilisation, Some Did It for Their Country: A Revised View of the Boxer War* (Hong Kong: The Chinese University Press, 2002).

56. Elliott, *Some Did It for Civilisation,* 530.

57. Boxer Protocol, 7 September 1901; text online in Joseph V. O'Brien, *Boxer Protocol (Peking)* (New York: History Department, John Jay College of Criminal Justice, n.d.), http://web.jjay.cuny.edu/jobrien/reference/ob26.html, accessed 23 February 2007.

58. James L. Hevia, "Leaving a Brand on China: Missionary Discourse in the Wake of the Boxer Movement," *Modern China* 18.3 (1992): 304–32.

59. Quoted in Douglas R. Reynolds, *China, 1898–1912: The Xinzheng Revolution and Japan* (Cambridge, Mass.: Council on East Asian Studies, Harvard University, 1993), 13.

60. Some historians question the empress dowager's sincerity in pursuing reforms and learning from the West. See Immanuel C. Y. Hsu, *The Rise of Modern China,* 6th ed. (Oxford: Oxford University Press, 2000), 411–2. Regardless of her sincerity, or lack thereof, significant reforms did take place in her last years.

61. Reynolds, *China, 1898–1912,* 149–50.

62. Hsu, *The Rise of Modern China,* 410–1.

63. Chuzo Ichiko, "Political and Institutional Reform, 1901–1911," in Fairbank and Liu, eds. *The Cambridge History of China, Vol. 11,* 396–7.

64. Edward J. M. Rhoads, *Manchus and Han: Ethnic Relations and Political Power in Late Qing and Early Republican China, 1861–1928* (Seattle: University of Washington Press, 2000), 164–5.

65. Marinus Johan Meijer, *The Introduction of Modern Criminal Law in China* (Batavia: De Unie, 1950), 118–9, 125.

66. Rhoads, *Manchus and Han,* 129–30.

67. Ralph L. Powell, *The Rise of Chinese Military Power, 1895–1912* (Princeton: Princeton University Press, 1955), 172, 239–40.

68. Zou Rong, "The Revolutionary Army," trans. John Lust, *The Revolutionary Army: A Chinese Nationalist Tract of 1903,* (Paris: Mouton, 1968); excerpts online in *Zou Rong: The Revolutionary Army* (Indiana: College of Humanities and Social Sciences, Indiana University of Pennsylvania, n.d.), http://www.chss.iup.edu/baumler/zourong.html.

69. Quoted from Patricia Buckley Ebrey, *Chinese Civilization: A Sourcebook,* 2nd ed. (New York: The Free Press, 1993), 344.

70. Bergère, *Sun Yat-sen,* 132–4.

Part II

THE ROAD TO WEALTH AND POWER, 1911–PRESENT

Chapter 3   STRUGGLING TO

                              BUILD A NATION

The 1911 Revolution

and the

Early Republic, 1912–1926

On 9 October 1911, a revolutionary conspirator in the Yangzi port city of Wuchang enjoyed a cigarette while he and his comrades worked on some bombs and ammunition in their headquarters, a house in the Russian-leased area of the city. When an accidental explosion injured one of the men, the plotters fled, leaving behind a membership list and other documents, which the police soon discovered. The revolutionaries, whose plans for an armed rebellion had already been delayed more than once, now faced arrest and severe punishment. With nothing left to lose, they staged their uprising the next day, 10 October.[1]

This poorly planned local military uprising set off a chain reaction of re-bellion that toppled the once-mighty Qing. The revolutionaries established a new country, the Republic of China, which replaced the Qing dynastic government and inherited Qing territory and international obligations—including the unequal treaties, indemnities, and foreign debt. But the leaders of the new Chinese republic were unable to establish a strong government or to transform the huge territory and disparate ethnic groups of the former Qing Empire into a cohesive nation-state. In its early years, the Republic of China endured the troubled presidency of Yuan Shikai (1859–1916), a for-mer Qing official, from 1912 to 1916. After Yuan's death the new country descended into a period of political turmoil from 1916 through 1927, in which hundreds of strongmen, or warlords, controlled their own armies and territories and fought with each other in a constantly shifting pattern of enmities and alliances.

Although the 1911 Revolution failed to establish an effective government and did nothing at all to address rural poverty or other social issues, it did open the way for a period of intensified intellectual, cultural, and social change. Musicians, artists, educators, and writers searched for the causes of China's continued weakness and for ways to construct a robust modern Chinese national identity. Domestic and international events also contributed to the development of new ideologies and new, more effective forms of political organization. The revolutionaries of 1911 had not been members of a single, organized revolutionary movement, had no common ideology, and had not even planned the events that became the 1911 Revolution. By 1926, China had not one but two relatively well-organized, disciplined revolutionary political parties: the Guomindang (Nationalist Party) and the much smaller Chinese Communist Party. Each had its own ideological vision of China's future. One of them, the Guomindang, also had its own army.

The 1911 Revolution

By 1911, the Qing Empire was like a house full of gunpowder and bombs. A single spark in the wrong place would be enough to set off a catastrophic explosion. Tensions between the Han Chinese elite and their Manchu rulers had reached the breaking point. The New Policies had been intended, in part, to address this problem, but the elimination of the civil service examination and the court's attempts to create a modern, Manchu-dominated central government only fed the fires of anti-Manchu feeling. Even measures to create a constitutional system with elected local, provincial, and national assemblies led only to increased alienation of Han elites from the Manchu court.

Chinese voters—men twenty-five years of age who had met minimum standards of education and wealth—voted for their representatives to their provincial assemblies in 1909. The provincial assemblymen, mostly forty- to forty-five-year-old men with traditional examination degrees, immediately clashed with the court-appointed provincial governors. The Qing court expected the assemblies to act as consultative organs which would advise and support the governors. The assemblymen wanted to act as legislators, and disputed with their governors over their role and the extent of their power.[2]

The National Assembly, composed of a hundred court-appointed members and a hundred representatives chosen from among the provincial assemblymen, convened in Beijing on 3 October 1910. Here too, the assemblymen's ambitions ran counter to the court's expectations. Prince Regent Zaifeng (1883–1951) viewed the National Assembly as an advisory body whose suggestions he could accept or reject as he saw fit.[3] The assemblymen thought otherwise. They tried to impeach members of the Qing Grand Council for ignoring their recommendations, petitioned the court to convene a true parliament, and demanded that Zaifeng appoint a cabinet.

Prince Regent Zaifeng ignored the National Assembly's denunciations of the Grand Council. He agreed reluctantly to advance the schedule for the convention of a parliament, from 1916 to 1913, but no earlier. And on 11 May 1911, he did appoint a cabinet, but one that consisted of nine Manchus (including five imperial princes) and only four Han. In the same month, Zaifeng, apparently caring nothing for the opinions of the assemblymen, made two very controversial decisions: to nationalize existing rail lines and to take out a large foreign loan to finance the construction of a unified national rail network.

Zaifeng's plan for a national railway system quickly became the focal point for Chinese anger. Control of railways and of the natural resources adjacent to the rail lines was one of the most obvious and intrusive aspects of Western and Japanese imperialism. Since the early 1900s, Chinese landowners and merchants had been creating provincial railway companies to buy out foreign-owned railways or build competing lines. The prince regent's decision to nationalize these provincial railway companies (with funds borrowed from foreign banks, no less) provoked public outrage.[4] In Sichuan, protesters accused the Qing court of selling their province to foreigners, encouraged students, ordinary townspeople, and farmers to take to the streets, and enlisted the support of a quasi-criminal group, the Elder Brother Society. In September 1911, with angry mobs taking to the streets and armed militia attacking government offices, Qing commanders transferred army units from Wuchang upriver to Sichuan to restore order.

Wuchang was one of three cities (Wuchang, Hankou, and Hanyang, now known collectively as Wuhan) located at the confluence of the Yangzi and Han Rivers. Revolutionary groups, both civilian and in the New Army units, had been active throughout the area since the early 1900s. Revolutionary Alliance members, especially Sun Yat-sen's rivals Huang Xing and Song Jiaoren, had contacts with many such groups and hoped that the region might become a springboard for revolution sometime in the future. But some of the revolutionary groups had their own plans, independent of the Revolutionary Alliance. A coalition of civilian and New Army revolutionaries in Wuchang was, in fact, planning its own uprising.[5]

It was members of these underground civilian and New Army revolution-ary groups who caused the accidental explosion that took place in Wuchang on 9 October 1911. On 10 October, they staged an uprising, taking over the city of Wuchang, with its arsenal and treasury. Since they did not have a leader of national stature, they captured the local commander, Li Yuanhong (1864–1928), and forced him to declare Hubei Province independent of the Qing Empire. Li had always suppressed any signs of revolution among his men, but with the revolutionaries now in charge and issuing edicts over his signature, he accepted his fate and became a revolutionary leader himself.

News of the events in Wuchang spread by telegraph across the Qing Em-pire and around the world. In province after province, coalitions of New Army units, provincial assemblymen, merchants, and secret society elements formed military governments and declared independence from the Qing. With seven provinces seceding by the end of October, and fourteen, includ-ing all of south China, Shanxi, and Shaanxi, by early December, the revolu-tionary leaders gathered in Nanjing to impose some order and leadership over what had, so far, been an entirely unorganized and leaderless series of events. The assembly of revolutionary delegates agreed that the Qing must be replaced by a new republican government. But who should be their new leader? Li Yuanhong vied for power with long-time revolutionaries Song Jiaoren and Huang Xing. As the debate unfolded, Sun Yat-sen finally appeared on the scene.

Sun, who had been on a speaking and fundraising tour of the United States, learned about the Wuchang uprising when he opened his morning newspaper in Denver, Colorado.[6] He had rushed off to Washington, London, and Paris, trying to convince foreign governments that he was leading the revolution in China, and that they should support him—both diplomatically and with generous bank loans. Foreign governments, maintaining a neutral attitude toward the revolution, would not help Sun: they preferred to watch as events in China unfolded.

So when Sun finally arrived in Shanghai in December, he had no foreign support, only a motley entourage of freelance foreign hangers-on and his reputation. Both were mixed blessings. Revolutionary leaders like Song Jiaoren had little respect for the physician and his shady underworld con-nections. His foreign camp followers struck the Chinese as an unimpressive lot: among them were Australian and Japanese journalists and adventurers, and Homer Lea (1876–1912), a Stanford-educated, Chinese-speaking, but physically deformed self-appointed "general" whom Sun had retained as a military advisor.[7] But with the struggle for leadership of the revolution

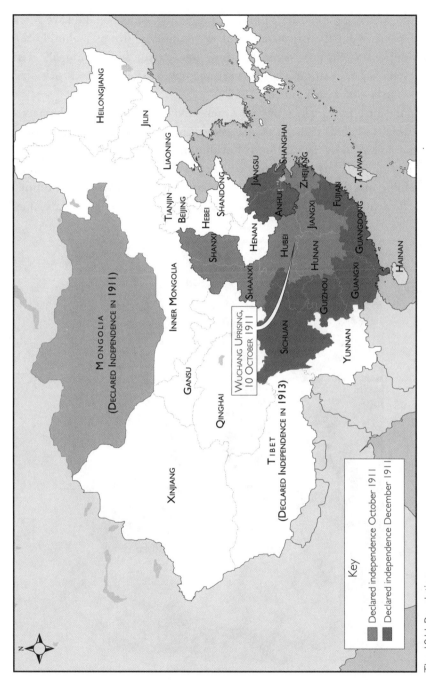

The 1911 Revolution.

deadlocked, Song and others put their misgivings aside. Sun did have years of experience in the organization of revolutionary groups including the Revolutionary Alliance (no matter how ineffective) and a national, even international, reputation. Thus Sun became the President of the Provisional Republic of China on 1 January 1912.

In the meantime, Prince Regent Zaifeng and the Manchu leadership faced the worst (and last) crisis of their careers. Over half the Chinese provinces of the empire were in rebellion. Revolutionary mobs were attacking and massacring Manchus in the Banner Quarters of major cities.[8] The National Assembly, meeting again in Beijing, was renewing its calls for a constitution, a parliament, and a cabinet. The Manchu court needed help. Desperate, they

The three-year-old Qing emperor Xuantong, better known by his personal name, Puyi, is on the right. On the left is Puyi's father, Zaifeng, who served as regent, holding the emperor's younger brother.

turned to Yuan Shikai, the man they had forced into retirement only two years earlier. Yuan was willing to serve the court—but only if he were made prime minister.

As prime minister, and commander of the powerful, modernized Beiyang Army, Yuan alone had the power to bring the revolution to an end. First, he conducted successful counterattacks on revolutionary forces in Hubei. Then, having demonstrated his military prowess, he held his forces back and began to negotiate between the Manchu court and the revolutionaries in Nanjing. To the Manchu nobles, he offered an end to the anti-Manchu violence and generous treatment in return for the emperor's abdication. To the revolutionaries, he offered achievement of their dream—a Chinese republic— without the need for a potentially disastrous civil war. His price was simple: in return for arranging the emperor's abdication, he would become president of the Republic of China.

Both the Qing court and the revolutionaries had reservations about Yuan, but in the end, both agreed to deal with him. On 12 February 1912, the court announced the abdication of Aisin Gioro Puyi (1906–67), the "last emperor." On 15 February, Sun Yat-sen resigned his presidency, and Yuan Shikai took his place. The foreign powers, which had been looking on with intense interest (and concern for their various investments) were much relieved. They knew Yuan well. He was a modernizer and a proven leader. Yuan was just the man to restore order, stability, and "business as usual." Or so it seemed in February 1912.

Yuan Shikai and the Warlords

The 1911 Revolution swept the Qing Empire from the stage and "opened the way for a long series of redefinitions" in which the characteristics and identity of the new nation-state of China would take shape.[9] The first stages of this often contentious process of nation-building took place during the presidency of Yuan Shikai (1912–16) and the "warlord period" (1916–27). As we will see later, these were years of significant change for culture, society, and everyday life. These changes took place in the context of years of weak government, militarism, and war.

Reformers from Li Hongzhang, Kang Youwei, and Liang Qichao to the empress dowager, Prince Regent Zaifeng, and the revolutionary Sun Yat-sen had all believed that only a strong central government leading a unified people could achieve the goals of national wealth and power. President Yuan Shikai certainly agreed. But the 1911 Revolution was the work of local forces: provincial assemblies, provincial army units, merchant organizations, secret societies, and fragmented revolutionary organizations. Though committed to the ideal of national strength, many provincial leaders believed that national strength could best be achieved on the basis of provincial autonomy. National leaders like Sun Yat-sen and Song Jiaoren agreed with Yuan on the need for a strong central government, but though they supported the compromise that made Yuan president, they did not trust him. All of this made for weak government throughout Yuan's presidency and beyond.

Disagreements between Yuan and the revolutionaries began almost at once. Yuan had promised to make Nanjing the capital of the new Republic of China. Then, as president, he insisted on establishing the capital in Beijing—his power base. But it was in the matter of elections and the role of the National Assembly that Yuan's clash with the revolutionaries and with provincial elites became deadly serious.

In 1912, the Revolutionary Alliance remade itself into a political party, the Guomindang (GMD, or Nationalist Party). Sun Yat-sen's partner and competitor Song Jiaoren was party leader. The Guomindang adopted Sun's "Three People's Principles" (Nationalism, Democracy, and People's Livelihood) as its basic platform. "Nationalism," originally anti-Manchuism, was now redefined as loyalty to a "Chinese nation" which included Han, Manchu, Mongol, Tibetan, Muslim and all the other ethnic groups of the former Qing Empire. "People's Livelihood" was purposely left vague. Song correctly understood that his party would never win the moral or financial support of merchants and large landowners on a platform that included any form of socialism. For similar reasons of political strategy, the Guomindang refused to include women's rights in its platform, much to the disgust of women who had participated in the 1911 Revolution, some of them in all-women's military units.[10]

Song Jiaoren may have compromised on revolutionary principle, but he proved to be an adept political strategist. In the elections of winter 1912–13, the Guomindang won 269 of the 596 seats in the lower house of the Parliament. With control of the Parliament assured, Song planned to use his parliamentary muscle to organize a cabinet, appoint a prime minister, and ease Yuan Shikai out of power. But on 20 March 1913, a gunman shot and fatally wounded Song as he prepared to board a train from Shanghai to Beijing for the inaugural session of the National Assembly. Apparently, the killer had acted on orders from Yuan Shikai's office.

The assassination of Song Jiaoren was part of Yuan's attempt to concentrate power in his own hands. When southern provincial and military leaders

Sun Yat-sen.

launched a "second revolution" in the summer of 1913, he defeated them. Sun Yat-sen and other Guomindang leaders who had been involved fled, again, to Japan. Between 1913 and 1916, Yuan outlawed the Guomindang, disbanded the National Assembly, provincial assemblies, and local councils, appointed his own governors and military commanders to most provinces, instituted press censorship, and created secret police forces that suppressed and sometimes assassinated political opponents.

Yuan did all this not simply because he was power-hungry, but because he sincerely believed that only a powerful central government could save China. As he saw it, strong provincial governments prevented tax revenue from flowing to the center, politicians were incompetent talkers, and entrusting the vast, uneducated majority of the Chinese people with the vote would only lead to chaos. His Chinese and foreign advisors and the foreign powers tended to agree.

As president, Yuan continued to pursue the style of centralizing, conservative reform that he had helped to design in the last years of the Qing and to work with government institutions and personnel inherited from the Qing state. He tried to suppress opium cultivation, held modern civil service examinations, and promoted universal primary education in basic literacy, Confucian morality, and the importance of obeying the government. He reduced the size and expense of the military and strengthened institutions of civil government in the provinces. He encouraged the development of civil rituals, such as the celebration of the "Double Ten" holiday (the anniversary of the 10 October Wuchang Uprising) and elaborate military parades, all designed to instill Chinese with the concepts of national unity and the central role of the president himself.[11] Many observers, Chinese and Western, were impressed with Yuan's accomplishments. Why, then, has Yuan Shikai gone down in Chinese history as a failure and as a traitor to the Revolution?

For all his strengths, Yuan had some remarkable weaknesses. Some of them were inherent in his position as president of a weak government that had inherited the crippling treaties, debt burdens, economic challenges, and environmental pressures that had plagued the Qing imperial government. He had to cut back on key modernization programs, notably on plans for modern courts and police, in order to balance the government's budget.[12] He continued to allow strong military leaders in many provinces.[13] His attempts to increase tax revenue alienated merchants and the landowning elite. And like the Qing, he was unable to present a strong front to the foreign powers. From the beginning of his presidency, Yuan was criticized for negotiating loans with foreign bankers under conditions that further compromised Chinese sovereignty. On top of all these problems came World War I, the Japanese invasion of Shandong, and the "Twenty-One Demands."

In 1914, Japan, Britain's ally in World War I, captured the German naval base, the city of Qingdao, and other concession areas on the Shandong peninsula. In January 1915, the Japanese followed up by presenting Yuan with a list of twenty-one demands regarding Japanese interests in China. The demands included recognition of Japan as successor to Germany's privileges in Shandong and various Japanese strategic and economic interests elsewhere in China. Chinese and Western diplomats, none of whom wanted to see Japan become the dominant power in China (though for quite different reasons), forced Japan to back down from some of the most onerous of the demands. But in the end, Yuan had to accept Japan's newly acquired sphere of interest in Shandong and grant the Japanese new economic privileges in Manchuria.

The affair of the Twenty-One Demands was only the most dramatic example of a problem that dogged Yuan throughout his presidency: his government's weak bargaining position repeatedly forced him to capitulate to foreign interests. This only confirmed his belief that China needed a stronger central government which could command both popular loyalty and national economic resources. Yuan concluded that in a poor country with a history of monarchical government, only a constitutional monarchy could achieve the goals of national unity, progress, and modernization. His Chinese and foreign advisors (including a respected American political scientist) laid out the theoretical arguments for monarchy. Yuan engineered "popular demand" and arranged for a "Representative Assembly" to elect him as emperor in November 1915. Ignoring Japanese and British advice to the contrary, Yuan accepted his "election" on 11 December 1915 and made plans for a grand coronation.[14]

The attempt to become emperor turned out to be the pitiful end of Yuan's ill-fated presidency. Monarchists, who still revered the Qing, were disgusted. Republicans, even those who had supported Yuan's dictatorship, denounced him. Provincial military leaders rose in rebellion. In March 1916, Yuan, in ill health, suspended his plan to assume the throne. He passed away in June. He left behind no institutions or individuals capable of unifying the many provincial military leaders and his own subordinates in the Beiyang Army. From June 1916 through 1927, regionally based strongmen, soon to acquire the pejorative label "warlords," competed with each other for control of territory. The national government in Beijing, while still recognized by the foreign powers and able to raise loans, was otherwise powerless, a pawn for the major warlords to fight over.[15]

There were hundreds of warlords. The major warlords whose actions and lifestyles defined the "warlord period," held territories comprising one or more provinces. Serving under these major figures were hundreds of minor warlords and subordinate officers who commanded smaller units and controlled territories ranging from substantial portions of a province to as little as one or more counties. Loyalties within warlord armies and of the commanders serving under major provincial warlords were all highly conditional.

The most powerful of the warlords came from a variety of backgrounds. Duan Qirui (1865–1936), a native of Anhui province, protégé of Yuan Shikai, and prime minister of China in June 1916, led a warlord coalition, the Anhui Clique. Several of Yuan's other protégés, including the Confucian-educated Wu Peifu (1874–1939) and the self-educated peasant (and Christian convert) Feng Yuxiang (1882–1948), formed the rival Zhili Clique. Zhang

Zuolin (1873?–1928), a hard-drinking, mahjong-playing Han Chinese former bandit and Qing army officer dominated his native Manchuria as leader
of the Fengtian Clique. Zhang Zongchang (1881–1932), a crude, ruthless,
illiterate bandit, rose to become master of Shandong province. Yan Xishan
(1883–1960), educated in a Japanese military school and a former member
of the Revolutionary Alliance, ruled his home province of Shanxi. A coalition
of three warlords, including the Muslim Bai Chongxi (1893–1966) and Han
Chinese Li Zongren (1890–1969), worked together to control the mountainous southwestern Guangxi province.

The great warlords all talked of patriotism and the need to unite China,
but each wanted to achieve national unity on his own terms. Their armies,
the best of which were well-equipped with Western and Japanese weapons,
and even airplanes, sold by international arms dealers, were the instruments
with which they hoped to achieve their goals.[16] As a result, the warlord period
saw hundreds of small conflicts. From 1920 to 1927 three major warlord
confederations fought four major wars in 1920, 1922, 1924, and 1926. In
these wars, the Zhili Clique, the Anhui Clique, and Zhang Zuolin's Fengtian
Clique battled for control of northern China, and for Beijing. In the brutal
fighting and constant politicking, small units, brigades, and sometimes entire armies switched sides. For example, in 1924, the Manchurian warlord
Zhang Zuolin used money provided by Japan to buy Feng Yuxiang away from
the Zhili Clique, with which Zhang's Fengtian Clique was fighting at the time.
Two years later, in 1926, the Fengtian Clique was allied with the Zhili Clique
in a war against Feng Yuxiang.

Warlords were not all brutal comic-opera characters, nor can the warlord
period be adequately understood as nothing more than anarchic violence.
Some of the major warlords were intelligent, capable men who proposed (although they did not always follow through with) progressive reforms in their
territories. The Guangxi warlords Li Zongren and Bai Chongxi were known
for their attention to the training, care, and discipline of their soldiers. Feng
Yuxiang, the "Christian Warlord," forbade his men from smoking opium,
gambling, and swearing and set them a rigorous schedule of training, prayer,
and hymn singing. Yan Xishan issued laws against foot-binding.

To the extent that they did behave as professional soldiers and reformers,
men like Li Zongren, Bai Chongxi, Feng Yuxiang, and Yan Xishan were ex-
ceptional. Most warlords were more notable for their crudity and cruelty,
for the operatic flamboyance of their uniforms and their lifestyles, and for their
undisciplined and sometimes downright vicious troops. Warlords including
Yan Xishan used "opium suppression" bureaus to run their own lucrative

opium monopolies. The unbacked, worthless paper currency that warlords forced civilians to accept in payment for goods and services and the unpredictable, punitive taxes and requisitions of goods took an incalculable toll on farmers and merchants. Warlord soldiers were permitted to carry out orgies of destruction, looting, and rape during and after battle. When not in combat, soldiers extorted or stole goods and services from civilians, rode the trains for free, and killed civilians with impunity.

Rural poverty, especially in parts of China already characterized by banditry or feuding, generated a steady supply of young men who were willing to answer the call of warlord army recruiters. Army life held the promise of better and more reliable income, regular meals, less work, and more opportunity for pleasure (sex, gambling, and opium) than life on the farm. And if a man found army life too hard or too dangerous, it was easy to desert, become a bandit, change sides, or just go home.[17]

The New Culture Movement

Before 1911, Han Chinese revolutionaries proclaimed that China was weak because it was a despotic monarchy run by the inferior Manchu race. The 1911 Revolution swept monarchy and Manchu rule into the dustbin of history, but China was still weak. Neither the revolutionaries nor Yuan Shikai nor any of the warlords were able to make the former Qing territories and their many ethnic groups into a cohesive nation-state or establish a government that could assert Chinese dignity and sovereignty in the face of foreign imperialism. As it became clear that the 1911 Revolution had failed to resolve China's problems, a new generation of intellectuals looked for the root causes of, and solutions for, national weakness. Their exploration and debate, running from around 1915 to 1925, is called the "New Culture Movement."[18]

The New Culture Movement began in 1915 when Chen Duxiu (1879–1942), a French-educated former revolutionary and fierce critic of Yuan Shikai, published the first issue of his monthly magazine *New Youth* in Shanghai.[19] Chen and the writers of his generation were intellectual inhabitants of two worlds: their initial education had been in the classical examination curriculum and their later education in the Western tradition, often in the West or in Japan. Consequently, Chen and the other writers whose work he published were in a position to pick up on intellectual trends that had already begun in the late 19th century, to push them farther than anyone had before. The basic elements of the *New Youth* formula were a commitment to socially (and sometimes politically) engaged literature, an exuberant, iconoclastic critique of Chinese culture, and the determination to write in the vernacular.

Young people, educated in modern, Western-style schools instead of in the old civil service examination system, gave *New Youth* the kind of audience that would not have existed a generation earlier. Copies of *New Youth* were circulated from hand to hand and read and discussed in study groups: the magazine achieved a circulation of sixteen thousand after 1917.[20] Many other magazines imitated, competed with, or attacked the combination of cultural critique, translations, theoretical articles, essays, and short stories that appeared in its pages. *New Youth* is, then, representative of an epoch and of a whole wave of writing and publishing during the New Culture period.

While Shanghai continued to be important, Beijing soon emerged as the epicenter of the New Culture Movement. In 1917, Cai Yuanpei (1868–1940), a German-educated intellectual and former minister of education in Yuan Shikai's government, took over as chancellor of Beijing University. Cai deliberately fostered an atmosphere of intellectual vitality and creativity by encouraging academic freedom and welcoming the expression of many different points of view. He also brought in staff and instructors who shared his interest in constructing a "new civilization."[21] These included Hu Shi (1891–1962), a student of John Dewey's at Columbia University Teachers' College; Li Dazhao (1888–1927), who had studied Western philosophy in Japan; the author Lu Xun (1881–1936); and Chen Duxiu (1879–1942), who moved the editorial offices of *New Youth* up to Beijing with him.

The New Culture intellectuals believed optimistically that human history is a tale of progress. "The evolution of human civilization is replacing the old with the new, like a river flowing on, an arrow flying away, constantly continuing and constantly changing," said Chen Duxiu.[22] The trouble was, as Hu Shi once put it, that the West had crossed the finish line on the racetrack of human history.[23] China was lagging behind. Why? And what would China need to do in order to catch up?

The New Culture intellectuals found the fundamental causes of China's poverty, weakness, and the failure of the 1911 Revolution in China's own culture: its family system, its Confucian philosophy, its art and music, its religions, and its manners. In short, the cultural identity in which Chinese scholars had taken such pride was the main problem: "I would rather see the ruin of our 'national quintessence,'" said Chen Duxiu, "than have our race of the present and future extinguished because of its unfitness for survival."[24] Chen enthusiastically led the charge against Confucianism, hierarchy, Chinese religions, respect for elders, and the family system. He urged youth to reject tradition, to "smash the Confucian family shop."

As they condemned the past, the New Culture intellectuals also suggested at least the general outlines of China's path to the future. The Chinese people would need to adapt to the spirit of the modern epoch and learn from the West and Japan. As he rejected Confucius, Chen urged China's youth to learn from "Mr. Science" and "Mr. Democracy." China needed not just modern technology, but also in the thought and culture that lay behind the development and the application of technological things. A few of the areas in which the New Culture intellectuals looked for improvement were in the production of a new, socially engaged vernacular literature and in the status of women and family life in general.

Hu Shi, an American-educated writer, took the lead in advocating the creation of a new vernacular Chinese literature as key to changing China's culture. Hu Shi published articles demonstrating and advocating the use of the vernacular in his friend Chen Duxiu's *New Youth*. The "literary revolution," he said, could be summed up in four points:

1. Speak only when you have something to say.
2. Say what you have to say, and say it as it is said.
3. Speak your own language, not the language of others.
4. Speak the language of your own time.[25]

As Hu Shi saw it, the goal of the literary revolution was to democratize education, to spread literacy, and so to enlighten and modernize the Chinese people. Chen Duxiu and Hu Shi wrote brilliant and highly readable essays. But many other men and women contributed to the beginning of the new Chinese vernacular literature. Of these, the most influential was Lu Xun.[26]

Lu Xun was born into a declining scholar-official family in the town of Shaoxing in Zhejiang province. Like many young men of his generation, Lu's education began in the traditional mode, then switched to modern schooling: in his case, a naval academy, a school of mines and railways, and then medical school in Japan. Unhappy in Japan (and evidently doing poorly in his studies), Lu Xun dropped out in 1906 to become a writer. A physician, he later argued, could cure only one body at a time. As a writer, he could treat the spiritual illness which lay at the heart of the Chinese people's weakness and humiliation. In stories like "Diary of a Madman," "Medicine," "My Old Home," and "The True Story of Ah Q," Lu Xun painted the Chinese as a people mired in superstition and ignorance, vainly comforting themselves with empty boasts about their long, glorious history and their morally superior civilization—a civilization that Lu Xun satirized as a barbarous "man-eating" culture hiding behind a façade of Confucian self-righteousness.

As they attacked Chinese culture and held up the West as a model for emulation, authors like Lu Xun and Hu Shi paid particular attention to the "woman problem." In the late 19th century, reformers like Kang Youwei and activists like Qiu Jin had worked for women's rights and education. Now, intellectuals saw women and their position as symbolic of China: both were rendered weak and defenseless because they were enslaved by Confucianism, their humanity denied, and their individual creativity stifled.[27]

The cultural criticism of the New Culture era was also a high tide for Chinese feminism. Men and women appropriated Western feminist theory to launch a withering critique of the way Chinese culture treated women. Pointing to things like low literacy levels and to women committing suicide rather than be forced into arranged marriages, the culture critics condemned the Confucian cult of chastity and the Chinese family structure. They advocated freedom of choice in marriage, women's education and co-education, voting rights, and equal pay.

Nora, the main character in Henrik Ibsen's play "A Doll's House," translated by Hu Shi, became a heroine to the new generation of women for her determination to walk out of her husband's house and her oppressive marriage to a stolidly bourgeois man. Chinese audiences saw Nora as a symbol of women's freedom, identity, and determination: just the sort of thing they believed not only women, but the Chinese nation needed.[28] Lu Xun, with typical cynicism, pushed the discussion further by asking "What happens after Nora leaves?" In China, he answered, she would either become a prostitute or return to her family: Chinese society had no place for an independent woman.

But despite Lu Xun's pessimism, Chinese society was changing, though too slowly to suit many. There were now significant numbers of modern-educated young men and women who were ready to respond to feminist ideas by changing the way they lived. Modern education led to the emergence of women professionals who pursued careers in teaching, writing, medicine and other professions, and sports (the first Chinese women's basketball team, established in 1925, played in Japan, winning six of ten games against a Japanese women's team).[29] The growth of modern industry (which we will discuss below) led to the development of a new class of working women, especially in the textile industry. Moreover, some women were ready to put feminism into action by starting a women's movement led by women.

These changes in women's roles, in family structure, and in women's education and organization were significant, but they were only a start. Changes that swept urban society in the coastal areas and the Yangzi Valley scarcely touched rural inland villages. And even in the cities, the changing spirit of the age ran ahead of women's and men's ability to change their own lives, even when they were vocal advocates of change themselves. Lu Xun, an ardent critic of tradition, bowed to his mother's insistence that he enter into an arranged marriage, demanded respect and obedience from his younger brothers, and, when he remarried a younger intellectual woman, expected her to give up her career to keep house and look after their child. Many men and women, though deeply influenced by or even leaders of the New Culture movement, still accepted that men could divorce and have multiple sexual partners, while disapproving of women who did the same.[30] It was often easier to criticize the values and habits of generations than to throw them off!

Whatever their weaknesses and hypocrisies, the New Culture intellectuals reached a generation of educated youth with their powerfully worded critique of tradition and their advocacy of Western individualism, humanism, liberalism, utilitarianism, and the allegedly aggressive, activist, modern nature of the West. But they were not the only voices in the intellectual world of the 1910s and 1920s: other writers leapt to the defense of Chinese civilization.

Liang Qichao, earlier a great admirer of the West, argued in the aftermath of World War I that Western culture was defined by a selfish, individualistic, materialist, hedonistic spirit that lead directly, not to the realm of individual freedom and human dignity, but to aggression and brutality. China should reject Western culture and embrace the values of its own "national character": familism, reciprocity, and respect for rank.[31] The Confucian philosopher Liang Shuming (no relation to Liang Qichao) argued in 1921 that while Western science and technology could improve the material standard of living, China's Confucian values were the cure for the Westerner's painful spiritual emptiness. The Chinese should hold onto their spirit of harmony, compromise, yielding, and intuition, and, as Confucius had recommended, maintain social order through ritual and music instead of law and punishment. Indeed, in these things, Westerners should learn from China.[32]

The cultural conservatives had few supporters. Their arguments often seemed irrelevant to the younger generation, and their scholarly classical prose was more difficult to read than the essays of the New Culture iconoclasts, whose passions and excitement shone forth in the easily accessible vernacular language. Debates between these defenders of Chinese culture and the New Culture intellectuals were part of a tension between old and new, modernity and tradition, and between different visions of how to make China competitive in the modern world. This same tension pervaded those most modern of places—the cities, and the art, entertainment, and literature consumed by city-dwellers in their everyday lives.

Cities, Arts, and Entertainments, 1911–1926

There were roughly four hundred million Chinese in 1911.[33] Perhaps twenty percent of them lived in the cities. China's major cities—Chengdu and Chongqing, Wuchang, Hankou and Hanyang, Beijing, Tianjin and Qingdao, Guangzhou, and especially Shanghai—were conglomerations of foreign concession areas and Chinese-administered sections. Urban population rose dramatically. Shanghai, for example, went from 1.1 million in 1921 to 2.8 million in 1929.[34] Migration fueled this growth rate: men (and, in smaller numbers, women) left the countryside in search of a better life in the urban industrial and service sectors. Many found a better life. Some became beggars, criminals, or prostitutes (and still may have been better off than they would have been in their villages).

Many of China's major cities also included large concession areas, the homes of European, American, and Japanese businesses, factories, religious and civic organizations, and political and military power. For their foreign residents, the concession areas were places to live and work; for some, particularly missionaries, but also many other Westerners, they represented "beachheads" of Western civilization. For Chinese, the treaty ports, their foreign communities, and their foreign businesses represented the humiliations of colonialism, the attractions of modern products, technologies, and lifestyles, and opportunities to make money.

The economic impact of the treaty ports should not be exaggerated. As late as 1933, China's modern industrial output accounted for only 3.4 percent of total domestic product. Total employment in factory industry, modern mining, and utilities was around four percent of the total nonagricultural labor force.[35] Still, foreign communities and businesses had a substantial economic impact in certain sectors and markets as well as leaving their mark in the realms of culture and politics. Some foreign companies did very well: British American Tobacco, for example, made creative use of a network of Chinese sales representatives, natives of their sales areas, in order to control the lion's share of the cigarette market. The Swedish Match Company, on the other hand, unwilling to delegate much authority to Chinese sales agents, was relegated to a small market share by the more successful China Match Company.[36] Japanese companies were highly competitive in a number of markets, particularly in textile manufactures.

Foreign-owned and Chinese factories, trading companies, department stores, and places of entertainment together created a new commercial culture in China's major cities. Foreign companies like British American Tobacco hired Chinese graphic artists to produce Chinese-style advertising for their products.[37] Cantonese entrepreneurs adapted the Western fixed, one-price department store model of merchandising to the needs of Chinese consumers to create major Shanghai department stores like the Sincere Company and the Wing On Company.[38] Chinese architects and builders in Shanghai combined Western and Chinese design principles to build *shikumen,* stone-framed, wooden-doored, two-story row houses that became one of the most common forms of housing for ordinary Chinese residents of Shanghai.[39]

As cities grew and became centers of trade, industry, and entertainment, government officials were presented with new challenges.[40] From their perspective, the cities were both an administrative and a moral problem. Organized crime and street beggars, the opium trade, traffic jams, public education, sanitation (or the lack thereof) . . . the list of challenges was seemingly endless. And if China were to convince the foreign powers to give up their extraterritorial privileges, Chinese would need to show that they could administer modern cities and maintain social order with institutions of policing and punishment that foreigners would accept as rational, modern, and just.

Beginning in the late 19th century and accelerating rapidly in the first two decades of the 20th century, the Qing and then the Republican governments drafted and promulgated Western-style law codes and built Western-style prisons. Municipal officials in major cities worked to develop modern police forces, though often with a distinctly Confucian flavor. A reformer in Chengdu advised the Qing court in the early 1900s that the police should "serve as models of correct behavior for the people."[41] In practice, modern laws, police, and administrative measures were still, in the 1920s, no more than a thin veneer on the surface of a teeming modern urban life in which police routinely worked with (or were members of) secret societies and organized crime syndicates and in which government regulation never really reached the small shopkeepers, the beggars, the opium dens, and the shantytowns of cities like Shanghai.

One of the things that bothered city officials was the world of entertainment, which was developing in ways quite beyond their expectations and their control. For most Chinese, of course, cheap (or free) entertainment was the only entertainment they could afford. Even in the great city of Shanghai, the average working family spent only one yuan per year on entertainment.[42] For the average person, traditional operas, singers, acrobats, storytellers, trained-monkey shows, martial arts demonstrations, and more could be seen on the streets. For those with bigger budgets, there were teahouses and bars, opium dens and prostitutes, Western-style plays and motion pictures. In Shanghai, the Great World Amusement Center, opened in 1917, boasted ten theaters, a main stage, ice-skating, and four stories of bars, teahouses, and shops.[43]

Intellectuals were both of this urban world and suspicious of it. On the one hand, they saw the cities as places of progress, enlightenment, science, democracy, industry, and opportunity. On the other hand, the cities were the centers of Western and Japanese imperialism and exploitation, of moral degradation, crime and corruption, ignorance and superstition.[44] For the New Culture intellectuals, the city was where one found the best of what the modern world had to offer, but it was also where the worst of tradition and modernity were rolled into one big chaotic mess, spilling exuberantly from the bars and bordellos, opium-houses and factories, into the streets, and into the minds of impressionable young people.

Socially conscious intellectuals hoped to use high-minded literature to move the Chinese masses further along the road of progress and enlightenment. Serious-minded readers could, and did, read the essays and stories of Hu Shi, Chen Duxiu, Lu Xun, and the like. But the serious and the less serious-minded readers alike absolutely devoured lighter brands of literature. Romantic stories of young lovers, known as "mandarin drake and butterfly literature," were tremendously popular. So were detective stories and romantic fiction featuring martial arts heroes defending the weak against powerful evildoers.[45] This popular literature was not completely divorced from the cultural politics of the 1910s and 1920s. Martial arts stories and "butterfly literature" romanticized the premodern Chinese past, and in so doing, rejected modern culture, its moral ambiguities, changing gender roles, and foreign influence.[46]

The huge market for cheap fiction and magazines opened up new avenues not only for professional writers, but also for the artists who drew the illustrations and designed book and magazine covers.[47] Most of these artists made little permanent impression on the Chinese art scene. But some did. After 1911, Western art was no longer an exotic flower to be nurtured in the Manchu court. It became a part of the mainstream. The Chinese scholar-official amateur ideal no longer exercised hegemony over the Chinese art world. Chinese artists now faced a choice: work in the Western tradition, or stay with Chinese painting, now known as *guohua* (national painting).[48] Because aesthetics was so closely connected to national identity, one's choice of artistic expression also signaled a stance as to one's position on the most effective way of constructing a Chinese identity for survival in the modern world.

Many amateur artists took a strong conservative stance, proudly staying within the confines of the scholar-amateur ideal as it had developed up to the 19th century. Most, however, searched for innovation within the *guohua* tradition. From the 1910s through the 1930s, Cantonese painters known as the Lingnan School, deeply influenced by Japanese adaptation of Western art techniques, brought touches of Western realism to Chinese *guohua* works like Gao Jianfu's (1879–1951) "Two Monsters of the Modern World," in which a tank sits in a Chinese landscape and an airplane flies overhead.[49] In Beijing, Qi Baishi (1863–1957), a man of humble farming background, brought a distinctive originality to the *guohua* genre with his use of strong color. Qi consciously avoided imitation of ancient masters and developed his own unique style of portraiture and landscape. By working with *guohua,* artists like Gao Jianfu and Qi Baishi were trying to develop a national identity both distinctively Chinese and, at the same time, modern.[50]

Artists more closely associated with the New Culture iconoclasts looked to Western oil painting for the sources of a new Chinese cultural identity. Cai Yuanpei led a successful movement to incorporate Western art into art education in Chinese schools, and encouraged young Chinese artists to study in Europe in the 1920s.[51] One of those young painters, Xu Beihong (1895–1953), went to France in 1919 on a government scholarship. Xu was convinced that he had discovered the key to reforming China's art, China's spirit, and China's reality in the 19th century realism of Delacroix and Rembrandt: "the departing point of art," he said, "lies in observing all things precisely and reflecting them properly."[52] Realism, he believed, was the appropriate remedy for what he saw as the self-indulgent intellectual abstraction that characterized China's art since the Song dynasty.

Not all students of Western art agreed. French-educated Lin Fengmian (1900–91) and the self-educated Liu Haisu (1896–1994) were admirers of Cezanne, van Gogh, Impressionism, and Post-Impressionism. Liu and his students put on their own shows in the 1920s, and were roundly criticized for displaying nudes.[53] The rivalry between Liu Haisu and Xu Beihong, modernism and realism, defined the politics of art in China from the late 1920s through the 1970s. This and other rivalries in the worlds of art, literature, and music became more politically charged, and more dangerous to the participants, from the late 1920s through the late 1970s, as all aspects of Chinese life were drawn into a series of political struggles.

Musicians in post-1911 China faced choices similar to those of artists: cling to "pure" Chinese forms, use Western techniques to "modernize" Chinese forms, or go for all-out Westernization. Here too, Cai Yuanpei played a key role, using his influence as president of Beijing University to encourage Chinese musicians to "improve" a "backward" Chinese music. Chinese musicians began to use violin techniques on the one-stringed *huqin* (a popular folk instrument), to move away from oral tradition to music notation, to standardize the intonation of instruments, to substitute harmony for heterophony, and to introduce Western-style resonant voicing to Beijing opera.[54]

The Communist Party, the Guomindang, and the First United Front

When they began to work together on *New Youth* in 1917, Chen Duxiu, Li Dazhao, Hu Shi, and other leaders of the New Culture Movement at Beijing University pledged not to engage in politics.[55] Their job would be to focus on cultural and educational issues. As Hu Shi said, they would "build a political foundation by means of nonpolitical factors."[56] But events from 1918 to 1921 brought some of them, particularly Chen Duxiu and Li Dazhao, into the midst of politics. China's experience in World War I, the Versailles Conference, and the Russian Revolution all contributed to the politicization of the New Culture Movement and to intellectuals' participation in two political parties: the Chinese Communist Party and the Guomindang (Nationalist Party).

For Chinese, World War I represented an opportunity to join the Allies on equal terms.[57] In 1914, Yuan Shikai offered to help Britain in joint operations against German positions in Shandong, including the port city of Qingdao. Britain rejected the proposal. When Japan, Britain's ally, took Qingdao and other German concessions and followed up with the Twenty-One Demands, Chinese diplomats renewed their efforts to join the war on the side of the Allies. China supported the Allies diplomatically, sold weapons to them, and sent one hundred forty thousand laborers to France, many of whom worked under dangerous conditions in battle zones.[58] In August 1917, when the West and Japan were finally ready to accept China as an ally, the Chinese government declared war on Germany and the Austro-Hungarian Empire.[59]

China's war aim, of course, was not to defeat Austria-Hungary and Germany in battle. It was to regain control of Austro-Hungarian and German concessions in China, including those now held by Japan. Beyond that, the Chinese hoped to win respect and equal treatment from the Allies and to do away with the concession areas, spheres of interest, extraterritoriality, and fixed tariffs—that is, the entire apparatus of foreign privileges created by the "unequal treaty" system since 1842.

The American president Woodrow Wilson's public commitment to peace, equality, and national self-determination as articulated in his "Fourteen Points" gave Chinese diplomats and the Chinese public reason to be optimistic. But Chinese hopes were dashed at the Paris Peace Conference. The Allies had no intention of treating China as an equal, and they had already agreed that Japan could keep the former German concessions, port, railways, and other interests in Shandong. The fact that the Chinese government had, in an exchange of diplomatic notes with Japan in 1918, agreed in principle to recognize Japan's interest in Shandong helped to justify the Western position.

When news of the Chinese delegation's failure to recover Shandong reached China, students in Beijing erupted in anger. On 4 May 1919, over three thousand young men and women, led by students from Beijing University, gathered in Tiananmen Square. With banners bearing slogans like "Return Qingdao," "Refuse to Sign the Peace Treaty," "China Belongs to the Chinese," and "Down with Traitors," they marched to the closed gates of the Foreign Legation Quarter, and then ransacked and burned the house of a Chinese Foreign Ministry official who had signed the secret correspondence recognizing Japan's claim to the German concessions.[60]

Government attempts to suppress the protestors and the arrest of student leaders led to weeks of student protests and a general strike in Beijing and in hundreds of other cities. College faculty and administrators, merchants, intellectuals, and even some warlords voiced support for the students. The student protests finally wound down in July, after the Chinese delegation in Paris refused to sign the treaty with Germany. But the May Fourth Movement had already begun to give an identity and a sense of purpose to a generation of students. It had also further politicized New Cultural intellectuals who were now no longer content to confine themselves to cultural critique and the promotion of vernacular literature. For some, notably Chen Duxiu and Li Dazhao, the times seemed to call not for more essays, but for political action. But what kind of action? What kind of politics?

The political scene was as eclectic and creative as the cultural and literary world. There were hundreds of journals and newspapers published throughout

China. Intellectuals and students in towns and cities had been organizing study groups (many of them inspired by reading *New Youth*), publishing their own writings, and participating in the May Fourth protests. There were devotees of Kant, Hegel, and Rousseau, fans of American or British democracy, followers of Kang Youwei, of Liang Qichao, of Sun Yat-sen, Chen Duxiu, and Hu Shi.

Socialism and anarchism were particularly influential in this mix of political ideas. Chen Duxiu, Li Dazhao, and many others were especially attracted by socialist and anarchist theories that suggested that education would enable people to reject capitalism and form the voluntary cooperative organizations that would take the place of oppressive government without the need for class struggle and violent revolution.[61]

Because they knew little about Marxism and nothing of Lenin's modifications of Marxist doctrine, Chinese leftists initially understood the Russian Revolution from an anarchist point of view. Chen Duxiu hailed the overthrow of the czar as a great victory for democracy—the only real victory to come out of World War I—but he ignored the October Revolution, which brought Lenin's Bolshveiks to power. Li Dazhao celebrated the October Revolution, which he saw as having laid the foundations for an anarchist society of workers' mutual aid groups. But despite their initial confusion, Chen, Li, and young men and women in a loose network of anarchist and leftist study groups around China worked to learn more about the events that had taken place in Russia and how they might be relevant to China's foreign relations and its internal politics.

As leftist intellectuals like Chen Duxiu and Li Dazhao became more and more involved in overtly political speech and action, Hu Shi and other liberals drew away from them. In the summer of 1919, Hu Shi criticized his leftist colleagues for paying too much attention to abstract social and political theories and too little attention to finding concrete solutions to specific problems:

> We don't study the standard of living of the rickshaw coolie but rant instead about socialism; we don't study the ways in which women can be emancipated, or the family system set right, but instead we rave about wife-sharing and free love; we don't examine the ways in which the Anfu Clique [the militarist power group then in control of the Beijing government] might be broken up . . . but instead we rave about anarchism.[62]

Hu Shi's attack on "isms" had no effect on Li Dazhao or Chen Duxiu. In the months before, during, and after the May Fourth Movement, Li organized a

Marxist study group at Beijing University. Mao Zedong (1893–1976), a bright but distinctly provincial library assistant from Hunan, was one of the members. Chen Duxiu, who fled to Shanghai to avoid arrest for his political activities during the May Fourth Movement, continued to be interested in a wide variety of thought: anarchism, guild socialism, the Korean Christian Socialist movement, and Chinese movements for cooperative societies. Essentially, Chen was curious about any ideology of social change that promised economic development in a collective society, free from the selfishness, the decadence, the cruelty, and the exploitation that seemed to be an inevitable part of economic growth under capitalism, whether in London or in Shanghai.[63]

While leftist Chinese intellectuals were interested in the Russian Revolution, the new Russian government (the Soviet Union after 1922) and Communist Party were intensely interested in China. As revolutionaries, Vladimir Lenin (1870–1924), Leon Trotsky (1879–1940), and the other Soviet leaders saw China as a place where they could strike a blow against the capitalist world powers. As leaders of the Soviet Union, they were keenly aware of China's strategic importance. The long Soviet-Chinese border, the status of Mongolia, and control over Chinese rail lines linking the Trans-Siberian Railway to Vladivostok made China as important to the Soviet Union as it had been to imperial Russia. In order to advance Russian interests and to spread Bolshevik revolutionary doctrine, the Soviet leaders sent Gregory Voitinsky (1893–1956), an agent of the Communist International (Comintern), to China.

Voitinsky's assignment was to make contact with leftist intellectuals, particularly Chen Duxiu. In 1920 Chen, acting on Voitinsky's advice, turned his Shanghai Marxist-Leninist study group into China's first Communist Party cell. Other anarchist and socialist study groups around China followed suit. They were encouraged not only by their interest in the Bolshevik ideology, but also by the fact that the Soviet Union had recently renounced all the imperialist privileges that Czarist Russia had wrung from China. In July 1921, thirteen men representing seven Chinese Communist Party cells held the First National Congress of the Chinese Communist Party in Shanghai. Half of those attending later quit the party, but some, including Mao Zedong, made it their life's career. Chen Duxiu, though not present, was chosen to lead the party as its first secretary-general.

As they worked to build a Chinese Communist Party, the Soviet leaders were keenly aware of the need to explore other options in China. They maintained relations with the warlord government in Beijing; at the same time, they sent Comintern agents to make contact with Dr. Sun Yat-sen. Sun had been trying since 1917 to build a base area in Guangdong province, from which he planned to strike north, defeat the warlords, and take over the national government in Beijing. So far, his efforts had been fruitless. The merchants of Guangzhou had no interest in funding Sun's adventures. His Guomindang was a loosely organized, faction-ridden party of around a thousand members. He had no army, just the services of mercenaries who were reliable only to the extent that he paid them. The Western powers and Japan regarded him as an incompetent political opportunist and rebuffed his requests for support.

Where other world leaders saw an unreliable political con man, Lenin saw opportunity. Following a series of preliminary contacts, Sun Yat-sen welcomed a Comintern agent, Mikhail Borodin (1884–1951), to Guangzhou in October 1923.[64] Borodin's task was to become Sun's advisor and to forge an alliance between the Guomindang and the Chinese Communist Party. Comintern agent Hendricus Sneevliet (1883–1942) had already, in 1922, begun to pressure the reluctant Chinese Communist Party leadership into accepting the idea of joining the Guomindang in a common struggle against the warlords and foreign imperialism.[65] The Communist Party had little choice. It was organizationally, ideologically, and financially dependent on the Comintern, and had made little progress in organizing the workers of Shanghai.

Many Guomindang members were also resistant to the idea of a "United Front." But Sun Yat-sen was eager to accept much (though not all) of Borodin's advice. Borodin and the Soviet Union offered him the essential support that he had failed to get elsewhere. On the key issues of ideology and plans for China's economy, Borodin was willing to agree that China was not yet ready for Soviet-style socialism. So in 1923, the Chinese Communist Party and the Guomindang formed an alliance that historians refer to as the "First United Front." Communist Party members joined the Guomindang as individuals, but maintained their Communist Party membership.

The First United Front served Sun's interests well. Comintern advisers reorganized the Guomindang into a stronger, more disciplined, centralized political party, focused, like the Soviet Communist Party, on a strong leader and his ideology. This gave the Guomindang a political outlook and organizational style that had much in common with the Chinese Communist Party. The difference was that in this case, the ideology was not Bolshevism or Marxism-Leninism: it was an updated version of Sun Yat-sen's Three People's Principles: Nationalism, Democracy, and People's Livelihood.

In the Three People's Principles of the 1920s, "Nationalism" was no longer the nationalism of Han Chinese as defined against Manchu minority rulers.

That struggle was long over. Nationalism now meant the assertion of the dignity and territorial sovereignty of the Chinese nation—implicitly and sometimes explicitly understood as the Han people, but now extended in an attempt to construct a sense of Chinese national identity that would include all the peoples and territories of the former Qing Empire: Han, Manchu, Mongol, Tibetan, Muslim, and others.

"Democracy," the second of the Three People's Principles, was still seen as the political system most suited to the Chinese nation-state, but Sun and his followers saw the realization of democracy as a long-term goal. China would first need a nationalist revolution. It would then go through three stages of political development. First there would be a period of military government. This would be followed by an indeterminate transitional stage of "tutelage" in which an authoritarian regime would educate and uplift the Chinese masses to the point at which they would be capable of being responsible citizens. Only then would China reach the final stage of establishing representative democracy. "People's Livelihood" remained a vaguely defined sort of socialism, to be achieved without class struggle and without much sacrifice on the part of the Guomindang's wealthy supporters.

With a stronger party organization and an ideological platform, the Guomindang could train a cadre of dedicated, politically indoctrinated party leaders and its own army. The newly created Canton University was linked directly to the Guomindang and its goals, establishing a model for the politicization of higher education.[66] Soviet instructors, weapons, and money helped to establish a Guomindang officers' training school, the Whampoa Military Academy, on an island downriver from Guangzhou. The academy turned out hundreds of officers who formed the core of the Guomindang's new army. The commandant, Chiang Kai-shek (1887–1975), was a young Japanese-educated career officer who, though he went through a brief training course in the Soviet Union, was deeply suspicious of the Soviets, and of the Chinese Communist Party.

The Political Parties, the Masses, and the May Thirtieth Movement

In 1925, China stood on the brink of yet another episode of revolutionary change. In the autumn of 1924, a major war between the Zhili Clique, the Manchurian Zhang Zuolin's Fengtian Clique, and the "Christian General": Feng Yuxiang had gravely weakened all the major warlord factions of northern

China and the Yangzi Valley. The fighting had also undermined the already shaky national government in Beijing and thrown China's urban economy into turmoil.[67]

The situation played right into the hands of Guomindang and Communist Party leaders, who, in 1924–25, were preparing to carry out Sun Yat-sen's plan for a "Northern Expedition" to unite China under a new, Guomindang-led government. The two parties worked together within the United Front to achieve that goal. But for the Communists, the creation of a Guomindang-dominated government was only the first step. Their next task would be to continue to organize farmers and workers in order to carry out a socialist revolution in which the Guomindang would be overthrown.

In preparing for the Northern Expedition, the Guomindang trained army officers and political leaders at the Whampoa Military Academy and Canton University. They raised money, built an army, and recruited supporters inside China and among overseas Chinese. Because they were more interested in working-class issues, Communist Party members played a leading role in United Front efforts to build support for the Northern Expedition among farmers and industrial workers. These organizational efforts helped the Communist Party to recruit new members and gave party leaders experience that some of them would draw on in the decades to come.

One of the lessons that at least some Communists learned was that rural work held great potential for the future. Marxist theory regards the industrial proletariat as the class that will carry out socialist revolution. But in the mid-1920s, the Comintern directed the Chinese Communists to work with farmers as well as with industrial workers. The reality was that around eighty percent of China's people lived in the rural villages. Most of them made their living from a combination of farming, crafts, and small-scale trade, and by selling their labor. Chinese farmers typically cultivated relatively small plots of land, using the labor-intensive, highly efficient, but premodern techniques that their ancestors had perfected over the centuries. Those living close to major transportation routes and cities were increasingly integrated into regional, national, and international markets.

Average farm income was very low. Under ideal conditions, traditional agriculture could be highly productive. But economic and environmental conditions were often less than ideal. Land tenure patterns varied, but many farmers rented all or some of their land from wealthier neighbors, large absentee landlords, or powerful clans. All farmers were vulnerable to natural disaster, banditry, extortionate taxation from warlord governments, and the pillaging of warlord troops. Their lives were made more precarious by the

Major warlord factions, 1924.

fact that the weak national government was unable to effectively deliver relief from famines or natural disasters. In some areas, farmers took the initiative to organize peasants' associations in an effort to resist rent increases or
protest against mistreatment at the hands of powerful landholding families.
Left-wing Guomindang members, socialists, anarchists, and even some conservative Confucian intellectuals were all intensely interested in rural issues,

but it was the Communists whose work in the countryside proved to have the most significant long-term consequences.

Two Communist Party members, Peng Pai (1896–1929) and Mao Zedong (1893–1976), were particularly interested in rural work.[68] Peng Pai, a Japanese-educated landlord's son from Guangdong province's mountainous and notoriously bandit-ridden Haifeng county, began to work with the farmers in his home area in 1921. Peng soon learned that if he was to be effective, he would need to dress simply, speak plainly, and listen to the peasants and accept their ideas. He also soon found that his own family would need to lower the rents on their fields before the peasants of Haifeng would accept him as a leader for peasants' rights. Peng won the respect and trust of the peasants, played a leading role in setting up a peasants' association, worked with farmers to demand rent reduction, and organized peasant support when Chiang Kai-shek's Guomindang army fought to capture Haifeng and neighboring areas of Guangdong from a local warlord.

Mao Zedong became interested in rural issues only in 1925 in the wake of the patriotic "May Thirtieth Movement" (to be discussed below).[69] Mao explained his understanding of the peasants' role in the national revolution in his "Report on an Investigation of the Peasant Movement in Hunan." In the "Report," Mao portrays peasants as a powerful force for revolution, but one that a true revolutionary must lead and direct. He emphasizes that "it is necessary to go to extremes" and describes approvingly how poor peasants break into landlords' houses, help themselves to grain and money, and trample on the landlords' feather beds: "Revolution," he explained, "is not a dinner party, or writing an essay, or painting a picture, or doing embroidery; it cannot be so refined, so leisurely and gentle, so temperate, kind, courteous, restrained and magnanimous. A revolution is an insurrection, an act of violence by which one class overthrows another."[70]

Peng Pai and Mao saw great revolutionary potential in the countryside, but they were odd ducks in the Chinese Communist movement of the mid-1920s. Party leaders viewed peasants as part of the bourgeoisie. They looked down on rural work. The real business of socialist revolution, they believed, was to work in the cities to organize the industrial workers.

The main problem with organizing industrial workers was that there were not very many of them. China's modern industrial economy got off to a slow start with the Self-Strengthening enterprises of the mid- to late 19th century. Chinese state-owned and private modern businesses found it difficult to compete with foreign imports and with foreign-run enterprises on Chinese soil, which enjoyed privileges under the "unequal treaties" and advantages in access to technology, capital, and managerial talent.

World War I gave Chinese businessmen their first significant window of opportunity to compete. With Western capital, manpower, and resources drawn into the conflagration in Europe, Chinese entrepreneurs were able to expand production to meet both domestic and international demand for everyday household products (such as matches and soap) and for textiles. The resulting "Golden Age" of the Chinese bourgeoisie lasted until a serious business downturn in 1923.[71]

The growth of Chinese and foreign-owned, especially Japanese, industry led to the development of a larger and more politically sophisticated Chinese urban working class. Most were first-generation migrants from the countryside. In 1919, there were roughly 1,489,000 workers in China, with the greatest concentration being in the city of Shanghai.[72] In Shanghai and other industrial cities, rural migrants found higher (or at least more stable) income, a more exciting environment, and better food, but also very harsh working conditions and the possibility of unemployment. Shanghai, China's modern city *par excellence,* was host to workers from everywhere, but especially from Guangzhou, from the Zhejiang provincial city of Ningbo, and from Jiangsu.

Migrants tended to live in neighborhoods much like the ethnic conclaves of early-20th-century Chicago. Workers from particular localities tended to dominate particular professions (Guangzhou men in carpentry, for example) and to find solidarity and protection in native place organizations.[73] Some sought protection and a higher income through involvement in organized criminal gangs. The most famous of these, the Green Gang, had its origins in a salvationist Buddhist sect that had offered spiritual and material sustenance to boatmen along the Grand Canal during the Qing dynasty.[74] By the 1920s, the Green Gang was the dominant criminal syndicate in Shanghai, with activities ranging from opium and prostitution to protection, gambling, kidnapping, and armed robbery.

In foreign-owned plants and in the foreign concession areas of the cities, workers also encountered firsthand the everyday humiliations of imperialism and the casual arrogance and brutality of foreign employers. Some factories subjected Chinese workers to body searches before they were allowed to leave the premises, to prevent them from taking away anything, even scraps. The attitude of foreigners was that such measures were necessary because of the "low state of civilization which the Chinese mill operatives occupy."[75] By 1923, Chinese workers already had a long history of involvement

The Bund in Shanghai in 1928, showing a view of the World War I memorial.

in strikes, protests, machine-smashing, and boycotts in which workplace issues combined with nationalist expressions of resentment against foreign imperialism.

In the spring of 1925, workers in Shanghai held a series of strikes against Japanese textile mills. Their concerns were not unusual. They demanded higher pay and protested harsh treatment at the hands of Chinese and Japanese foremen.[76] These strikes were led by Chinese Communist Party organizers, who had been working hard to gain a position of leadership over the labor movement as a whole. So when a Chinese worker (and Communist Party member) was killed in a violent clash with Japanese guards at a cotton mill in mid-May, the Communist Party worked to build on the incident by calling for a protest in Shanghai's International Concession, thus linking the labor issue to the struggle against imperialism. On 30 May 1925, thousands of Chinese workers, students, and townspeople took to the streets. When a British police officer ordered his men to open fire on the crowd, four were killed on the spot; eight more died of their wounds afterward.[77]

This brutal shooting of unarmed protesters caused a nationwide reaction known as the May Thirtieth Movement. Urban China was hit by months of strikes, boycotts of British and Japanese goods, demonstrations, and petitions. Workers, shopkeepers, clerks, intellectuals, artists, and writers joined the patriotic movement. Many Chinese businessmen, who blamed foreign (especially Japanese) competition for the post-1923 economic decline that had hit them particularly hard, supported the May Thirtieth activists. So did a number of warlords, including the notoriously brutal Zhang Zongchang in Shandong and the Japanese-supported Zhang Zuolin in Manchuria.

The businessmen's support soon waned (especially when strikes began to hit Chinese as well as foreign firms). The warlords, too, quickly returned to form, violently suppressing demonstrators and arresting protest leaders. The May Thirtieth Movement died down by the end of the summer of 1925, but the burst of activity had convinced many ordinary urban Chinese that the fate of the nation was at stake: standing aside from political issues and simply tolerating imperialism and warlord rule were no longer acceptable. For urban China, the May Thirtieth Movement marks an increasing level of politicization of cultural and intellectual life which some historians see as marking the end of the freewheeling, iconoclastic atmosphere of the "New Culture Movement."[78]

The Communist Party benefited immensely from this new high tide of patriotic feeling. Communist Party membership jumped from one thousand to ten thousand by November 1925, and to fifty-eight thousand by the spring of 1927. The Communist Youth League made similar strides, with youth from worker rather than intellectual background becoming the majority for the first time.[79] With its increased membership and stronger appeal to workers, the Communist Party now became the leading force in the Chinese labor movement. The Guomindang, too, recruited new members who believed that service to the Nationalist Party would be the most effective way of making a meaningful contribution to the betterment of their country.

The rising tide of patriotism energized the Guomindang at a crucial juncture in its history. Dr. Sun Yat-sen had died of liver cancer on 12 March 1925 in Beijing, where he had gone in an attempt to negotiate a national unity government with the warlord Duan Qirui (1864–1936). Before his death, he signed a "Political Testament" drafted by Wang Jingwei, an early anti-Manchu activist and close collaborator of Sun's, which reaffirmed the goal of a national revolution to "restore to China its liberty and a rank equal [to that of the other nations]" and called upon his comrades to "continue to struggle for this victory."[80] But with Sun gone, who would lead the Guomindang, and the United Front, to victory? And who would be the president of a newly reestablished Republic of China?

The Communist Party, the junior partner in the United Front, was growing rapidly, particularly as a result of its recruiting among urban workers. The Guomindang itself was split between left and right factions. On the left, Wang Jingwei, now chairman of the Guomindang, laid claim to be the successor to Sun Yat-sen. On the right, a group of men known as the "Western Hills Faction" (after their first meeting place in the Western Hills outside of Beijing, where Sun's body was temporarily laid to rest) pledged to take the Guomindang in a more conservative, anti-Communist direction.

In the middle, still supported by Russia (some called him the "Red General"), but already deeply suspicious of the Chinese Communist Party and of the Soviet Union, was Chiang Kai-shek, commandant of the Whampoa Military Academy. Chiang had already taken steps to consolidate control of Guangzhou. He could not immediately solve the problem of political succession, but as the creator of the Guomindang's army, he was the man to lead the Northern Expedition. The issue of the political leadership and direction of the country would be decided in the context of the armed struggle against the warlords. As commander of the National Revolutionary Army, Chiang would clearly have an advantage.

Notes

1. Vidya Prakash Dutt, "The First Week of Revolution: The Wuchang Uprising," in Mary Clabaugh Wright, ed., *China in Revolution: The First Phase 1900–1913* (New Haven: Yale University Press, 1968), 395–6.

2. Chuzo Ichiko, "Political and Institutional Reform, 1901–11," in John K. Fairbank and Kwang-Ching Liu, eds., *The Cambridge History of China, Vol. 11: Late Ch'ing, 1800–1911, Part 2* (Cambridge: Cambridge University Press, 1980), 399–401.

3. This description of Prince Regent Zaifeng's clash with the National Assembly is based on Edward J. M. Rhoads, *Manchus and Han: Ethnic Relations and Political Power in Late Qing and Early Republican China, 1861–1928* (Seattle: University of Washington Press, 2000), 157–70.

4. Frederic Wakeman, Jr., *The Fall of Imperial China* (New York: The Free Press, 1975), 247–8.

5. This and the following draw on Dutt, "The First Week of Revolution," 383–416.

6. This description of Sun and his role in 1911 is based on Marie-Claire Bergère, *Sun Yat-sen* (Stanford: Stanford University Press, 1998), 207–13. Bergère's account (p. 207) suggests that Sun was in Denver when he read the news of the Wuchang Uprising. Other accounts suggest that he was on a train en route from Denver to Kansas City.

7. The revolutionaries found Lea's physical deformity—a hunchback—particularly unsettling. Some regarded it as a bad omen. Bergère, *Sun Yat-sen*, 212. See also Eugene Anschel, *Homer Lea, Sun Yat-sen and the Chinese Revolution* (New York: Praeger, 1984).

8. Rhoads, *Manchus and Han*, 187–205.

9. Mary Backus Rankin, "State and Society in Early Republican Politics, 1912–1918," in Frederic Wakeman, Jr., and Richard Louis Edmonds, eds. *Reapprais-*

ing Republican China (Oxford: Oxford University Press, 2000), 6.

10. Ono Kazuko, *Chinese Women in a Century of Revolution, 1850–1950* (Stanford: Stanford University Press, 1989), 74–5, 83–9.

11. Peter Zarrow, "Political Ritual in the Early Republic of China," in Kai-wing Chow, Kevin M. Doak, and Poshek Fu, eds., *Constructing Nationhood in Modern East Asia* (Ann Arbor: The University of Michigan Press, 2001), 149–88.

12. Ernest P. Young, *The Presidency of Yuan Shih-k'ai: Liberalism and Dictatorship in Early Republican China* (Ann Arbor: The University of Michigan Press, 1977), 163.

13. Ibid., 158–9.

14. Ibid., 221–2.

15. For a discussion of warlordism, see Edward A. McCord, *The Power of the Gun: The Emergence of Modern Chinese Warlordism* (Berkeley: University of California Press, 1993).

16. Bruce Elleman, *Modern Chinese Warfare, 1795–1989* (London: Routledge, 2001), 163. For a discussion of warlord conflict and politics, see Arthur Waldron, *From War to Nationalism: China's Turning Point, 1924–1925* (Cambridge: Cambridge University Press, 1995).

17. For warlord soldiers and recruiting, see Diana Lary, *Warlord Soldiers: Chinese Common Soldiers, 1911–1937* (Cambridge: Cambridge University Press, 1985).

18. Historians differ on the definition of the "New Culture" period. Most begin the period with the publication of Chen Duxiu's *New Youth* in 1915. Some regard the foundation of the Chinese Communist Party as marking the end of the New Culture Movement. I am following Wang Zheng in seeing the rise of nationalism with the May Thirtieth Movement of 1925 as marking the end of the New Culture period. See Wang Zheng, *Women in the Chinese Enlightenment: Oral and Textual Histories* (Berkeley: University of California Press, 1999), 23. Like most such dividing lines, this one is subject to debate: the literary trends begun in the late 1910s and 1920s, for example, developed throughout the 1930s, so that Philip Williams, for example, defines the "May Fourth New Culture Movement" in literature as extending from 1917 to 1937. Philip Williams, "Twentieth-Century Fiction," in Victor H. Mair, ed., *The Columbia History of Chinese Literature* (New York: Columbia University Press, 2001), 744.

19. Leo Ou-fan Lee and Merle Goldman, "Introduction: The Intellectual History of Modern China," in Goldman and Lee, eds., *An Intellectual History of Modern China* (Cambridge: Cambridge University Press, 2002), 87.

20. Chow Tse-tsung, *The May 4th Movement: Intellectual Revolution in Modern China* (Cambridge, Mass.: Harvard University Press, 1960), 73.

21. Ibid., 50.

22. Quoted in Leo Ou-fan Lee, "Modernity and Its Discontents: The Cultural Agenda of the May Fourth Movement," in Kenneth Lieberthal, Joyce Kallgren, Roderick MacFarquhar, and Frederic Wakeman, Jr., eds., *Perspectives on Modern China: Four Anniversaries* (Armonk: M. E. Sharpe, 1991), 162.

23. For this, and for the tension between optimism about human progress and pessimism about China's failure to progress, see Lung-kee Sun, "The Presence of the Fin-de-Siècle in the May Fourth Era," in Gail Hershatter, Emily Honig, Jonathan N. Lipman, and Randall Stross, eds., *Remapping China: Fissures in Historical*

Terrain (Stanford: Stanford University Press, 1996), 195.

24. Quoted in Chow, *The May 4th Movement,* 46.

25. Quoted in Jerome B. Grieder, *Hu Shih and the Chinese Renaissance: Liberalism in the Chinese Revolution, 1917–1937* (Cambridge, Mass.: Harvard University Press, 1970), 81.

26. "Lu Xun" was a pen-name; the author's real name was Zhou Zuoren. This and subsequent discussion on Lu Xun draw on David E. Pollard, *The True Story of Lu Xun* (Hong Kong: The Chinese University Press, 2002).

27. Wang, *Women in the Chinese Enlightenment,* 46.

28. See the discussion in Elisabeth Eide, *China's Ibsen: From Ibsen to Ibsenism* (London: Curzon Press, 1987).

29. Wang, *Women in the Chinese Enlightenment,* 156–7.

30. Ibid., 183–4.

31. Lee and Goldman, "Introduction," 53.

32. Guy S. Alitto, *The Last Confucian: Liang Shu-ming and the Chinese Dilemma of Modernity* (Berkeley: University of California Press, 1986), 82–125.

33. Ping-ti Ho, *Studies on the Population of China, 1368–1953* (Cambridge, Mass.: Harvard University Press, 1959), 73–9. Describing the widespread inefficiency and falsification of census data, Ho concludes that "all the official population figures between 1902 and 1927 were the result of governmental self-deception" (79). The figure of four hundred million Chinese in 1911 is simply a rough guess based on the unreliable figures of 341,913,497 from the Qing census of 1908–11 and 419,640,279 for the census of 1912. (See Ho, 73, 79.)

34. Zhang Kaizhi, ed., *Zhongguo lishi: wan Qing Minguo juan* (Chinese history: late Qing and Republic volume) (Beijing: Gaodeng jiaoyu chubanshe, 2001), 241.

35. Rhoads Murphey, *The Treaty Ports and China's Modernization: What Went Wrong?* Michigan Papers in Chinese Studies 7 (Ann Arbor: Center for Chinese Studies, University of Michigan, 1970), 66.

36. Sherman Cochran, *Big Business in China: Sino-Foreign Rivalry in the Cigarette Industry, 1890–1930* (Cambridge, Mass.: Harvard University Press, 1980); Sherman Cochran, "Three Roads into Shanghai's Market: Japanese, Western, and Chinese Companies in the Match Trade, 1895–1937," in Frederic Wakeman, Jr., and Wen-hsin Yeh, eds., *Shanghai Sojourners* (Berkeley: Institute of East Asian Studies, University of California, 1992), 35–75.

37. Liang Dingming, Hu Boxiang, Ni Gengye, and Zhang Guangyu, "Artists at British American Tobacco," in Ellen Johnston Laing, ed., *Selling Happiness: Calendar Posters and Visual Culture in Early-Twentieth-Century Shanghai* (Honolulu: University of Hawaii Press, 2004), 171–98.

38. Wellington K. K. Chan, "Selling Goods and Promoting a New Commercial Culture: The Four Premier Department Stores on Nanjing Road, 1917–1937," in Sherman Cochran, ed., *Inventing Nanjing Road: Commercial Culture in Shanghai, 1900–1945* (Ithaca: Cornell University East Asia Program, 1999), 23–4.

39. Hanchao Lu, "'The Seventy-two Tenants': Residence and Commerce in Shanghai's *Shikumen* Houses, 1872–1951," in Cochran, ed., op. cit., 133–84.

40. On issues of urban administration and modernization, see Kristin Stapleton, *Civilizing Chengdu: Chinese Urban Reform, 1895–1937* (Cambridge, Mass.: Harvard

University East Asian Center, 2000). For law, punishments, and policing, see Frank Dikötter, *Crime, Punishment, and the Prison in Modern China* (New York: Columbia University Press, 2002); and Michael Dutton, *Policing and Punishment in China: From Patriarchy to "the People"* (Cambridge: Cambridge University Press, 1992).

41. Stapleton, *Civilizing Chengdu*, 84.

42. E. Perry Link, Jr., *Mandarin Ducks and Butterflies: Popular Fiction in Early Twentieth Century Chinese Cities* (Berkeley: University of California Press, 1981), 190.

43. Hanchao Lu, *Beyond the Neon Lights: Everyday Life in Shanghai in the Early Twentieth Century* (Berkeley: University of California Press, 1999), 115. On urban life generally, in addition to Lu, see Di Wang, *Street Culture in Chengdu: Public Space, Urban Commoners, and Local Politics, 1870–1930* (Stanford: Stanford University Press, 2003); David Strand, *Rickshaw Beijing: City People and Politics in the 1920s* (Berkeley: University of California Press, 1989); and Madeleine Yue Dong, *Republican Beijing: The City and Its Histories* (Berkeley: University of California Press, 2003).

44. Yingjin Zhang, *The City in Modern Chinese Literature and Film: Configurations of Space, Time, and Gender* (Stanford: Stanford University Press, 1996), 9–12.

45. For "butterfly literature," see Link, *Mandarin Ducks;* on detective fiction, Jeffrey Kinkley, *Chinese Justice, the Fiction: Law and Literature in Modern China* (Stanford: Stanford University Press, 2000).

46. Leo Ou-fan Lee, "Literary Trends I: The Quest for Modernity, 1895–1927," in John King Fairbank, ed., *The Cambridge History of China, Vol. 12: Republican China, 1912–1949, Part 1* (Cambridge: Cambridge University Press, 1983), 462–3.

47. Julia F. Andrews, "Commercial Art and China's Modernization," in Julia F. Andrews and Kuiyi Shen, eds., *A Century in Crisis: Modernity and Tradition in the Art of Twentieth Century China* (New York: Guggenheim Museum), 1998, 181.

48. Julia F. Andrews, "A Century in Crisis: Tradition and Modernity in the Art of Twentieth-Century China," in Andrews and Shen, eds., op. cit., 4.

49. Michael Sullivan, *Art and Artists of Twentieth Century China* (Berkeley: University of California Press, 1996), 55.

50. David Der-wei Wang, "In the Name of the Real," in Maxwell K. Hearn and Judith G. Smith, ed., *Chinese Art: Modern Expressions* (New York: The Metropolitan Museum of Art, 2001), 40.

51. Mayching Kao, "Reforms in Education and the Beginning of the Western-Style Painting Movement in China," in Andrews and Shen, eds., *A Century in Crisis,* 153–5.

52. Quoted in Wang, "In the Name of the Real," 30.

53. Sullivan, *Art and Artists,* 72–4.

54. Tsui Ying-fai, "Ensembles: The Modern Chinese Orchestra," in Robert C. Provine, Yoshiko Tokomaru, and J. Lawrence Witzleben, eds., *The Garland Encyclopedia of World Music, Vol. 7, East Asia: China, Japan, and Korea* (New York: Routledge, 2002), 228–9; Stanley Sadie, ed., *The New Grove Dictionary of Music and Musicians,* vol. 4 (New York: MacMillan Publishers, 1980), 248–9.

55. Chow, *The May 4th Movement,* 57.

56. Ibid.

57. This and the discussion of China in World War I in general follow the interpretation presented in Guoqi Xu, *China and the Great War: China's Pursuit of a New National Identity and Internationalization*

(Cambridge: Cambridge University Press, 2005).

58. Ibid., 130.

59. Ibid., 164.

60. Chow, *The May 4th Movement,* 99–116.

61. On Chen Duxiu and Li Dazhao's transition from anarchism to Marxism-Leninism and on the founding of the Chinese Communist Party in general, I follow Arif Dirlik, *The Origins of Chinese Communism* (Oxford: Oxford University Press, 1989).

62. Quoted in Grieder, *Hu Shih and the Chinese Renaissance,* 124.

63. Lee Feigon, *Chen Duxiu: Founder of the Chinese Communist Party* (Princeton: Princeton University Press, 1983), 145–6.

64. Bergère, *Sun Yat-sen,* 318.

65. S. A. Smith, *Like Cattle and Horses: Nationalism and Labor in Shanghai, 1895–1927* (Durham: Duke University Press, 2002), 148.

66. Bergère, *Sun Yat-sen,* 343–4.

67. As described in Arthur Waldron, *From War to Nationalism: China's Turning Point, 1924–1925* (Cambridge: Cambridge University Press, 1995).

68. For Peng Pai, see Fernando Galbiati, *Peng Pai and the Hai-Lu-Feng Soviet* (Stanford: Stanford University Press, 1985).

69. Stuart Schram, *The Thought of Mao Tse-tung* (Cambridge: Cambridge University Press, 1989), 35.

70. Mao Zedong, "Report on an Investigation of the Peasant Movement in Hunan," in *Selected Reading from the Works of Mao Tse-tung* (Peking: Foreign Languages Press, 1971), 30.

71. Marie-Claire Bergère, "The Chinese Bourgeoisie, 1911–1937," in Fairbank, ed., *The Cambridge History of China, Vol. 12,* 746–51, 788.

72. Jean Chesneaux, *The Chinese Labor Movement 1919–1927* (Stanford: Stanford University Press, 1968), 42–3.

73. Elizabeth J. Perry, *Shanghai on Strike: The Politics of Chinese Labor* (Stanford: Stanford University Press, 1993), 19–27.

74. Brian G. Martin, *The Shanghai Green Gang: Politics and Organized Crime, 1919–1937* (Berkeley: University of California Press, 1996), 10–17.

75. A. S. Pearse, *The Cotton Industry of Japan and China* (Manchester: International Federation of Master Cotton Spinners and Manufacturers Associations, 1929), 172, quoted in Richard W. Rigby, *The May 30th Movement: Events and Themes* (Canberra: Australian National University Press, 1980), 15.

76. Smith, *Like Cattle and Horses,* 162. See also the discussions of the May Thirtieth Movement in Perry, *Shanghai on Strike;* and Rigby, *The May 30th Movement.*

77. C. Martin Wilbur, "The Nationalist Revolution: From Canton to Nanking, 1923–1928," in Fairbank, ed., *The Cambridge History of China, Vol. 12,* 547–9.

78. Wang, *Women in the Chinese Enlightenment,* 23.

79. Lucien Bianco, *Origins of the Chinese Revolution 1915–1949* (Stanford: Stanford University Press, 1971), 55–6.

80. Quoted in Bergère, *Sun Yat-sen,* 406.

革

Chapter 4   YEARS OF TURMOIL

China Under
Chiang Kai-shek's
Guomindang Government

In 1926 Chiang Kai-shek sent the Guomindang's National Army forth on the Northern Expedition to defeat the warlords and re-unite China. In 1927, he proclaimed the establishment of the new government in Nanjing. From then until 1949, Chiang led the Republic of China through twenty-two dramatic, chaotic, and, for many Chinese, miserable years. Finally, his regime weakened by years of war with Japan and defeated on the battlefield by the Communist Party's People's Liberation Army, Chiang, his government, and his army fled to the island of Taiwan.

The Nationalist period (1927–49) left a mixed legacy. Ruling from the capital of Nanjing from 1927 to 1937—the "Nanjing Decade"—Chiang's government presided over a period of economic growth, development of a Western-style legal system, and progress toward ending the galling provisions of the "unequal treaties." But Chiang's autocratic leadership style, his willingness to use violence, even murder, to further his political goals, his partnerships with organized crime, the undisguised corruption of the leading men and women of his government and his family all tarnished the image of Chiang's Nationalist Party (Guomindang) regime and contributed to its loss of the mainland.

The Northern Expedition

When Sun Yat-sen died, both the Guomindang and the Communist Party were riding a high tide of nationalist, anti-imperialist fervor sparked by the May Thirtieth Incident (see Chapter 3). With anti-foreign protests, strikes, and boycotts sweeping the nation and support for national unity running high, the Guomindang stood at a crossroads. Should the party commit its energy to continued anti-foreign, especially anti-British, strikes and boycotts in order to force the foreign powers to give up their colonial privileges? Or should it carry out Sun Yat-sen's idea of a Northern Expedition to defeat the warlords and give China a strong central government? The question became entangled with the issue of who would follow Sun as leader of the Guomindang.

Three elements within the Guomindang competed for control after Sun's death. The left wing of the Guomindang, led by Wang Jingwei, favored continued cooperation with the Soviet Union and the Chinese Communist Party. Standing against Wang was the more conservative Guomindang right wing, some of whom had taken an oath in the presence of Sun's body as it lay in state at a temple in Beijing's Western Hills. This Western Hills Faction wanted to see an immediate end to relations with the Communists and the Soviet Union. Circumstances initially favored the Guomindang Left. In Guangzhou, the leftist and Communist Party delegates combined to elect Wang Jingwei as party chairman. Wang, the Communist Party, and the Comintern advisors did not support the idea of a Northern Expedition. They preferred to continue with the strikes and boycotts, which were hitting hard at British interests in Hong Kong and Guangzhou and could potentially lead to a broader social revolutionary movement.

Chiang Kai-shek during a radio address, 1947.

Chiang Kai-shek, the man who led the Guomindang's army, stood in the middle. Maneuvering artfully between left and right, Chiang pushed the Northern Expedition to the top of the Guomindang's agenda. He played especially on the fears of Guangdong merchants and landlords, who were deeply suspicious of the Guomindang Left's radical social programs (strikes, work-slowdowns), which were as likely to undermine Chinese capitalists as they were to weaken the British. In a key incident, the truth of which remains unclear, leftist party members aboard the Guomindang's naval vessel the *Zhongshan* allegedly tried to kidnap Chiang on 18 March. Chiang used the "*Zhongshan* Incident" to purge the Guomindang leadership of Communists, drive off several influential Comintern advisors, and weaken leftist opposition to his proposed campaign. The restructured Guomindang leadership approved the Northern Expedition, with Chiang as its commander-in-chief, in June.

The purpose of the Northern Expedition was to defeat the warlords and bring all Chinese territory under the authority of a strong central government. But from the beginning, Chiang's strategy was to win some warlords over to his side by allowing them a high degree of control over their own armies and autonomy within their own areas. For example, Chiang's preparations for the Northern Expedition included an agreement under which the leading generals of the "Guangxi Clique," including Li Zongren (1890–1969) and the Muslim general Bai Chongxi (1893–1966), incorporated their forces into Chiang's National Revolutionary Army.[1] As the National Revolutionary Army struck north from Guangdong to attack the warlord Wu Peifu (1874–1939), Chiang bought off and incorporated key local warlords who were willing to shift their support from Wu's Zhili Clique to the Guomindang.

Chiang's strategy was successful. The National Revolutionary Army, its ranks strengthened with warlord troops and experienced warlord generals, swept north to Wuhan, which it took in October 1926 after fierce fighting with Wu Peifu's forces. The Nationalist armies then proceeded down the Yangzi, taking Nanjing, and then Shanghai, from warlord Sun Chuanfang (1885–1935). In their campaigns, Chiang's armies were accompanied by Soviet military advisors who contributed significantly to the planning and execution of Nationalist operations. The army also benefited from the support of farmers and workers, some of them organized and mobilized by the Communist Party. But as the revolutionaries approached Shanghai, the Guomindang's cooperation with the Soviet Union and the Chinese Communist Party was already unraveling.

革

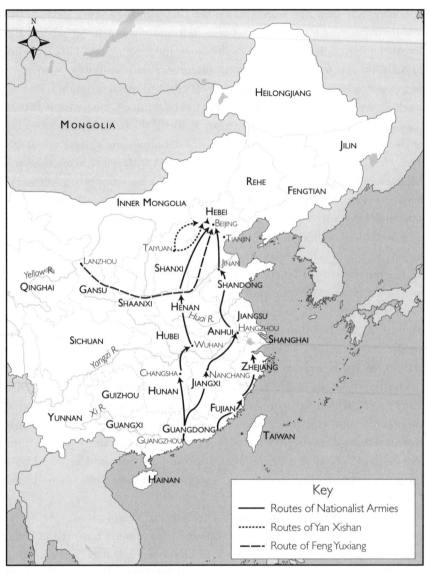

The Northern Expedition, 1926–28.

The Northern Expedition had not been good for the Guomindang Left.
Chiang had ordered an end to the anti-British strikes and boycotts in
Guangzhou and Hong Kong; while undermining British businesses, the anti-
imperialist movement was also harming the Guomindang's two main sources
of revenue: import taxes and the active support of Chinese merchants.
Police raids on the Soviet Embassy in Beijing and consulates in Tianjin and

Shanghai on 6 April 1927 brought the release of documents that showed how Comintern agents gave advice and support to the Communist Party and the Guomindang Left.[2] Warlord Zhang Zuolin's men in Beijing arrested and executed Li Dazhao, one of the leaders of the New Culture Movement and of the Chinese Communist Party. The Guomindang Left–Communist Party coalition seemed in mortal danger, but Wang Jingwei was still chairman of the Nationalist Party. In March and April, the Guomindang's Central Executive Committee, meeting in Wuhan, passed a series of resolutions reducing Chiang's power and establishing a new government, to be headed by Wang Jingwei.

Chiang responded by setting up a rival national government in Nanjing. On 12 April, with his control over Shanghai still tenuous and his armies suffering defeat as they tried to march north from the Yangzi, Chiang took violent measures to weaken the Guomindang Left and destroy the "United Front" with the Communists. On his orders, Guomindang agents, assisted by members of Shanghai's notorious Green Gang, rounded up Communist Party members and labor organizers around Shanghai. Perhaps three to four thousand Communist Party members were killed in Shanghai and other cities and towns across China during the "White Terror." Estimates for total deaths of party members, peasants' association members, and others branded as leftists from March through August 1927 are as high as around thirty thousand.[3] The United Front and the era of close cooperation with the Soviet Union came to a bloody end.

In Wuhan, Wang Jingwei and the Guomindang Left struggled on for a few months longer. Members of the Chinese Communist Party, who had played a major role in setting up the Wuhan government, had orders from Joseph Stalin (1878–1953) to advance the revolution to the next stage, in which the Guomindang would be subordinated to Communist Party leadership. When Wang Jingwei saw a copy of Stalin's telegram, he was understandably disturbed. In July 1927, the Guomindang Left finally ended their cooperation with the Soviet Union, split with the Chinese Communist Party, and cast their lot with the Nanjing government. By 1 January 1928, Chiang Kai-shek was in control of the Nationalist Party, the army, and the government in Nanjing. He had used the Northern Expedition and the mass murder of Communists to consolidate his position as supreme leader. He had also strengthened his status by marrying into one of China's premier business and political families: the Song family.

Charles Song (1863?–1918), the patriarch of the Song clan, had been educated in America courtesy of the Methodist church. Returning to China as a missionary in 1886, he soon switched to the far more lucrative business world, dealing in cigarettes, cotton, and running a publishing company which printed Bibles and anti-Qing revolutionary literature. Mr. Song made a fortune and became an influential supporter of Sun Yat-sen and the Guomindang.[4] His daughters, Ailing (1890–1973), Qingling (1893–1981), and Meiling (1897–2003), and son Ziwen (1894–1971), all went to college in the United States. The eldest daughter, Song Ailing (who had firmly rejected Chiang Kai-shek's advances in the early 1920s), was the wife of the banker H. H. Kong (1881–1967). The second daughter, Song Qingling, had run off to marry Sun Yat-sen, against her father's wishes.

In 1927 Song Ailing arranged to marry her youngest sister, Meiling, to the now powerful leader of the Northern Expedition.[5] Chiang, already divorced and re-married once, cast aside his second wife, agreed to study Christianity (he later was baptized as a Methodist), and prepared for a splendid wedding ceremony in Shanghai. His young bride, Song Meiling, intelligent, ambitious, and fluent in English, would soon play a significant role in national and world politics. Her sister Ailing, brother-in-law H. H. Kong, brother Song Ziwen (T. V. Soong), and their immediate circle of friends would make their careers—and their fortunes—from their close connection with Chiang. Meiling's second sister, Sun Yat-sen's widow Song Qingling, for her part, would come to despise Chiang and her sisters both for their corrupt personal lives and their right-wing politics.

With his alliances with the Shanghai elite and the Shanghai underworld on solid ground, the Wuhan regime eliminated, and the Communists purged, Chiang continued with the second phase of the Northern Expedition. In order to raise desperately needed cash, his secret police and Green Gang thugs had already extracted money from the Shanghai business world through a combination of threats, outright violence, and kidnapping (sometimes disguised as arrest on suspicion of being a Communist). The money generated by these crude but effective techniques helped to fund the National Revolutionary Army as it struck north of the Yangzi in the autumn and winter of 1926–28, engaging in heavy combat with warlord armies. There were some defeats along the way, but in the end, the National Revolutionary Army was victorious. With history apparently favoring the Guomindang, northern warlords Feng Yuxiang and Yan Xishan agreed to put their territories and their forces under the authority of Chiang and the Nanjing government.

There remained the Japanese-supported Zhang Zuolin in Manchuria. Believing that a unified China would be bad for their national interests, the Japanese urged Zhang to resist. Japanese forces in Shandong even fought against Nationalist units as they tried to advance toward Manchuria.[6] Then, in 1928, some ultranationalist Japanese officers overreached. Believing that Zhang Zuolin was too weak to stand against Chiang and hoping that a bloody incident would prompt their own government to intervene in China, young officers in Japan's Kwantung Army blew up a railroad bridge outside Shenyang as Zhang's private train passed over. The old bandit died, but the Japanese officers had underestimated his son. Zhang Xueliang (1901–2000), the "Young Marshal," set aside his playboy lifestyle and took command of his father's army, assassinating those few of his father's former officers who stood in his way. Much to the dismay of the Japanese, Zhang raised the flag of the Republic of China over his headquarters in December 1928. Manchuria had escaped from Japan's grasp to become part of Chiang's now reunified Republic of China.

The Nanjing Decade

With the success of the Northern Expedition, China was once again united under a central government—or so it appeared. Chiang Kai-shek strove to fulfill Sun Yat-sen's goals as he understood them: to establish an effective central government and make China a rich country with an army capable of defending its territory. Chiang firmly believed that this required an authoritarian government under his own personal leadership. He justified his vision and his methods by constant reference to Sun's "Three People's Principles" and Confucian concepts like filial piety and benevolence. But he also had some more tangible sources of power.

First and foremost, Chiang had the loyalty of the professionally trained units that formed the core of the National Army. Their commanders were his former students at the Whampoa Military Academy. They received the best equipment and the best assignments. In return, these "Whampoa Clique" commanders gave Chiang their unstinting support in the political struggles that continued to pit Chiang against left- and right-wing opponents in the Guomindang. Whampoa Clique officers created a number of more or less secret organizations to serve Chiang. The most significant of these was a secret police organization called the Military Bureau of Investigation and Statistics. Dai Li (1897–1946), a devoted supporter of Chiang, built the BIS into an extensive domestic and international operation with agents in the Guomindang, in the military, in towns and cities across China, and in overseas Chinese communities.[7]

Chiang also had the support of key units in the Guomindang: his friends, the brothers Chen Lifu (1899–2001) and Chen Guofu (1892–1951), the leaders of the "CC Clique," ran the party's Organization Department, which appointed, promoted, and demoted officials. They also ran the Guomindang's Bureau of Investigation and Statistics (not to be confused with their rival Dai Li's Military Bureau of Investigation and Statistics), which they used to investigate, threaten, and punish political enemies.[8] The CC Clique and the Whampoa Clique were each suspicious of the other and engaged in political turf battles, which occasionally turned violent. Both looked down on the "Political Study Group," which, being made up entirely of policy experts who enjoyed a close relationship with Chiang, had no secret police force with which to engage in the kind of hard-knuckle politics in which the CC and Whampoa men excelled.

In addition to organizational and military power, backed up by secret police, Chiang also had financial resources that his rivals within the Guomindang could not touch. Chiang had privileged access to Shanghai money in the form of loans, taxes, and the ability to float bonds. His personal relationships with leaders of the Shanghai business world were solidified by his marriage with Song Meiling, which brought him the Song family's financial power and contacts (including Song Ailing's husband, the banker H. H. Kong). These contacts in the "legitimate" business world were supplemented by the support of Green Gang boss and drug baron Du Yuesheng (1887–1951). Du was appointed to multiple positions in the Nanjing government, including chief of the Opium Suppression Bureau. This gave the Green Gang a monopoly on the drug trade, from which it funneled a generous share of the profits to the Nanjing government.

Chiang used his sources of strength effectively in the factional struggles that continued to roil the Guomindang throughout the Nanjing Decade. The divisions were not simply a matter of personality and personal interest, although those were clearly involved. Chiang Kai-shek and his chief rival, Wang Jingwei, had fundamentally different ideas as to how to make China into a strong, modern state, capable of dealing with two specific threats: the Communists and the Japanese.[9]

Wang Jingwei and others (including Chiang's brother-in-law and minister of finance, Song Ziwen) believed that the government should focus on economic growth and modernization. Their vision, which had broad support from the business community, called for the use of government credit and government-supported cooperatives to increase agricultural production. The goal was to make the Chinese countryside into a reliable source of cheap raw materials (cotton and other industrial crops) for Chinese industry and a strong domestic market for Chinese-made goods. Wang had a significant degree of support within the Guomindang—enough to force Chiang to accept him as prime minister in a coalition government in 1932.

Wang, Song, and others used their positions to design and implement government programs designed to offer cheap credit in rural areas, help to organize farmers' cooperatives, and improve agricultural technology. They also worked to establish new standards for industry (businessmen were not so enthusiastic about this part of their program). Wang and his supporters hoped that these programs would strengthen the economy, make the Communists' radical programs less appealing to farmers, and generate increased tax revenue for the government. Their efforts failed. Rural elites manipulated the credit programs and cooperatives. Businesses refused to submit to government attempts to rationalize and modernize management and production. Government corruption exercised a corrosive influence on everything. But most importantly, the programs did not have Chiang's support.

Chiang completely rejected Wang and Song's "economist" prescription for national wealth and power. As he saw it, the key to domestic and international power was military strength, moral rectification, and firm control of political life. In the tug-of-war for government funds, Chiang consistently won, forcing through regular increases in the military budget. Chiang won these struggles because he used his sources of power wisely. Access to money, domination of the Guomindang's Organization Department, the use of secret police to gather information and pressure opponents, and the loyalty of the army won the day.

Chiang had the power and the political acumen to prevent Wang Jingwei and other competitors from controlling the party and carrying out their policies, but he did not have enough strength to translate his own vision of China's future into reality. One problem was money. Chiang had access to more money than his competitors, but he and his government never had enough money to be truly effective. The Chinese government ran deficits throughout the Nanjing Decade. The Nanjing government's perpetual deficits were related to the heavy debt burdens which it had inherited, some of them indemnities and loans from the late Qing years. The government's fiscal problems were also related to the simple fact that it did not actually control much of China's territory, and was thus unable to collect taxes effectively.

During the Northern Expedition, Chiang had made deals with a number of major warlords. As a result, men like Zhang Xueliang, Feng Yuxiang, and Yan Xishan still commanded their own armies and had substantial control over their own territories, tax revenue, railroads, ports, and "opium suppression bureaus." Conflicts between Chiang's government and the warlords led to several full-scale wars during the first years of the Nanjing Decade. As with the Northern Expedition, Chiang achieved "victory" partly by defeating enemies on the battlefield, and partly by using "silver bullets" to keep major warlords on his side. One of the main beneficiaries was the Manchurian "Young Marshal" Zhang Xueliang, whose ongoing support for Chiang had to be purchased at the price of 10,000,000 yuan and the promise of substantial control over north China.[10]

The continued power of the warlords was one reason that Chiang never had money enough to carry out the military modernization necessary to deal with the Communists or, especially, the Japanese. Another reason for the Nanjing government's problems lay with Chiang Kai-shek himself. Chiang was a short-tempered man with an autocratic leadership style. He made a fetish of self-discipline, living simply, rising early every day to meditate and exercise, and keeping a strict vegetarian diet. In his mind, the military solution to China's problems would be successful if he could impose strict military discipline, moral rectitude, unity, and cohesion on the entire Chinese population.

Chiang's goal—a unified, disciplined people who think and act as one—had been a goal of national leaders from Confucius himself to the Manchu reformers to Liang Qichao to Sun Yat-sen. As Chiang searched for ways to remake the Chinese people, he found inspiration in the Italian fascist and German Nazi movements of the 1920s–1940s. What he liked about them was their emphasis on a disciplined, unified people under a strict, powerful, efficient, militaristic government. But unlike Hitler and Mussolini, Chiang had no interest in creating mass movements.[11] His style was to play the Confucian patriarch, cajoling and haranguing his bureaucrats, his army officers, and the people at large, demanding shrilly that they be loyal, self-disciplined, self-sacrificing, and united under his leadership. The people did not necessarily listen.

Chiang's greatest attempt to impose discipline and morality on China's society was the New Life Movement, which he inaugurated with much fanfare in 1934. This movement, he said, was to "militarize thoroughly the lives of the citizens of the entire nation so that they can cultivate courage and swiftness, the endurance of suffering and a tolerance for hard work, and especially the habit and ability of unified action, so that they will at any time sacrifice for the nation."[12]

The New Life Movement generated immense amounts of propaganda. The Chinese were urged to kill flies and mosquitoes, do calisthenics, stop smoking, stop spitting on the street, queue up nicely, dress neatly, and show proper respect for their elders. Rickshaws were to line up in an orderly way in front of the hotels, and pedestrians to walk on the right-hand side of the street. The government re-instituted the ritual worship of Confucius, with Chiang performing the ceremonies in person. The Whampoa Clique founded a new organization, dubbed the "Blue Shirts," in imitation of Mussolini's "Black Shirts" and Hitler's "Brown Shirts." The "Blue Shirts" were the strong-arm enforcers of New Life regulations and a part of Chiang's attempt to bring to the Guomindang the kind of internal discipline that he admired in European fascism.[13]

The "New Life Movement" was a failure. Government officials were on their best behavior when they knew Chiang would be around. They cleaned streets, painted buildings, and enforced public order in towns and along routes when Chiang and Madame were expected to pass through. Otherwise, life went on in its accustomed chaotic, corrupt way. High-ranking government and military leaders continued to make insider stock market deals, Du Yuesheng's opium business still generated profits for the Green Gang and the government, Chiang's family members still lived the high life, and Madame Chiang kept right on smoking foreign cigarettes.[14] Observers were not blind to the hypocrisy.

Although it was weak, permeated with corruption and roiled by internal power struggles, the Nanjing government did preside over some successes. The regime's economic record was mixed. Economic growth continued, perhaps in spite of, rather than because of, government policies. The industrial sector saw particularly strong growth, 6.7 percent annually from 1931 to 1937, although from a very low starting point.[15] The agricultural sector, which still employed four-fifths of the work force and produced sixty-five percent of the gross domestic product, was another story. Average tenancy rates of around fifty percent, rents amounting to fifty to seventy percent of the crop, and too many people farming too little land using essentially pre-modern technology combined to produce rural poverty and some of the highest death rates in the world.[16] Like many developing countries, then and later, Republican China was characterized by tremendous disparities in the distribution of wealth, and between the rural and urban worlds.

Chiang Kai-shek's efforts to build modern governmental institutions, too, had much in common with the state-building policies of other developing countries. Like Sun Yat-sen, Chiang believed that weak, inefficient government was one of China's fundamental problems. Continuing work begun in the late Qing and early Republic, the Guomindang enacted Western-style legal codes (criminal and civil) and built modern police forces, courts, and prisons. Foreign advisors, including a police officer from Berkeley, California, contributed to these efforts.[17] These reforms were designed to convince foreign governments to give up the extraterritoriality and other privileges that they had gained in the "unequal treaties" stretching back to the Opium War.

Chinese negotiators did, in fact, convince the Western powers to give up some of their treaty privileges and to return almost two-thirds of the concession areas in Chinese cities back to Chinese control. Chinese diplomats also convinced foreign powers not to extend diplomatic recognition to the Dalai Lama's Tibetan regime and fended off the Soviet Union's advances on Xinjiang.[18] The Nanjing government also achieved considerable success in suppressing one of its most troublesome internal enemies: the Chinese Communist Party.

The Chinese Communist Party: From Shanghai to Yan'an

The year 1927, Chiang Kai-shek's year of triumph, was a year of disaster and defeat for the Chinese Communist Party. Chiang's Guomindang and Green Gang strong-arm men slaughtered thousands of Communists. Thousands more were arrested or simply cut their ties with the party. Joseph Stalin compounded the problems when he concluded that a high tide of revolution was sweeping China and that the Communists must do their part by taking over towns and cities, which were the strongholds of Guomindang supporters. Assaults on several major cities and a series of "Autumn Harvest uprisings" in rural Hunan all ended in failure. A brief Communist occupation of Guangzhou led to a brutal government suppression and the arrest and execution of the Cantonese Communist leader Peng Pai. In Hunan, Mao Zedong was arrested after the failed Autumn Harvest uprisings. A bribe paid to his jailers allowed him to escape, with a price on his head and some bitter experience under his belt. Mao, as we will see later, went to the countryside to build an army and a base area. But the core party membership and the party Central Committee remained underground in Shanghai, trying to organize workers and students there and in China's other major cities.

Working underground was not easy. Chiang Kai-shek's police forces continued to spy on, arrest, imprison, and execute Communist Party members and Communist sympathizers. Party members also faced resistance, or at least a lack of interest, on the part of workers. China's urban working class consisted of a number of distinct groups, each with its own identity. Many of them were migrants, moving into the cities in the tens of thousands, settling in poor neighborhoods or building shantytowns. The provincial folk who flocked to Beiping (as Beijing was called after 1927 when Chiang designated the city of Nanjing as the Chinese capital), the despised but essential Subei people (from north of the Yangzi) who came to Shanghai—these were the cooks and cleaners, the rickshaw-pullers, hired laborers, servants, and factory workers without whom economic growth and the service industries would have ground to a halt. Beyond the reach of the state, they organized themselves into communities based on their own clan and native-place identities. As a result, they lacked any broader working-class identity.[19] In addition, labor unions controlled by the Guomindang and/or by organized crime syndicates competed with the Communists for the loyalty of the working class, focusing their efforts on the kind of bread-and-butter economic issues that had more immediate appeal to workers than the Communists' ideological messages of resistance to warlords and anti-imperialism.[20]

Communist Party leaders in Shanghai did have some success in recruiting new members, building support among workers, and linking their nationalist, anti-imperialist rhetoric to more fundamental economic issues.[21] Some non-Communist radicals, too, helped to get members of the younger generation of students and workers interested in issues of social justice and revolutionary thought. For example, Deng Yuzhi (Cora Deng), head of the YWCA Labor Bureau in Shanghai, although not a Communist, established night schools for women workers. The curriculum included studies of industrialism, trade unionism, labor legislation, and imperialism, as well as basic courses in writing, arithmetic, geography, history, and recent events.[22] Deng could get away with her work because her Christian identity and association with foreigners protected her from the police. Communist Party members, on other hand, lived with the constant threat of arrest—or worse. By December 1934, there were no more than around 450 active Communist Party members in Shanghai.[23]

While the Party Center struggled on in Shanghai, Mao Zedong began developing a new strategy for revolution in the countryside.[24] After his narrow escape from jail in 1928, Mao led a small number of soldiers to the remote Jinggang Mountains in the Jiangxi-Hunan border area. A former Guomindang commander and Communist Party member named Zhu De (1886–1976) and his troops joined Mao at Jinggangshan. Together, Mao and Zhu began to build a Communist Party army. Zhu served as commander; Mao was the army's political commissar—the Communist Party representative, whose job it would be to make sure that the army served the needs of the party. This would be an army under party leadership. Officers and men would be taught to understand that they were fighting for long-term political goals: not only to unite the nation, but also to remake it through a social revolution that would redistribute wealth from the rich to the poor.

Mao and Zhu required from their troops not only loyalty, but also discipline. Their Red Army could not afford to behave like warlord soldiers, laying waste to the countryside and then returning to their urban barracks. The Communists needed to build base areas where they could stay for months or years. They needed to develop methods to draw material support, intelligence, and new recruits from the villages while winning and keeping the support of the vast majority of the people. Red Army soldiers cultivated the image of "an army of sons and brothers" who cared for the common folk, never taking from them without paying, respecting local traditions and local women. But discipline alone could not generate food, clothing, other supplies, and recruits. To do that, the party would have to transform rural life and the rural economy.

In 1927 Mao Zedong, then a leader of the Guomindang's Peasant Training Institute, had observed the peasant movement in his native Hunan province. In his "Report on an Investigation of the Peasant Movement in Hunan," Mao suggested that farmers could be a powerful force for revolution. This idea was a radical one, contradicting Karl Marx's belief that the industrial working class would be the motive force of socialist revolution. In the 1930s, Mao took those lessons and applied them systematically to the creation and maintenance of rural base areas. Moving his base area headquarters from Jinggangshan east to the Jiangxi-Zhejiang-Fujian border area, Mao directed an intense program of land reform. Party work teams were sent to the villages, where they were to make contact with politically reliable villagers (generally understood to be the poor tenant farmers) and to make a thorough investigation and analysis of the local economy. Villagers would be placed in categories: landlord, rich peasant, middle peasant, lower peasant, landless, and "bad element" (local criminals). Party activists would mobilize the poor and landless families to denounce the landlords and the rich, and to confiscate and redistribute their land, houses, draft animals, other property, and wealth. A portion of confiscated landlord wealth also went to the party.

Mao's Jiangxi Soviet, with its capital in the Jiangxi town of Ruijin, was the largest of a half dozen Communist rural base areas. The Communist Party's Central Committee in Shanghai criticized Mao's reliance on the rural poor and his relatively moderate policies toward "rich peasants" as departures from the orthodox Marxist theory of revolution. But in 1932, the Party Center was forced to flee Shanghai and take refuge in the Jiangxi Soviet. These included Comintern advisor Otto Braun (1900–74), party General Secretary Wang Ming (1904–74), and other Soviet-trained members of the party leadership. Among Wang's supporters was Zhou Enlai (1898–1976), the Paris- and Moscow-trained son of a wealthy family and a senior member of the party Central Committee. Mao and Zhu De were now no longer in command: the men from the Party Center outranked them, and continued to disagree with Mao on matters of social policy and of military strategy.

Mao's military strategy had been one of the keys to the continued survival of the Jiangxi Soviet. Between 1930 and 1934, the Nanjing government had carried out five "encirclement campaigns" against the Communist "bandits." Facing an enemy with superior numbers and weapons, Mao and Zhu had used guerilla warfare. Their principles were to avoid battle unless they were sure of victory, to lure enemy units deep into their territory, cut them off, and annihilate them, and to make full use of the mountainous terrain and local intelligence. Mao's strategy worked well against the first two encirclement campaigns (1931 and 1932), for which Chiang had deployed warlord units that were simply not up to the task. The third (July–October 1932), which drove deep into Communist territory, was cut short because of the need to deal with Japanese aggression (discussed below). Zhou Enlai, who had replaced Mao as the Red Army's political commissar, directed a successful defense against the fourth encirclement campaign (1933).

The fifth encirclement campaign, begun in September 1933, was successful. Chiang's armies systematically cleared one sector after another of the Communist base area, sealing off each cleared sector with "a line of multi-storey blockhouses . . . spaced close enough together to permit overlapping fields of fire."[25] The numerically inferior and poorly armed Communists were now forced to fight head to head with an enemy who would not be lured in and cut off. Continued defense of the Jiangxi Soviet was impossible. In October 1934, facing certain defeat, the party leaders called for a withdrawal. Leaving a small army behind to continue the fight against the Guomindang, the Communist main force of around eighty thousand broke out of the encirclement.[26] Though they did not know it, this retreat was the beginning of the Communist Party's Long March of 6,000 miles (10,000 km) from Jiangxi in the southeast to Yan'an in northern Shaanxi province.

The Long March proved to be a defining experience for a generation of party leaders. Within two months, heavy casualties and desertions had reduced the Communist ranks from eighty thousand to around thirty thousand.[27] In January 1935 the Communists paused at the town of Zunyi, in

Guizhou province, long enough for the Central Committee to discuss the causes of their defeat and to decide on a strategy and direction for the future. Wang Ming, Otto Braun, and their supporters came in for severe criticism. With the support of Zhou Enlai and others, Mao Zedong emerged from this meeting as a member of the five-man Standing Committee of the Communist Party's Politburo. Soon afterward, he was appointed political commissar of Zhu De's Front Command Headquarters, which effectively put him in charge of the Central Red Army. These were Mao Zedong's first steps toward becoming the supreme leader of the Communist Party.[28]

From Zunyi, the Communists continued their march through Guizhou, into Yunnan, north to Sichuan, and across Gansu and Ningxia. Government forces pursued the Communists throughout their year-long trek. In the southwest, Chiang Kai-shek made a point of using the pursuit of the Communists to increase his influence over warlord territories and warlord troops.[29] Local warlords, for their part, were often willing to let the Communists pass through their territory as quickly as possible in order to avoid any trouble with either the Communists themselves or the government armies that were chasing the Communists. Mao and other Communist leaders spent many of their days being carried in sedan chairs while they slept. By night, they dealt with radio communications, evaluated incoming intelligence, and planned the route and operations for the next day's march.

Mao and his forces crossed mountains, rivers, and swamps. In November 1935 the Long Marchers arrived in the area of Yan'an in Shaanxi Province. Of the more than eighty thousand who began the Long March, only seven to eight thousand were left. Some had split from Mao's ranks to join a rival Communist leader, Zhang Guotao, whose army later re-joined Mao in Shaanxi.[30] Some had been left behind, unable to continue the difficult journey. Many had died from the hardships en route. These included Mao's two-year-old son, left behind at the beginning of the Long March, and a daughter, born during the march and left with a peasant family. Neither child was found again afterwards.[31]

Those who completed the Long March shared an experience that would become one of the founding myths of the People's Republic of China and a defining characteristic of a generation. Long March veterans would dominate Communist Party politics until the mid-1990s. But for the moment, Yan'an would be the capital of their base area and Mao's headquarters. Here, Mao would consolidate control over the Communist Party, establish his credentials as an interpreter of Marxism-Leninism for the Chinese revolution, and enhance his already solid reputation as a master of guerilla warfare. As he did so, his fate, and that of the Chinese Communist Party, would once again become entangled with that of Chiang Kai-shek and the Guomindang, this time in reaction to a common enemy: Japan.

Japanese Imperialism in the Nanjing Decade

Japan had begun acquiring parts of Chinese territory with the Sino-Japanese War of 1894–95, when the Qing ceded the island of Taiwan to the Japanese Empire. With that victory, Japan became a significant competitor against Russia for influence in the Chinese northeast (Manchuria) and Korea. Japan then defeated Russia in the Russo-Japanese War (1904–1905). This gave Japan a free hand in Korea, which it annexed in 1910. It also gave Japan control of key territories in Manchuria that had been leased to Russia: the ice-free port of Lüshun (known in English as Port Arthur) at the southern tip of the Liaodong Peninsula, and control of the South Manchurian Railway, which ran from Lüshun to Shenyang (then known as Mukden). Japan stationed a military force, the Kwantung Army, in Shenyang to protect the railway and other Japanese interests.

These acquisitions heightened Japan's strategic competition with the Russian Empire—a competition that took on an ideological dimension after 1917 when capitalist Japan faced the Communist Soviet Union. This strategic and ideological competition made Japanese political, military, and business leaders of the 1920s deeply interested in resources beyond Lüshun and the South Manchurian Railway. Manchuria had coal, iron, and productive agricultural land that could bring profits to Japanese business and enhance Japan's strategic position vis-à-vis the Soviet Union.

The question that the Japanese government faced was not whether to extend Japanese influence in Manchuria, but when and how. In 1931, the Japanese prime minister and cabinet preferred a deliberate, diplomatic strategy. But in Manchuria itself, some young officers in Japan's Kwantung Army decided to force their government into action. On 18 September 1931, they set off a small explosion along the railway on the outskirts of Shenyang (Mukden). Asserting the need for action against this "Chinese" outrage, the Kwantung Army took over the city, and then all of Manchuria. The Japanese government and emperor, initially taken by surprise, acquiesced in this unplanned expansion of the Japanese Empire.[32] Zhang Xueliang, acting on orders from Chiang, withdrew his Northeast Army from Manchuria without a fight.

The Chinese public responded to events in Manchuria with public demonstrations and boycotts of Japanese goods. In January 1932, the Japanese

landed marines in Shanghai to secure their concession area, which they believed was threatened by Chinese demonstrators. This led to five weeks of
intense fighting between Chinese and Japanese forces and a Japanese aerial
bombardment of the city (which caused tremendous civilian casualties).[33]
Chinese units fought bravely, but they were no match for Japan's well-trained
and well-equipped forces. Foreign governments had been willing to criticize
Japan for the "Mukden Incident," but no more. Japan shrugged off the inevitable League of Nations investigation and condemnation by withdrawing
from the League in 1933.

Facing no significant Chinese military resistance, Japan declared that it had
liberated the Manchu homeland from Chinese rule and established the state
of "Manchukuo." In 1932 Aisin Gioro Puyi, the last Qing emperor (a child
in 1911, now a young man of twenty-six), was brought in to reign over the
"Manchu homeland" (an anachronistic concept, since the vast majority of the
Manchurian population was Han Chinese) as a puppet emperor. The Japanese-
controlled "Manchukuo" government set up an educational system to teach
children that "Manchukuo" was a special place, different from China, and historically linked to Japan.[34] Korean farmers were brought in to farm land confiscated from Chinese. Japanese capital invested heavily in Manchurian coal
mines, iron and steel works, and factories, making the area one of the largest
industrial bases in the world. In 1935, Japan further expanded its power
when it forced Chiang's government to allow Japanese troops freedom of
movement in areas bordering "Manchukuo": Hebei, Chahar, and Inner Mongolia, where Japan supported Mongolian nationalist movements.

Chiang's reaction to Japanese aggression in Manchuria, Shanghai, north
China, and Inner Mongolia was to negotiate disengagement with the Japanese.
He was not willing to fight battles that he knew his armies could not win. Instead, he focused on military modernization and the fight against the Communist Party. Chiang's decision to delay confrontation with Japan and focus
first on eliminating the Communists was militarily sound, but politically
disastrous. The government's concessions to Japan inspired criticism from
intellectuals, students, and from the Communists themselves, who were
quick to question Chiang's credentials as a defender of national sovereignty
and to express their own view that Chinese should fight their common enemy,
not each other.

In the meantime, Chiang was using the twin threats of the Communists
and the Japanese as weapons in his ongoing struggle to keep his many warlord allies weak and divided. In 1935 he assigned two potentially troublesome

warlords and their armies to surround the Communist base area of Yan'an in the northwestern Shaanxi province: Yang Hucheng (1893–1949), commander of the Northwestern Army, and Zhang Xueliang, commander of the Northeast Army. Aware that Chiang had put them on the front lines, facing both the Communists and the Japanese, in order to weaken them, Yang and Zhang began talking with Communist Party representatives about forming an anti-Chiang "Northwestern Alliance."[35]

Concerned about the loyalty of his warlord allies, Chiang flew to the Shaanxi provincial capital of Xi'an in December 1936 to take them in hand. Chiang stayed at the hot springs resort outside the city—the same springs that Tang Xuanzong and the charming Yang Guifei had enjoyed so much. There, on the night of 12 December, Zhang Xueliang's bodyguards shot their way into the compound and captured Chiang (who had hidden in a cave, in his bathrobe and minus his false teeth).[36]

Having captured Chiang Kai-shek, Zhang Xueliang now consulted with the Communists: What should they do with their important prisoner? Rejecting their initial impulse, which was to execute the Generalissimo, the Communist leadership, acting on directives from the Soviet Union, instructed Zhang to make a deal: Chiang could gain his freedom in return for a promise to relieve pressure on the Communists and take a stronger stand against Japanese encroachment on Chinese territory—encroachment that the Soviet Union viewed as a strategic threat. Chiang, the Communists, and the Young Marshal reached an unwritten agreement. On 25 December, Chiang was released to Madame Chiang and his advisors, who had flown in from Nanjing, thus ending the "Xi'an Incident."[37] Yang Hucheng and Zhang Xueliang surrendered themselves and were sent back to Nanjing for trial. Yang was executed in 1949. Zhang remained under house arrest until 1991.

Chiang's deal with the Communist Party became fully operative when war broke out in 1937. As with the occupation of Manchuria, the war began with a minor incident. On the night of 7 July 1937 Japanese troops on patrol near Marco Polo Bridge, on the outskirts of Beiping (Beijing), were searching for a missing soldier when they exchanged shots with Chinese whom they suspected of having taken the man. The soldier later showed up, but after some internal debate, the Japanese government decided that this was their opportunity to solve the "China problem" once and for all. Confident that an aggressive campaign would bring north China under control and Chiang Kai-shek to his knees within three months, Japanese troops moved south from Beiping toward the Yellow River.[38] This time, Chiang Kai-shek would not negotiate disengagement.

Nationalists and Communists in the
War of Resistance Against Japan

China endured staggering losses and suffering during the War of Resistance Against Japan (1937–45): an estimated fifteen to twenty million dead, ninety-five million refugees, and property damage of upward of one hundred billion dollars.[39] In order to get a better understanding of the way in which the War of Resistance developed and how it changed China, we can divide it into two stages. In the first stage, from 1937 to 1941, Chiang's government fought the Japanese with relatively little foreign support. During these years, the Guomindang, the Communist Party, and regional warlords, although not abandoning their mutual suspicion, worked more or less cooperatively in a national struggle against the Japanese invader. The years 1941 through 1945 were marked by a collapse of mutual cooperation within China. These years also saw a significant increase in foreign involvement. With Japan's attack on the American fleet at Pearl Harbor on 8 December 1941, China's War of Resistance Against Japan became a part of World War II.

During the first stage of the war (1937–41), Chiang Kai-shek and his government worked against heavy odds to mobilize China's resources and armed forces to resist the Japanese. With Japanese troops on the offensive in north China, Chiang opened a second front with a bombing raid on Japanese ships in the river off of Shanghai on 14 August 1937. The purpose of the second front was to force the Japanese to fight in the Shanghai area, where Chiang's best German-trained armies outnumbered the Japanese by ten to one.[40] Nationalist units fought bitterly for ninety days to defend Shanghai against the vastly better-armed and better-trained Japanese troops, whose field artillery and complete control of the air gave them a tremendous advantage. By mid-November, the Japanese were advancing rapidly from the coast toward the Chinese capital of Nanjing, mercilessly slaughtering the retreating Chinese troops.[41]

As they advanced pell-mell toward Nanjing, Japanese units outran their supply lines and began to requisition food and other goods from Chinese civilians, beating and killing any who resisted. When they captured Nanjing itself on 13 December, Japanese officers allowed their men to carry out a massive, indiscriminate slaughter of surrendered Chinese soldiers and Chinese civilians and to commit uncountable acts of rape, torture, and looting. The chaotic nature of the circumstances makes it impossible to gauge the precise extent of the brutality: reasonable estimates for the soldiers and civilians killed in the "Rape of Nanjing" range from around one hundred thousand to over three hundred thousand.[42]

With Nanjing lost, the Nationalist government moved up the Yangzi River to the city of Wuhan. From January through October 1938, Chinese armies between the Yangzi and the Yellow Rivers fought bitterly to defend the routes to Wuhan, including the crucial railway junction city of Xuzhou.[43] Despite a brave showing, the Chinese ultimately retreated in the face of superior Japanese force. North of the Yangzi, warlord commanders fell before the Japanese without a struggle. In desperate attempt to slow the Japanese advance, Chiang ordered his troops to breach the Yellow River dikes at Huayuankou. The resulting flood swept over extensive parts of three provinces. An estimated half a million people were killed, and millions more became refugees.[44]

The breaching of the Yellow River dikes did little to slow the Japanese as they advanced south from the Yellow River and west up the Yangzi toward Wuhan. With the Japanese forces pressing ever closer, Chiang Kai-shek withdrew from Wuhan on 25 October 1938, retreating beyond the mountains to Sichuan, where the city of Chongqing became his wartime capital. By the end of 1938, Japan was well on its way to controlling large parts of eastern China. University faculty, government offices and government personnel, and over six hundred factories were moved into China's interior, beyond the reach of the Japanese. Nonetheless, Chiang's government had lost most of China's industrial infrastructure and its main sources of prewar tax revenue.[45]

From 1938 to 1945 there were three Chinas. The Japanese-occupied areas in the east, the more rural interior regions of the west under Chiang Kai-shek's Chongqing government, and the Communist base area centered on Yan'an in the northwest. In the occupied areas, a number of regional warlords and their armies chose to collaborate with the Japanese, who hoped to establish a cooperative Chinese government in the occupied areas as an alternative to Chiang Kai-shek. In December Wang Jingwei, Chiang's longtime competitor for power, chose to go over to the Japanese. In 1940, he was formally inaugurated as president of an alternative national government in Nanjing. Wang evidently believed that with Japan's support, he could finally realize Sun Yat-sen's dream of building a strong modern China. Many other Chinese, too, collaborated with the Japanese occupation. Some, like Wang, were convinced that with Japanese sponsorship, they could build a new modern China. Others, such as businessmen with factories and other enterprises in the Yangzi Valley, workers, and farmers stayed because they had no choice, or because they saw the possibility of profiting from cooperation with Japan.

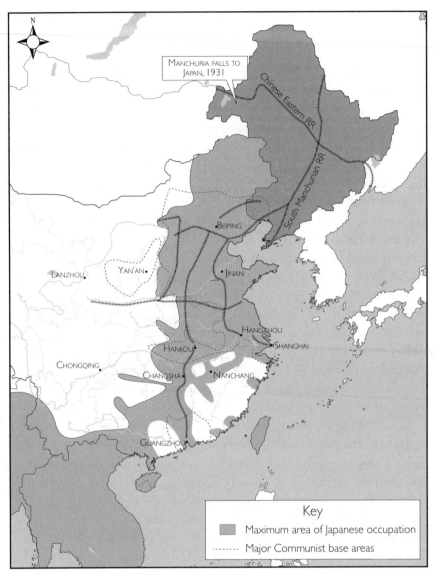

The War of Resistance Against Japan, 1937–45.

In the west and southwest, the Nationalist government in Chongqing and its warlord allies controlled territory amounting to around half of China's population (excluding Manchuria) and sixty percent of its rice production, but with very little industrial capacity.[46] From 1938 through 1941, Chiang's government worked to mobilize its limited resources for continued resistance against Japan, but with little success. Nationalist forces turned back a

Japanese attack on the city of Changsha in September 1939, but a winter offensive launched against the Japanese in late November ended in failure. Guomindang-sponsored guerilla armies operating behind Japanese lines also failed to make significant headway against the Japanese.

With the outbreak of war in 1937, China's Communist Party leaders had entered a "Second United Front" with the Guomindang and formally placed their forces under Chiang Kai-shek's overall command as the Eighth Route and New Fourth Armies. But Chinese Communist operations against the Japanese were on a smaller scale and no more effective than those of the Nationalist government. Communist guerillas could harass, but not defeat, Japan's armies. In August 1940, Communist forces under the command of General Peng Dehuai (1898–1974) abandoned guerilla warfare in favor of a series of attacks on Japanese positions across the northwest. This "Battle of the Hundred Regiments" inflicted some damage on the railways and put coal mines in Shanxi out of operation for a year, but at the cost of twenty-two thousand casualties. The Japanese responded with an intense counterattack, throwing the Communists on the defensive by October and bringing the Battle of the Hundred Regiments to an end in December.[47]

One of the reasons for launching the Battle of the Hundred Regiments had been to counter Nationalist arguments that the Communists were avoiding battle with the Japanese and spending most of their energy on expanding their base area—charges that had more than a little truth to them.[48] The Communist New Fourth Army had been using operations against the Japanese in order to establish a presence south of the Yangzi, which Chiang rightly saw as a threat to his control over that area. In January 1941, units of the New Fourth Army operating south of the Yangzi ignored orders from Chongqing and from Yan'an to move north of the river. The Nationalist army responded by attacking the New Fourth Army and wiping out an entire division. The "New Fourth Army Incident" had little effect on overall Communist strength, but it did make a dramatic end to Communist-Guomindang military cooperation.[49]

The collapse of the "Second United Front" caused serious difficulties for the Communist Party. Chiang Kai-shek's government cut off important material assistance to the Communist forces after the New Fourth Army Incident. Beginning in July 1941, the Japanese also put intense pressure on the Communist base areas in north China by mounting the "three alls" campaign (kill all, burn all, loot all), an operation that substantially reduced Communist strength by decimating guerilla forces and the rural communities on which they relied for support. All this, in combination with both Guomindang and Japanese blockades on the Communists and a drought in the Chinese

northwest threw the Communist base areas into a fiscal crisis that lasted from
1941 to 1943.[50] The party mobilized soldiers and party cadres (party officials) to grow their own food. Party leaders also attempted to alleviate their
fiscal crisis by turning to a tried-and-true warlord practice: growing and selling opium.[51]

The Guomindang government and armies suffered from the same fundamental problems as the Communists: how to face an enemy with superior
weapons and training while suffering from low industrial capacity and chronic
grain shortages. The Nationalist government had made intensive efforts to
increase industrial production early in the war. But by 1941, inflation, mismanagement of state-run industries, lack of access to imported equipment,
and shortages of raw materials and labor had slowed the government's industrial mobilization program.[52] Production of rice and wheat both plum-
meted in 1941, causing a deterioration of conditions in the rural areas. With
the countryside the main source of soldiers, deterioration of the rural economy led directly to declines in recruitment and in the quality of recruits. In
Chongqing, Japanese bombing raids took a toll on civilian morale, while inflation reduced the purchasing power of wages to fifteen percent of prewar
levels by 1941.[53]

Added to these challenges were the problems inherent in Chiang's deeply
divided armies. The Whampoa Clique "Central" units loyal to Chiang were
deeply distrustful of the various regional warlord armies that were theoretically also under Chiang's overall command. Because he himself distrusted
the regional armies, Chiang dispersed both regional and Central units widely
across his territory so that Central units could act as a check on the activities of the regional armies. All military units faced serious shortages of equipment and grain, shortages that their officers tried to address by engaging in
trade, smuggling, and preying on the civilian population.[54] With all these
challenges, it is little wonder that after 1941, "[a]lthough China continued to
resist Japan, both the Guomindang and the Chinese Communists conducted
mainly defensive actions. . . ."[55] In the final analysis, neither the Communists
nor the Nationalists had the weapons with which to defeat the Japanese or the
grain necessary to keep an army in the field for extended periods of time.[56]

If there was any bright side to the Chinese situation after 1941, it was the
substantial increase in foreign assistance. From 1937 to 1941, Chiang Kai-
shek and the Communists had faced the Japanese with very little help from
the Western powers. Germany's military assistance to the Chinese Nationalist government, which had included advisors, arms, and over a dozen dive
bombers, ended in February 1938 when Hitler decided that the relationship

with Japan better served his interests.[57] From 1937 to 1939 the Soviet Union offered significant assistance—arms, aircraft, and advisors—to China as part of its strategic competition with Japan. This aid (which was directed to Chiang Kai-shek's government armies, not to the Chinese Communists) was cut off when Stalin signed the Nazi-Soviet Pact in August 1939. Neither German nor Soviet aid had been enough to significantly increase China's ability to fight the Japanese.[58]

In 1941, as Japan's China War and the war in Europe became increasingly intertwined, Britain and the United States of America became more interested in offering assistance to China. In 1941, British special operations officers initiated a "China Commando Group" program designed to train thirty thousand guerilla fighters for Chiang Kai-shek (the program soon ended as when the British advisors' ill-disguised contempt for the Chinese military and their use of the program to infiltrate British agents into China became unbearable).[59] In the same year, the retired American air force pilot Claire Chennault, who had come to China in 1937 as an air-power consultant, received permission from the United States government to create a special air force unit in China: the American Volunteer Group, better known as the Flying Tigers.[60] In their seven months of existence, the Flying Tiger pilots racked up an impressive record: 299 Japanese airplanes destroyed and around 250 damaged, at a cost of only twelve American airplanes and ten pilots lost in combat.[61]

The British guerilla training project and the Flying Tigers had both begun as unofficial operations: neither Britain nor the United States was at war with Japan. This changed in December 1941, when the Japanese attack on Pearl Harbor and on American and British positions in East and Southeast Asia made the war in China a part of World War II. Lend-lease aid from the United States was increased, though it still fell far short of meeting China's needs. American agents worked with Chiang's secret police boss Dai Li on joint intelligence operations. Chiang Kai-shek took his place at international conferences as one of the "Big Four" alongside American president Franklin Roosevelt (1882–1945), British prime minister Winston Churchill (1874–1965), and Soviet leader Josef Stalin (1878–1953). China's armies were now involved in joint operations with the Allies in their common fight against Japan.

As China was incorporated into the Western alliance against the Axis powers, it was also sucked into the morass of alliance politics. American assistance came with strings attached, and in the form of two Americans who cordially despised one another. Claire Chennault, already well-established in China, was a firm believer in air power. Given enough planes, he said, he could not only defeat Japan in China, but even bomb the Japanese home islands and force the Japanese to surrender. Chennault got along well with Chiang and Madame and thus had their support, but he never had enough airplanes to carry out his grandiose plans.

Facing Chennault was the man whom the Americans had sent to serve as Chiang's military advisor: General Joseph "Vinegar Joe" Stilwell (1883–1946). Stilwell, who despised Chennault, Chiang, and the British, was known more for his irascibility than his accomplishments. Stilwell's belief in "boots on the ground" matched Chennault's fixation on airpower.[62] Convinced (against all evidence) that northern Burma was the key to the defeat of Japan, Stilwell personally led some of Chiang's crack units in a misconceived and utterly unsuccessful campaign there in 1942. Even afterward, he kept valuable Chinese troops in India, returning for a second, more successful Burma campaign in 1944.[63] Stilwell's very negative assessment of Chiang and his abilities prompted President Roosevelt to instruct Chiang to put Stilwell "in unrestricted command of all your forces."[64] Stilwell gleefully delivered this message to Chiang on 19 September 1944—a victory in which he took intense pleasure.[65] But the general was no match for the Generalissimo. Personal pride and China's recent history of subjugation to imperialism meant that Chiang could not possibly accept the imposition of foreign command over Chinese troops. At Chiang's irate demand, Roosevelt called Stilwell back from China.

Chiang Kai-shek with his wife, Song Meiling, and General Stilwell.

Part of the tension between Chiang and the Americans revolved around the fact that some Americans (including Stilwell) believed that the Communists were doing a better job of resisting Japan than Chiang's Nationalist government. Their military operations against Japan may have been of no more significance than those of the Guomindang government, but both during and after the war, the Chinese Communist Party successfully created a mythical history that contrasted their stubborn guerrilla resistance with alleged Nationalist passivity. The Communists' self-discipline, the simple lifestyles of their leaders, their moderate land reform and rent reduction policies, and their consistent anti-Japanese propaganda were very impressive to a number of Americans. Left-leaning journalists like Edgar Snow and Anna Louise Strong wrote glowing reports on Mao Zedong and life in Yan'an. A

革

group of American military officers and diplomats calling themselves the "Dixie Mission" visited the Communist "rebel" base in Yan'an in July 1944, and though they were no leftists, they too concluded that the Communists' willpower and discipline made a striking contrast to the conditions of Chiang Kai-shek's corrupt "Free China."

Even positive reports like those of Edgar Snow and the Dixie Mission would not convince the American government to abandon Chiang Kai-shek and throw its support behind what was, after all, a Communist Party. Furthermore, the Allies regarded China as a minor part of the war against Japan. Operations in Burma had been a distraction and lend-lease assistance to China was minimal. When General Stilwell was recalled in October 1944, there were more than twenty different United States agencies active in China, none of them coordinating its efforts with the others, and some, like General Claire Chennault's Fourteenth Air Force (the successor organization to the Flying Tigers), operating virtually independently.[66]

The Japanese had dramatically underlined China's continued weakness after years of American aid when they launched a major new operation, the

Chinese Communist headquarters in Yan'an in April 1937. From left: Mao Zedong; Earl Leaf, U.P. Correspondent; Zhu De; and translator Wu Lili. © Bettman/CORBIS.

Ichigo Offensive, in April 1944. Ichigo was an all-out push to establish a rail connection from the Japanese-held areas of north China all the way to Vietnam and to strengthen Japan's position in potential negotiations with the Allies.[67] By the time the offensive was over in December, China had lost five hundred thousand to six hundred thousand men and parts of three provinces that had been the government's major sources of grain and conscripts.[68] In the first years of their struggle against Japan, Chiang Kai-shek, his armies, and his Nationalist Party government had successfully mobilized their limited resources to resist the Japanese. The initial stages of the war had produced a new sense of national unity in the face of foreign aggression. By the end of the war, the Chinese government's strength was sapped and the sense of national unity seriously undermined. This trend was evident not only on the battlefield, but also in development of art and literature from the Nanjing Decade to the end of the War of Resistance.

Art and Literature Go to War

The Nanjing Decade was arguably a high point for mass-produced, apolitical art and literature made for sale to a growing urban middle class with a strong appetite for entertainment. There was a great demand for serialized tales of martial arts heroes and Chinese historical fiction. There was also a demand for Western and Western-influenced (and particularly American-influenced) cultural products. American films and jazz were very popular, as were jazz-influenced Chinese pop music and Chinese films. Film, film magazines, and advertising played major roles in creating images of "modern" Chinese men and women. May Fourth intellectuals had tried to define "modern" young Chinese in terms of education, independence, and patriotism. In the consumer culture of the Nanjing Decade, advertising firms defined the "modern" man and woman in terms of consumption of (or association with) products: cigarettes, beer, makeup, hairstyles, and clothing. Along with "modernity," consumer culture also defined "Chineseness" by playing up filial piety, loyalty, and, for women, a certain modesty of dress, demure attitude, and perhaps the presence of a symbol of "Chineseness" such as a fan, a Chinese musical instrument, or an identifiably "Chinese" landscape, pavilion, or pagoda in the background.[69]

For many people, art, literature, and film were cheap escapes from the tension and dreariness of everyday life. The Nanjing Decade was the heyday of bars and dance halls, cinema, street entertainers, horse and dog racing, and of the Great World Entertainment Center—a multi-story entertainment palace offering operas, puppet plays, brothels, opium dens, chorus lines, wrestlers, restaurants, and more.[70] For some, art was politics, a struggle for social justice, a struggle for the soul of the nation. Some film studios, writers, and artists supported the Guomindang. But on the whole, politically engaged art and literature leaned to the left. Many of the most famous writers of the period were members of the League of Left-Wing Writers, a Communist-led writers' organization founded in 1930. Communist filmmakers worked through a "front organization" called the Left-Wing Dramatists League to infiltrate the Shanghai film world. Members edited "film supplements" attached to otherwise right-wing newspapers and worked as scriptwriters and directors in some of the major Shanghai studios.

In a sense, left-wing artists, writers, and film-makers had gone to war against Japan (and against the Guomindang) even before war broke out in 1937. Communists contributed to films that celebrated Chinese resistance to the Japanese invasion of Shanghai in 1932 (a thinly disguised criticism of Chiang Kai-shek's accomodationist policies). Communists also moved studios in the direction of making films that took up social issues. A movie based on Communist author Mao Dun's (1896–1981) story "Spring Silkworms," for example, dealt with the plight of a Zhejiang silkworm-raising family whose livelihood is destroyed by Japanese manipulation of the Shanghai silk industry. In the silent film *The Goddess,* a virtuous prostitute tries to send her son to school and struggles hopelessly against the corruption and prejudice that hit her from every side.[71]

Films like *Spring Silkworms* and *The Goddess* pushed the limits of what the Guomindang censors would allow. According to law, no film should "violate the political principles of the Guomindang," affect the "prestige of the nation," harm "morality in public places," or encourage "superstitious practices." Censors routinely banned or edited films they found in violation of these rules. Blue Shirt Society thugs smashed the facilities of the leftist Yi Hua Studio and threatened to do the same to any cinema that showed films that "promote class struggle [and] pit rich against poor."[72]

The Nanjing government's censorship was sometimes brutal, but it fell considerably short of total control. Established artists or writers like Xu Beihong (1895–1953) or Lu Xun (1881–1936) could get away with subtle digs at the Guomindang. Xu's huge oil painting of 1933, *Awaiting a Deliverer,* depicts a small group of men, women, and children standing in a desolate landscape, peering into the distance, waiting for a great leader to bring them out of their misery. China, Xu seemed to imply, did not then have such leadership.

Lu Xun's acerbic essays and his leading role in the League of Left-Wing Writers (he was sympathetic to, but did not join, the Communist Party) brought him a good deal of attention from the police, but he was never arrested.[73]

Less famous or less subtle artists than Xu Beihong often faced prison, execution, or assassination. Communist woodblock artists were given extremely harsh treatment. Lu Xun sparked the Nanjing Decade's woodblock print movement when he introduced European (particularly Soviet) woodblock prints to China. The direct, rough simplicity of these works and their vivid portrayal of the poor and downtrodden inspired a generation of leftist Chinese woodblock artists. Work like Zhou Xi's (1910–83) *Disputing With the Landlord* or Chen Tiegang's (1908–70) *The Meshes of the Law* dealt graphically with controversial issues: poverty, land reform, revolution, and police repression. These were politically sensitive themes. Many young wood-block artists themselves were caught in the "meshes of the law." A number were imprisoned, and some were executed. In reaction to the execution of twenty-three young male and female woodblock artists, Lu Xun lamented: "During the last thirty years, with my own eyes I have seen the blood of so many young people mounting that now I am submerged and cannot breathe. . . . What sort of world is this? The night is so long, the way is so long, that I had better forget, or else remain silent."[74]

Writers, too, were objects of police surveillance, harassment, and arrest. The atmosphere of inefficient repression, combined with the possibility of finding refuge (and publishers) in the foreign concession areas, may have stimulated artistic creativity. Famous leftist writers like Lao She (1899–1966), Guo Moruo (1892–1978), Shen Congwen (1902–88), and Ding Ling (1904–86) produced their best work in the tension-filled world of Nationalist China. Ding Ling's "Miss Sophie's Diary" (1928) expressed the sexual and occupational frustrations of a young urban woman—suggesting that patriarchy still ruled behind the modern veneer of Shanghai. Lao She, who grew up in an impoverished Banner family in Beijing, made his name with *Camel Xiangzi,* the tale of an honest, hardworking rickshaw puller from the countryside who is ultimately worn down and corrupted by urban Beijing. Shen Congwen, a former soldier, drew on his intimate knowledge of rural Hunan to produce a series of short stories and novels. Ba Jin (1904–2005), an anarchist, brilliantly portrayed inter-generational tensions in his novel *Family,* published in 1931.

When war did begin, writers, artists, and musicians, whether left, right, or centrist, put aside their differences and rallied under the banners of

"Resistance Literature," "Resistance Art," and "Resistance Music." As the Japanese occupied their accustomed haunts of Shanghai, Beijing, Tianjin, and other cities, China's composers and artists, writers, and filmmakers joined the mass migration of refugees fleeing west. At first, many of them headed for the rural western provinces: Guizhou, Yunnan, and Sichuan. In much of their work, the left-wing authors of the 1930s had romanticized the Chinese countryside. Villages were portrayed as the locus of good, old-fashioned "Chinese" qualities: honesty, hard work, moral virtue, and warm human feelings. The cities, by contrast, were Westernized cesspools of corruption in which cold, hard-hearted individuals pursued their own profit without scruple or pity. This romantic idealization of the countryside grew even stronger after the Japanese invasion, as intellectuals (many for the first time in their lives) absorbed the realities of rural life, drank in the new landscapes, and observed the customs of the non-Han ethnic groups of the southwest.

But from 1940 onward, as the war dragged on and as conflict between the Communist and Nationalist parties re-emerged in the wake of the New Fourth Army Incident of 1941, artists and writers began returning to the cities and expressing more discontent with the Guomindang leadership, often expressing their feelings through the medium of historical drama.[75] Many moved on to join the Communists in Yan'an. Here they would participate in new developments in art and literature, and in political struggles more intense than anything they had experienced during the Nanjing Decade, when they could always take refuge in Shanghai's International Concession. In Yan'an, art and politics were closely intertwined: and there was no place to escape to.

Art and Politics in Yan'an

While the Yangzi port city of Chongqing served as China's wartime capital, the small town of Yan'an became the capital of the Communist Party's Shaan-Gan-Ning Base Area. The base area itself was roughly the size of Ohio with a population of only 1.4 million.[76] Yan'an itself was a town of around seven thousand permanent residents and some thirty thousand Chinese Communist Party cadres, who constituted a society in most ways quite separate from the townspeople.[77] It was from Yan'an that Mao Zedong and the Party Center directed Communist military operations and social and economic policies. It was also in Yan'an that Mao Zedong pushed aside all competitors to become the unquestioned leader of the party and author of its guiding philosophy, "Mao Zedong Thought."

The Communist war effort has already been discussed briefly above. As they conducted guerrilla operations and built base areas across northwestern and northern China, the Communists needed to carry out social and economic policies that would win the support of the majority of the mostly rural population. When they first arrived in Yan'an in 1935, the party had carried out a full-fledged program of land reform: investigation of landholding, labeling of the population, and confiscation and redistribution of land above a certain maximum. But in order to work within the "Second United Front" and to disrupt the rural economy as little as possible, Mao and the other party leaders suspended land reform and instead pursued a policy of reducing rents and interest rates after 1937. For the time being, the party wanted the support of landlords, merchants, and the educated classes. Mao Zedong argued that in China, the working class could unite with and lead the "national bourgeoisie" (i.e., Chinese capitalists who were willing to cooperate with the Communist Party) on the basis of their common interest in throwing off imperialism and building a new, modern China.[78] Even when military cooperation with the Guomindang came to an end in 1941, the Communist Party continued to engage the "national bourgeoisie" under the rubric of the "United Front."

Mao's policies did not go unchallenged. Experienced generals like Peng Dehuai, who, unlike Mao, had been educated in military schools, criticized his emphasis on guerilla warfare. Upholders of Marxist-Leninist orthodoxy like Wang Ming and other Moscow-trained party members questioned his emphasis on rural issues and his willingness to make accommodations with landlords and merchants. Mao labeled his opponents as "dogmatists" who would blindly apply their Soviet book-learning to China's revolution.

Mao declared that Marxist doctrine needed to be adapted to China's concrete circumstances: an overwhelmingly rural population and a war with Japan. In his talk "On Contradiction," Mao argued that every phenomenon and situation is rife with contradiction. A revolutionary's task, he said, was to grasp and resolve the most important contradiction. For him, this meant focusing on the struggle with Japan and putting aside, for the moment, contradictions between the Communist Party and the Guomindang, between tenants and landlords, or between the proletariat and the bourgeoisie. In another talk, "On Practice," he suggested that dogmatic application of theoretically correct principles needed to give way to knowledge derived from practical experience: "Discover the truth through practice, and again through practice verify and develop the truth."[79]

By 1942, Mao had already eliminated Wang Ming and other rivals from the party leadership. But unless he could purge the party of all potential support for the Wang Ming line, his enemies might be able to stage a comeback. In order to conduct such a purge, Mao initiated the Party Rectification Movement of 1942. In this campaign, or "mass movement," as in many later campaigns, party leaders mobilized parts of the bureaucracy, the party, and/or the people (the "masses") to pursue a defined goal.[80] In this case, party members were to identify, criticize, and reform "dogmatists" (Wang Ming and other foreign-educated party members), "empiricists" (Zhou Enlai, Peng Dehuai, and others), and their supporters. All those targeted were forced to write self-criticisms.

While "dogmatists" and "empiricists" were the initial targets of the campaign, Mao also had his sights on writers and artists. Many young east coast urban intellectual party members had made the pilgrimage to Yan'an in the late 1930s and early 1940s. Their ideals brought them to the base area, but once there, many found conditions more difficult than they had imagined. The harsh conditions, lack of physical comfort, scarcity of entertainment, and, for the young men, the small number of single young women were all hard to bear. But more significantly, they chafed at the party's strict control over artistic expression and at the apparent hypocrisy of top party officials. Yan'an was not the egalitarian society that they had imagined. Higher-ranking people (like Mao Zedong) lived in better quarters, wore better clothes, and ate more and better food than the rank and file.

Some authors expressed their opinions in print. Their unofficial leader, Ding Ling, a woman writer and party member from Shanghai, called for leftist authors to continue the practice of writing satirical essays to point out injustice—even in Yan'an. As editor of the literary section of the party newspaper *Liberation Daily,* she had the power to get such work published. Ding Ling herself wrote and published "Thoughts on March Eighth," a scathing critique of the patriarchal attitudes and continued discrimination against women in Yan'an.[81] She also published her friend Wang Shiwei's (1906–47) "Wild Lilies," a bitter attack on elitist party leaders and their privileges: the special kitchens, better clothing, and even, indirectly, Mao Zedong's well-known fondness for the companionship of pretty young women.[82]

This sort of thing was unacceptable. The Rectification Campaign swung around to hit dissident intellectuals, broadly defined. When it became clear that denouncing others could win one praises—or at least protection from being denounced oneself—the denunciations, criticisms, and self-criticisms

flowed in. Thousands of intellectuals in Yan'an were forced to undergo multiple rounds of humiliating criticism and self-criticism at public meetings.
Most of them—including Ding Ling—renounced their views and participated in the criticism of Wang Shiwei.[83] The Party Rectification Movement
was a forerunner of other movements in which the Communist Party disciplined intellectuals—and in which some intellectuals avidly took part as they
helped the party to discipline the others.

As a part of this disciplinary exercise, Mao Zedong gave a pair of talks at
the opening and closing ceremonies of the "Yan'an Forum on Art and Literature." In these talks, Mao explained to the intellectuals that writing and art
always serve a political purpose, whether good or bad, progressive or reactionary. The party expected that its intellectuals would produce works
of art and literature that communicated party policy and the party's vision
of China's future to ordinary people (farmers and workers) in images, language, and performances that they could understand. Culture was a branch
of political work. As such, it must follow the principle of the "mass line":
derive goals and ideas from the masses, refine them in accordance with
the overarching revolutionary theory of Marxism-Leninism–Mao Zedong
Thought, and deliver them to the masses in ways that would allow the masses
to accept them as their own.

Writers, artists, musicians, and playwrights in the Communist base areas
working in accordance with the party's guidelines produced work with some
distinct aesthetic and political characteristics. Already inclined to draw inspiration from a romanticized countryside, creative artists in Yan'an now
drew directly on rural folk traditions. Xian Xinghai, a prolific composer of
anti-Japanese songs, used elements of folk music and work songs in his *Yellow River Cantata.* Playwrights drew on Yan'an's traditional *yang'ge* ("sprouts
songs") to create a new form of *yang'ge* drama—plays on subjects like land
reform, opening new fields, and resisting the Japanese.[84] Ding Ling did
penance by writing an epic novel of land reform. Artists, who found that rural people did not like the rough simplicity and rather pessimistic air of black-
and-white woodblock prints, drew on the styles of colorful traditional New
Year's prints to produce much more colorful, cheerful, and optimistic revolutionary art.

By 1945, the Chinese Communist Party was stronger than it had ever been.
Through art and literature, land reform and rent reduction, and limited
guerilla operations against the Japanese and "puppet government" troops,
the Communist Party created an image of itself as idealistic and honest,

A U.S. bomber on its way to bomb Japan, crossing the bows of some of the Flying Tigers' P-40 fighter planes in China, 1943.

concerned about social justice and resistance to Japan, and ready to talk with the Guomindang and with the United States. Mao Zedong and his supporters had used the war and the Rectification Campaign to solidify Mao's control over the party and to enshrine his ideas—"Mao Zedong Thought"—as part of the party's ideology. Party membership stood at 853,420 in 1945, up from 736,151 in 1942 and a mere 40,000 in 1937.[85] In the meantime, the Nationalist government, already weakened from war, loss of territory, inflation, and corruption, was reeling from Japan's Ichigo Offensive.

In the end, neither the Guomindang nor the Communist Party defeated the Japanese forces in China. Both parties traded with the occupied territories and maintained secret contacts with the Wang Jingwei government and the Japanese. American operations in the Pacific and bombing raids on the home islands brought Japan to its knees. American airplanes firebombed Tokyo on 9 March and dropped atomic bombs on Hiroshima and Nagasaki on 6 and 9 August, respectively. The Soviet Union declared war on Japan and entered "Manchukuo" on 8 August, quickly defeating Japanese troops there. The Japanese surrender came days later on 15 August.

The Civil War, 1945–1949

As they celebrated victory, both the Guomindang and the Communist Party scrambled to take advantage of Japan's sudden collapse. Both parties competed to move their troops into areas formerly under Japanese occupation and to take the surrender of the Japanese and collaborationist Chinese armies. For the next four years, the two parties would fight each other on the battlefield and in the diplomatic arena. Their competition unfolded in the context of the Cold War rivalry between the United States and the Soviet Union, each of which wanted to see a friendly government ruling over China.

The Communist Party's first significant move was to abandon the south, where they had only a few very weak base areas. Instead, they would focus on the north, especially the northeast. With Japan defeated, there was no government authority in "Manchukuo." In late August, Communist troops from north China began moving into the northeast. They traveled light, expecting to receive support from the Soviet Union's Red Army and to inherit weapons and supplies from the "Manchukuo" and Japanese armies. By mid-October, Communist troops had taken up positions at key rail lines, cities, and entry points into the northeast. The Party Central Committee ordered Lin Biao (1907–71), commander of the Communist forces in Manchuria, to prevent any Nationalist troops from entering the area.[86]

But the Guomindang government had not been idle. Chiang Kai-shek was equally determined to assert government authority over the northeast and all other Japanese-occupied areas. His strategy was to maneuver between the Soviet Union and the United States, extracting maximum benefit from each. On 8 August 1945, his diplomats agreed to the terms of a "Treaty of Friendship and Cooperation" with the Soviet Union. The Soviets would turn Manchuria over to Chinese government troops and officials in return for joint Soviet-Chinese management of the Manchurian railways and Soviet leases on key Manchurian ports (Dalian and Lüshun). Chiang now faced the task of getting the Soviets to follow through on their promises while using American support to move his troops into Manchuria. In the context of the developing Cold War, this strategy was doomed to failure: the more Chiang relied on the Americans for military support, the more concerned the Soviets became. In the end, the logic of the Cold War competition between the United States and the Soviet Union forced Chiang to take sides: as a result, he was forced into complete reliance on the United States.[87]

On paper, Chiang's armies were far superior to those of the Communists. But beneath the surface, the government was weak. Many units were under-strength and poorly trained. The army was rife with factional struggles: the rivalry between Whampoa Clique units and former warlord units was particularly strong. Many of the government officials and army officers who were assigned to areas recently recovered from Japanese occupation acted like occupiers themselves, taking whatever they could for their own personal profit. Inflation and corruption sapped civilian morale. The nation's economy was in shambles. Chiang's American allies were accordingly pessimistic about his chances of winning a full-blown civil war.

Hoping to save Chiang from defeat, President Harry Truman (1884–1972) appointed General George Marshall (1880–1959), who had commanded Allied operations during World War II, as special representative to negotiate a cease-fire and coalition government between the Guomindang and Communist parties. The Americans evidently believed that Chiang would compromise, and that the Communists would stop trying to overthrow the government if they were allowed to become a part of it. They were wrong on both counts: neither side was willing to settle for anything other than complete victory, which could be won only on the battlefield, not at the conference table.

The initial results of the war were encouraging for Chiang. In the winter of 1945–46, his well-equipped, American-trained motorized forces pushed the ragtag Communists out of most areas of southern Manchuria. By early June, Lin Biao's main force had retreated north of the Sungari River to Harbin. At this point, his troops already overextended, fearful of Soviet reaction, and facing pressure from Marshall, Chiang agreed to a cease-fire, which halted the fighting in Manchuria for four months. Chiang used this time to go on the offensive in China Proper, driving the Communists away from major rail lines and cities in North China, recovering parts of Shandong province, and even capturing the Communist headquarters town of Yan'an in March 1947.

But Chiang's victories in 1946 and 1947 left him weaker, not stronger. As both Marshall and the Communist commander Lin Biao had predicted, Chiang's troops, though better trained and equipped than the Communists, were now stretched thin and concentrated in major cities and along the rail lines upon which they depended for supplies and transportation. Beginning in 1947, Lin Biao's forces launched a counteroffensive in Manchuria. With the hopes of producing a coalition government rapidly fading, Marshall ended his mission to China in January 1947. The United States continued to extend limited support to Chiang's government. But as his armies suffered defeat after defeat, the Truman administration became convinced that the Nationalist

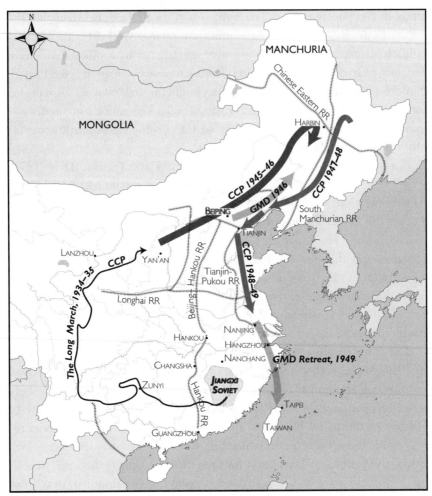

The Long March (1934–35) and the Civil War (1945–49).

government was incapable of carrying out the internal reforms necessary to win broad public support and that Chiang Kai-shek's armies were unable to defend their territory against the Communists.[88] In autumn and winter of 1948, the Communist armies went from strength to strength, incorporating captured or surrendered Guomindang units and their weapons (some government units joined the Communists voluntarily), capturing Manchuria, Tianjin, and Beiping, and then sweeping south to cross the Yangzi in late March 1949.

While defeating government forces on the ground, the Communist Party was also winning the struggle for the hearts and souls of rural and urban

Chinese. Party operatives in the countryside carried out a radical land reform program in which they mobilized poor farmers to confiscate land and other property from the wealthy and redistribute it to the poor—a process during which the Communist Party itself both won local support and appropriated a good deal of wealth for its own purposes. For educated urbanites, the Communist Party's promises of a "new democracy" in which workers, farmers, small business people, and even wealthy business families who supported the Communists would work together to realize the May Fourth/ New Culture Movement ideals of a reconstructed, modern Chinese culture and a strong Chinese nation, free of imperialism.[89] These ideals and the Communist Party's reputation for discipline and honesty were attractive to many urbanites disappointed with a Guomindang administration which, in many people's minds, was more and more associated with inflation and corruption.

In the autumn of 1949, as Chiang Kai-shek's government forces fell in one defeat after another, the Communists prepared to form a new government. On 1 October 1949, party Chairman Mao Zedong stood on the rostrum atop the old Qing imperial palace's Gate of Heavenly Peace and formally proclaimed the establishment of the People's Republic of China. As for Chiang Kai-shek, he was planning his final retreat. Guomindang forces had taken over the island of Taiwan after the Japanese surrender. Chiang now ordered gold, the art treasures of the Forbidden City, government offices, and army units to be transferred to Taiwan. He himself left the mainland in December, vowing to return someday.

Notes

1. This section on the Northern Expedition is based on the accounts in Donald A. Jordon, *The Northern Expedition: China's National Revolution of 1926–1928* (Honolulu: The University Press of Hawaii, 1976); and Hans Van de Ven, *War and Nationalism in China: 1925–1945* (London: Routledge, 2003).

2. Bruce A. Elleman, *Modern Chinese Warfare, 1795–1989* (London: Routledge, 2001), 173.

3. Hans Van de Ven, *From Friend to Comrade: The Founding of the Chinese Communist Party, 1920–1927* (Berkeley: University of California Press, 1991), 193.

4. Jonathan Fenby, *Chiang Kai-shek: China's Generalissimo and the Nation He Lost* (New York: Carroll & Graff Publishers, 2003), 134.

5. Ibid., 163–71.

6. Jordon, *The Northern Expedition,* 256.

7. Frederic Wakeman, Jr., *Spymaster: Dai Li and the Chinese Secret Service* (Berkeley: University of California Press, 2003), 4–6, 42–5.

8. Fenby, *Chiang Kai-shek,* 231; Lloyd Eastman, "Nationalist China During the Nanking Decade 1927–1937," in John K. Fairbank and Albert Feuerwerker, eds., *The Cambridge History of China, Vol. 13: Republican China, 1912–1949, Part 2* (Cambridge: Cambridge University Press, 1986), 142.

9. The following discussion draws on Margherita Zanasi, *Saving the Nation: Economic Modernity in Republican China* (Chicago: The University of Chicago Press, 2006).

10. Eastman, "Nationalist China During the Nanking Decade," 127.

11. Fenby, *Chiang Kai-shek,* 226; Frederic Wakeman, Jr., "A Revisionist View of the Nanjing Decade: Confucian Fascism," in Frederic Wakeman, Jr., and Richard Louis Edmonds, eds., *Reappraising Republican China* (Oxford: Oxford University Press, 2000), 141–78.

12. Chiang, quoted in Eastman, "Nationalist China During the Nanking Decade," 146.

13. Wakeman, "Confucian Fascism." See also Maria Hsia Chang, *The Chinese Blue Shirt Society: Fascism and Developmental Nationalism* (Berkeley: Institute of East Asian Studies, University of California), 1985.

14. Fenby, *Chiang Kai-shek,* 246–8.

15. Eastman, "Nationalist China During the Nanking Decade," 155.

16. Ibid., 151–5.

17. Frederick Wakeman, Jr., *Policing Shanghai 1927–1937* (Berkeley: University of California Press, 1995), 74–5.

18. William C. Kirby, "The Internationalization of China: Foreign Relations at Home and Abroad in the Republican Era," in Wakeman and Edmonds, eds., *Reappraising Republican China,* 183–7.

19. Emily Honig, *Creating Chinese Ethnicity: Subei People in Shanghai, 1850–1980* (New Haven: Yale University Press, 1982).

20. Patricia Stranahan, *Underground: The Shanghai Communist Party and the Politics of Survival, 1927–1937* (Lanham: Rowman & Littlefield, 1998), 75; Lawrence R. Sullivan, "Reconstruction and Rectification of the Communist Party in the Shanghai Underground, 1931–34," *The China Quarterly* 101 (March 1985): 92–3.

21. Sullivan, "Reconstruction and Rectification," 95.

22. Emily Honig, "Christianity, Feminism, and Communism: The Life and Times of Deng Yuzhi (Cora Deng)," in Cheryl Johnson-Odim and Margaret Strobel, eds., *Expanding the Boundaries of Women's History: Essays on Women in the Third World* (Bloomington: Indiana University Press, 1992), 132–6.

23. Stranahan, *Underground,* 122.

24. The following paragraphs draw on Lucien Bianco, *Origins of the Chinese Revolution 1915–1949* (Stanford: Stanford University Press, 1971); and on Jerome Chen, "The Communist Movement 1927–1937," in Fairbank and Feuerwerker, eds., *The Cambridge History of China, Vol. 13,* 204–8.

25. Edward L. Dreyer, *China at War, 1901–1949* (London: Longman, 1995), 190. Some historians credit Chiang Kai-shek's German advisors with devising the blockhouse strategy. Dreyer argues that it was based on the experiences of Zeng Guofan and Zuo Zongtang's campaigns against the Nian and Tungan rebellions of the mid-19th century. See Dreyer, 191.

26. Benjamin Yang, *From Revolution to Politics: Chinese Communists on the Long March*

(Boulder: Westview Press, 1990), 95–9; Gregor Benton, "Under Arms and Umbrellas: Perspectives on Chinese Communism in Defeat," in Tony Saich and Hans Van de Ven, eds., *New Perspectives on the Chinese Communist Revolution* (Armonk: M. E. Sharpe, 1995), 116; Otto Braun, *A Comintern Agent in China 1932–1939* (Stanford: Stanford University Press, 1982), 75–81. Braun describes the withdrawal from the Jiangxi Soviet as a well-organized, carefully planned breakthrough of the Communist main forces that "although it did take on the character of a retreat later on . . . was not initially regarded as such." Braun, 83.

27. Harrison E. Salisbury, *The Long March: The Untold Story* (New York: Harper & Row, 1985), 109.

28. Yang, *From Revolution to Politics*, 123–4.

29. Van de Ven, *War and Nationalism in China*, 150.

30. Mao and Zhang Guotao had both pursued rural revolution and been criticized by the Moscow-trained party leadership in the 1930s. But perhaps because of their similar approaches to revolution, Mao and Zhang became bitter rivals for influence within the Communist Party. See Yang, *From Revolution to Politics*, 129–30.

31. Bianco, *Origins of the Chinese Revolution*, 67–8; Chen, "The Communist Movement," 214–5; Salisbury, *The Long March*, 87; Jonathan Spence, *Mao Zedong* (New York: Penguin Putnam, 1999), 83–5.

32. Herbert P. Bix, *Hirohito and the Making of Modern Japan* (New York: HarperCollins Publishers, 2000), 239–41.

33. Elleman, *Modern Chinese Warfare*, 197.

34. Andrew R. Hall, "Constructing a 'Manchurian' Identity: Japanese Education in Manchukuo, 1931–1945," Ph.D. dissertation, University of Pittsburgh, 2003.

35. Van de Ven, *War and Nationalism in China*, 178–80.

36. Fenby, *Chiang Kai-shek*, 2.

37. Van de Ven, *War and Nationalism in China*, 188; Fenby, *Chiang Kai-shek*, 11.

38. Bix, *Hirohito*, 317–23.

39. Eastman, "Nationalist China During the Sino-Japanese War 1937–1945," in Fairbank and Feuerwerker, eds., *The Cambridge History of China, Vol. 13*, 547, 565; Hsi-sheng Ch'i, "The Military Dimension, 1942–1945," in James C. Hsiung and Steven I. Levine, eds., *China's Bitter Victory: The War with Japan 1937–1945* (Armonk: M. E. Sharpe, 1992), 179.

40. The bombing raid went tragically wrong when Nationalist pilots mistakenly dropped their bombs on Nanjing Road, the heart of Shanghai's commercial district. Fenby, *Chiang Kai-shek*, 295–6; Hsi-sheng Ch'i, *Nationalist China at War: Military Defeats and Political Collapse, 1937–45* (Ann Arbor: The University of Michigan Press, 1982), 41–2; Elleman, *Modern Chinese Warfare*, 203.

41. Ch'i, *Nationalist China at War*, 42.

42. Honda Katsuichi, *The Nanjing Massacre: A Japanese Journalist Confronts Japan's National Shame* (Armonk: M. E. Sharpe, 1999), 285. Questions regarding the number of casualties at Nanjing, the causes of the massacre, and the roles of Japanese commanders in acquiescing in, or even ordering, the violence are the subject of much scholarship and too complex to summarize here. In addition to Katsuichi, see Joshua A. Fogel, ed., *The Nanjing Massacre in History and Historiography* (Berkeley: University of California Press, 2000); Daqing Yang, "Convergence or Divergence? Recent Historical Writings on the Rape of Nanjing," *American Historical Review* 104.3

(June 1999): 842–65; and Daqing Yang, "Atrocities in Nanjing: Searching for Explanations," in Diana Lary and Stephen MacKinnon, eds., *Scars of War: The Impact of Warfare on Modern China* (Vancouver: UBC Press, 2001), 76–96. Iris Chang's *The Rape of Nanking: The Forgotten Holocaust of World War II* (Harmondsworth: Penguin, 1998), while respected for its moving descriptions of events, is not a reliable source on issues of causation or numbers of casualties.

43. Stephen R. MacKinnon, *Wuhan, 1938: War, Refugees, and the Making of Modern China* (Berkeley: University of California Press, 2008), 31–7.

44. Diana Lary, "Drowned Earth: The Strategic Breaching of the Yellow River Dyke, 1938," *War in History* 8.2 (2001): 191–207.

45. William C. Kirby, "The Chinese War Economy," in Hsiung and Levine, eds. *China's Bitter Victory*, 190–3.

46. Ibid., 191.

47. Lyman Van Slyke, "The Battle of the Hundred Regiments: Problems of Coordination and Control During the Sino-Japanese War" *Modern Asian Studies* 30.4 (Oct. 1996): 979–1005.

48. Ibid., 983–4.

49. Van de Ven, *War and Nationalism in China,* 245.

50. Chen Yong-fa, "The Blooming Poppy Under the Red Sun: The Yan'an Way and the Opium Trade," in Saich and Van de Ven, *New Perspectives on the Chinese Communist Revolution,* 265.

51. Ibid., 277.

52. William C. Kirby, "The Chinese War Economy," 197.

53. Van de Ven, *War and Nationalism in China,* 268–9.

54. Ibid., 284; Ch'i, *Nationalist China at War,* 103.

55. Elleman, *Modern Chinese Warfare,* 210.

56. Van de Ven, *War and Nationalism,* 295–6.

57. Maochun Yu, *The Dragon's War: Allied Operation and the Fate of China 1937–1947* (Annapolis: Naval Institute Press, 2006), 4.

58. Ch'i, *Nationalist China at War,* 59.

59. Yu, *The Dragon's War,* 64–5.

60. Daniel Ford, *Flying Tigers: Claire Chennault and the American Volunteer Group* (Washington: Smithsonian Institution Press, 1991), 19–27.

61. Yu, *The Dragon's War,* 44–5.

62. This analysis follows Hans Van de Ven, "Stilwell in the Stocks: The Chinese Nationalists and the Allied Powers in the Second World War," *Asian Affairs* 34.3 (Nov. 2003); and Van de Ven, *War and Nationalism in China,* 19–63. For more positive assessments of Stilwell, see Barbara W. Tuchman, *Stilwell and the American Experience in China 1911–1945* (New York: The Macmillan Company, 1971); and Theodore H. White, ed., *The Stilwell Papers* (New York: William Sloane Associates, Inc., 1948).

63. Van de Ven, "Stilwell in the Stocks, 243–59.

64. Tuchman, *Stilwell and the American Experience in China,* 493.

65. See Stilwell's diary entry for 19 September 1944, in White, ed., *The Stilwell Papers,* 333.

66. Yu, *The Dragon's War,* 177–8.

67. Van de Ven, "Stilwell in the Stocks," 253; Van de Ven, *War and Nationalism in China,* 48.

68. Hsi-sheng Ch'i, "The Military Dimension, 1942–1945," in Hsiung and Levine, eds., *China's Bitter Victory,* 165.

69. For further discussion and illustrations, see Leo Ou-fan Lee, *Shanghai Modern: The Flowering of a New Urban Culture in China, 1930–1945* (Cambridge, Mass.: Harvard University Press, 1999).

70. Hanchao Lu, *Beyond the Neon Lights: Everyday Shanghai in the Early Twentieth Century* (Berkeley: University of California Press, 1999), 184; Frederic Wakeman, Jr., "Licensing Leisure: The Chinese Nationalists' Attempt to Regulate Shanghai, 1927–49," *The Journal of Asian Studies* 54.1 (Feb. 1995): 19–42.

71. Yingjin Zhang, "Prostitution and Urban Imagination: Negotiating the Public and the Private in Chinese Films of the 1930s," in Yingjin Zhang, ed., *Cinema and Urban Culture in Shanghai, 1922–1943* (Stanford: Stanford University Press, 1999, 167–71). The screenplay for *The Goddess* was written by Wu Yonggang.

72. Jay Leyda, *Dianying: An Account of Films and the Film Audience in China* (Cambridge, Mass.: The MIT Press, 1972), 88.

73. David E. Pollard, *The True Story of Lu Xun* (Hong Kong: The Chinese University Press, 2002), 143.

74. Sullivan, *Art and Artists of Twentieth Century China,* 84.

75. Chang-tai Hung, *War and Popular Culture: Resistance in Modern China, 1937–1945* (Berkeley: University of California Press, 1994), 84.

76. This and the following draw on Lyman Van Slyke, "The Chinese Communist Movement During the Sino-Japanese War 1937–1945," in Fairbank and Feuerwerker, eds., *The Cambridge History of China, Vol. 13,* 609–723.

77. Gao Hua, *Hong taiyang shi zenyang shengqide:Yan'an zhengfeng yundong de lailong qumai* (How the red sun rose: the origins and development of the Yan'an rectification movement) (Hong Kong: Zhongwen daxue chubanshe, 2000), 211.

78. Mao Zedong, "On New Democracy," in *Selected Works of Mao Tse-tung,* Vol. 2 (Beijing: Foreign Languages Press, 1965), 339–42.

79. Mao Zedong, "On Practice," *Selected Readings from the Works of Mao Tsetung* (Beijing: Foreign Languages Press, 1971), 81.

80. Julia Strauss, "Morality, Coercion, and State Building by Campaign in the Early PRC: Regime Consolidation and After, 1949–1956," in Strauss, ed. *The History of the PRC (1949–1976)* (Cambridge: Cambridge University Press, 2007), 37–58.

81. Ding Ling, Tani E. Barlow, and Gary Bjorge, *I Myself Am a Woman: Selected Writings of Ding Ling* (Boston: Beacon Press, 1989). 8 March is International Women's Day.

82. Dai Qing, *Wang Shiwei and Wild Lilies: Rectification and Purges in the Chinese Communist Party 1942–1944* (Armonk: M. E. Sharpe, 1994); Timothy Cheek, "The Fading of Wild Lilies: Wang Shiwei and Mao Zedong's Yan'an Talks in the First CPC Rectification Movement," *The Australian Journal of Chinese Affairs,* 11 (Jan. 1984): 25–58.

83. Tony Saich, ed., *The Rise to Power of the Chinese Communist Party: Documents and Analysis* (Armonk: M. E. Sharpe, 1996), 983.

84. *The Garland Encyclopedia of World Music, Volume 7, East Asia: China, Japan and Korea* (New York: Routledge, 2002), 346, 384–5.

85. Van Slyke, "The Chinese Communist Movement," 621.

86. Harold M. Tanner, "Guerilla, Mobile, and Base Warfare in Communist Military Operations in Manchuria, 1945–1947," *Journal of Military History* 67.4 (Oct. 2003): 1177–1222.

87. Odd Arne Westad, *Cold War and Revolution: Soviet-American Rivalry and the Origins of the Chinese Civil War* (New York: Columbia University Press, 1993), 166, 171.

88. U.S. Central Intelligence Agency, "CIA Report on China (SR-8), November 1947 Section V: Military Situation," CIA Research Reports, China 1946–1976 (Frederick: University Microfilms of America, 1982), reel 1; Michael Schaller, *The United States and China: Into the Twenty-first Century,* 3rd ed. (New York: Oxford University Press, 2002), 115.

89. Saich, *The Rise to Power of the Chinese Communist Party,* 1205.

Chapter 5   THE PEOPLE'S
                        REPUBLIC OF CHINA

                            The Mao Era

On 1 October 1949, Mao Zedong stood triumphantly on the rostrum of the Tiananmen (the Gate of Heavenly Peace) in Beijing to announce the found-ing of the People's Republic of China to the enthusiastic crowd gathered in front of him in the very place where the May Fourth Movement had begun thirty years earlier.

Mao's announcement and the Communist victory over Chiang Kai-shek's Nationalist government spelled disaster for many Chinese. Some two mil-lion refugees, including Guomindang (Nationalist Party, GMD) members, government officials, wealthy families, and six hundred thousand soldiers fled with Chiang to Taiwan.[1] But many more Chinese welcomed the new government in Beijing. A wave of patriotic optimism invigorated left-leaning, nationalistic urban intellectuals and brought many educated professionals back from Hong Kong, Southeast Asia, North America, Europe, and Japan to participate in the construction of a new China. Ordinary people waited with mixed feelings to see what the new regime would do, and how long it would last. Would Mao Zedong and his Communist Party really transform China? Would they improve people's daily lives and make the country wealthy, powerful, and respected on the world stage? And if so, how?

The Communist Party, the Chinese State, and Mass Movements

Mao and his comrades employed three major institutions in their bid to make China a strong, industrialized socialist country: the Chinese Communist Party (CCP), the People's Liberation Army (PLA), and the Chinese state consisting of legislative, judicial, and executive branches. Because the Communist Party dominated the state, which party leaders viewed as an instrument to be wielded as they saw fit, analysts often refer to the system as the "party-state." In addition to these formal institutions, Chinese leaders also mobilized party members and ordinary citizens to participate in mass movements or "campaigns" to transform education, society, family life, and even the government and the party itself.

In 1949, the Chinese Communist Party had around five million members, the majority of whom were rural men with little education.[2] Its formal governing body, the National Congress of the Chinese Communist Party, was an unwieldy group of thousands of representatives of base-level party organizations that met on an irregular basis. The Party Congress delegated its authority to the party's one hundred– to two hundred–member Central Committee, which, in turn, delegated its authority to its fourteen- to twenty-member Political Bureau (Politburo). The Standing Committee of the Politburo, a group of around five or six men (no women), exercised day-to-day leadership over party, military, and government business. Party organizations at the provincial and local levels of government administration were similarly structured, with small party committees leading all government work.[3]

The People's Liberation Army was the second major institution through which the Communist Party leaders controlled and hoped to transform China. The PLA had 5.5 million soldiers in 1949.[4] When they first took control of China, the Communists divided the country into six military regions in which PLA officers performed the functions of civilian administration. This, however, was a temporary measure and was phased out during the early 1950s as the party built provincial and local civilian governments. The PLA's main mission was to defend the national territory. Ultimate power in the party was closely linked to leadership of the military. Mao Zedong served as the Chair of the Central Committee's Military Affairs Commission. PLA generals often served in the party's Central Committee and Politburo, and the army played significant roles in politics and in propaganda. However, although political power was closely linked to military leadership, the army was always subordinate to party leadership: military coups and military dictatorship did not become part of the Chinese political culture.

In theory, the real leaders of the People's Republic of China were the people themselves as represented in their elected local, provincial, and national People's Congresses as laid out in the Constitution of 1954.[5] The National People's Congress was responsible for legislation. Executive power was vested in the State Council, with a largely ceremonial president (Mao Zedong, until 1959, when he gave the position to Liu Shaoqi [1898–1969]) and a premier (Zhou Enlai) supervising the work of various ministries, including the Foreign Ministry, Public Security (police), Supreme People's Court, and Supreme People's Procuratorate (an oversight and prosecutorial agency).

Provincial and county governments were organized along the same lines, each with its own elected People's Congress, People's Government, Public Security office, court, procuratorate, and so on. It was a unitary, not a federal, system: each organ of government on each level was subordinate to the corresponding organ above it. For example, county Public Security, courts, and procuratorates accepted the oversight of the People's Government at the corresponding level, but were under the direct administrative authority of the provincial Public Security office, court, and procuratorate. At the county level, the secretary of the county's Communist Party committee exercised overall power in a way reminiscent of the Qing county magistrate.

The Party Center in Beijing supervised the work of party members and the work of the government through a system of provincial and local party organizations and of party cells in government organs. The party kept a list of government posts and other important positions (university presidencies, for example) to which only party members could be appointed, and corresponding lists of party members eligible for appointment to posts at various levels. The laws, the organs of the state, the police, and the army were considered to be instruments for carrying out party policy.

As it came into power, the Communist Party did not aim simply to restore stability. The idea was to transform the Chinese economy, society, family and culture. There would also be times when the party leadership would want to rectify the party itself, as it had in Yan'an in 1942. The "campaign" or "mass movement" was the ideal instrument for this sort of transformation. In a campaign, the party used its organization and propaganda to mobilize all or parts of the government, the party, and/or the entire Chinese population to achieve a particular goal.[6]

A campaign could be as simple as calling on everyone to swat flies—there would be announcements, meetings, and propaganda posters about the need to kill flies in order to improve public health, quotas established for schoolchildren to bring in set numbers of dead flies, public praise for people who killed record numbers of flies, and so on. The same technique could be used to mobilize people for land reform, to identify and punish "counter-revolutionaries," to produce more grain, to dig irrigation ditches, or to accomplish a host of other political, economic, or social goals.

There were many campaigns during the first twenty-six years of the People's Republic. A short list (each of which will be discussed briefly later in this chapter) includes:

Land Reform (1950–52)
Campaign to Resist America and Aid Korea (1950)
Campaign to Suppress Counterrevolutionaries (1951)
Campaign to Carry Out the Marriage Law (1951–52, 1953)
Three-Antis and Five-Antis Campaigns (1951–52)
Campaign to Criticize Hu Feng (1955)
Hundred Flowers/Anti-Rightist Campaign (1957)
Great Leap Forward (1958–60)
Socialist Education Campaign (1962–65)
Great Proletarian Cultural Revolution (1966–69)
Campaign to Criticize Lin Biao, Criticize Confucius (1973–74)

The Chinese people got to be quite adept at carrying out campaigns—writing and chanting slogans, holding mass rallies and political discussion meetings, and behaving (or appearing to behave) as expected. But at times, there could be a fundamental contradiction between the interests of the party-state bureaucracy and the technique of the mass campaign. If the "masses" mobilized for a campaign were not carefully directed and supervised, but allowed to adapt the campaign to their own purposes or to act spontaneously, the campaign itself could spin out of control. Party-state officials preferred campaigns to focus on narrowly defined targets and to unfold under the watchful eye and close supervision of party cadres (officials). The campaigns of the early and mid-1950s were indeed carefully managed events. In later campaigns, particularly the Hundred Flowers, the Anti-Rightist Campaign, and the campaigns of the Cultural Revolution years (1966–76), the targets were loosely defined and even included many party members themselves.

Revolutionary Change, 1949–1953

The Communist Party's first tasks in 1949 were to complete the conquest of China's national territory and to restore economic stability. Continued military operations against remaining Guomindang forces brought southwestern China under Communist control in February 1950, and Hainan Island in March. With the small and poorly armed Tibetan army collapsing and Lhasa occupied, the Dalai Lama and his government of Tibetan nobility signed a "Seventeen-Point Agreement" with China in 1951. The agreement allowed the Tibetan nobility and the Dalai Lama to retain their land, wealth, and power while obliging them to recognize Chinese sovereignty.

These victories were offset by the People's Liberation Army's inability even to capture the small Nationalist-held islands of Jinmen and Mazu, just miles off the coast of south China. Without a real navy, the PLA would need at least a year's preparation before attempting an invasion of Chiang Kai-shek's last sanctuary on Taiwan. At the time, the American government regarded the fall of Taiwan as inevitable.[7] The outbreak of the Korean War in 1950 (see below) changed the equation: the United States, now determined to defend Chiang Kai-shek, stationed the Seventh Fleet in the Taiwan Straits. This explicit American commitment to Taiwan's defense, which lasted until 1979, allowed the Nationalist Republic of China to pursue its own, capitalist path of economic development on Taiwan while the Communist Party moved forward with the construction of a socialist economy on the mainland.

In the economic sphere, the Communist Party's long-term goal was to draw on the model of the Soviet Union to build a modern socialist China. Party leaders realized that this could not be done overnight. Both Liu Shaoqi and Mao Zedong stated that the party would work with private enterprise to improve production and "enter the new era of socialism unhurriedly and with proper arrangements when our economy and culture are flourishing, when conditions are ripe, and when the transition has been fully considered and endorsed by the whole nation."[8] This cautious approach did not mean that the Communist Party had adopted a laissez-faire economic policy: the party moved quickly to assert state control over key areas of banking, price control, and currency in order to create conditions under which a mixed economy of state enterprises and private businesses could recover and increase production.

China's economy did recover quickly. By mid-1950, inflation was under control, bond issues and a unified tax system had put the government on a stable financial footing, and production was rising. Campaigns to eliminate prostitution and opium and to crack down on crime brought a new level of stability and public safety to major cities like Shanghai, Beijing, and Tianjin. With the restoration of public order, the establishment of a strong party-state regime, and assertion of firm central control over most of the territory of the former Qing Empire, the Communists had finally achieved the state-building goals that had eluded Chinese leaders since the mid-19th century. This achievement combined with the external threat of American involvement in the Korean War and in the Taiwan Strait (see below) strengthened the hand of those within the party who were convinced that they should move faster toward the destruction of the old economic, social, and cultural regime and the building of a thoroughly new socialist China.

Whether radical or moderate, all party members agreed that it was necessary to destroy the old China in order to create something new and better. From 1950 to 1953, the "Campaign to Suppress Counterrevolutionaries" and other campaigns targeted people still resisting or planning to resist the Communist Party, former Nationalist Party members, government officials, soldiers, leaders of religious secret societies, and people with real or suspected family connections or loyalties to the Guomindang. Millions of suspects were investigated and denounced at carefully stage-managed public rallies. Estimates of the number executed range from eight hundred thousand to two million.[9]

In the countryside, the Campaign to Suppress Counterrevolutionaries overlapped with a nationwide Land Reform Campaign (1950–52). Party work teams of three to thirty members entered villages and created mass movements intended to get landless and poor farmers to identify "rich peasants" and "landlords," punish them, and confiscate their wealth—land, houses, money, nonagricultural businesses, and personal possessions.[10] During this process, families were assigned to categories: landlord, rich peasant, middle peasant, poor peasant, or "bad element" (local toughs, rent collectors, and criminals). Those in the undesirable categories were publicly humiliated at mass meetings, which often involved beatings and other physical punishment. An estimated one to two million accused landlords died, many of them beaten to death or executed after quick, informal trials.[11]

While landlords and rich peasants were under attack in the countryside, corrupt party members and businessmen were the targets of twin campaigns. The Three-Antis Campaign (1951) trained its sights on party cadres guilty of corruption, waste, and bureaucracy. This carefully controlled exercise was followed by the Five-Antis Campaign (1951–52), which attacked businessmen accused of bribery, theft of state property, tax evasion, cheating on government contracts, and theft of state economic information. Some of those investigated were, no doubt, guilty of financial shenanigans. But with employees encouraged to denounce their bosses, anonymously if they chose, the movement soon developed into a reign of terror against the business class.

By the time the campaign was over, the Chinese business world had been thoroughly cowed. Millions of businesses were investigated. Thousands of businessmen were held prisoner in their offices. Some were tortured, and an unknown number committed suicide.[12] With the movement causing a drop in trade with Hong Kong, rising unemployment, and declining production, the party brought the campaign to a "victorious" conclusion in June 1952. Punitive fines had forced many businesses into unequal "partnerships" with the state. By one estimate, the government had taken over US$500,000,000 in fines or, according to Mao Zedong, enough to "see us through another eighteen months" of the Korean War, which had broken out in 1950 (see below).[13]

Campaigns against internal enemies like landlords, counterrevolutionaries, corrupt cadres, and dishonest businessmen overlapped with campaigns that were intended to clean up the cities; to reform Chinese artists, writers, college professors, lawyers and judges, and other intellectuals; and to change the place of women in family, society, and the workplace. Thought reform campaigns forced politically unreliable, but still desperately needed college professors, legal professionals, and government bureaucrats to participate in "criticism and self-criticism" and "study" sessions in order to purge their minds of their bourgeois Western orientation and re-orient themselves intellectually toward socialism, the Soviet Union, and obedience to the Communist Party.

The party established research institutions and organizations like the All-China Literature Organization, All-China Artists' Association, and All-China Music Association to bring art, music, and literature under state guidance. The leaders of these organizations were often well-known authors, musicians, and artists. Ding Ling and Guo Moruo played leading roles in the Writers' Association. Until his death in 1953, Xu Beihong played a leading role in the art world: party backing enabled him finally to make his fixation on 19th-century realism into a state-enforced aesthetic orthodoxy which imprisoned Chinese artists like an iron cage until the 1980s. But behind the famous names, there were always Communist Party cultural commissars calling the shots. Art and literature in the People's Republic developed in obedience to party policy.

The women's movement, too, was firmly subordinated to the party. The All-China Women's Federation, organized in 1949, helped to draft the Marriage Law of 1950. The law was designed to revolutionize China's culture and economy (especially in the rural areas). Arranged marriages (particularly those arranged when the future partners were still children) were banned, as the law defined marriage as a relationship "based on free choice of partners, on monogamy, [and] on equal rights for both sexes."[14] Husbands and wives were to have "equal rights in the possession and management of family property," and women were given significant rights to property, financial support, and access to their children after divorce. The provisions were so revolutionary that the campaign to carry out the law ran into significant resistance in the rural areas from some men and older women.[15] Party leaders moderated the implementation of the law in order to prevent rural men from becoming alienated from party rule. Nonetheless, the Marriage Law marks the beginning of a significant change in the legal and social status of Chinese women, particularly in the rural areas, where family life had been relatively untouched by the modernizing, Westernizing trends of the cities.[16]

All the campaigns of the early 1950s took place in the context of China's "War to Resist America and Aid Korea" (1950–53). Following consultations with the Soviet Union and China, North Korean leader Kim Il-Song ordered his forces to invade South Korea on 25 June 1950. This bid to unite the Korean peninsula came at an inopportune time for China. Nonetheless, Mao strongly supported the goal of Korean unification, applauding as North Koreans forced the South Korean and American troops into a small area surrounding the port of Pusan in the extreme south. When United Nations forces under General Douglas MacArthur (1880–1964) turned the tide in September, advancing nearly to the Yalu River (which forms part of the Chinese–North Korean border), Mao sent a Chinese "Volunteer Force" (in fact, regular PLA units and officers) to assist the North Koreans.[17] China would fight in Korea both for its own strategic interest and as a surrogate for the Soviet Union, which, though concerned about North Korea's fate, did not want the events in Korea to lead them into a war with the United States.[18]

The decision to send Chinese troops to Korea was made over the objections of a majority of Politburo members who thought it unwise to fight the United States. Unlike his more cautious comrades, Mao was convinced that superior numbers, guerilla operations, and sheer determination would enable the poorly equipped Chinese People's Volunteer Force (CPVF) to defeat the better-armed Americans.[19] At first, it seemed that he was correct. The CPVF under the command of Marshal Peng Dehuai, a Long March veteran, pushed the Americans back south of Seoul before the inherent technological and logistical weakness of the CPVF forced the Chinese and North Korean leadership to negotiate a ceasefire along the 38th parallel.

革

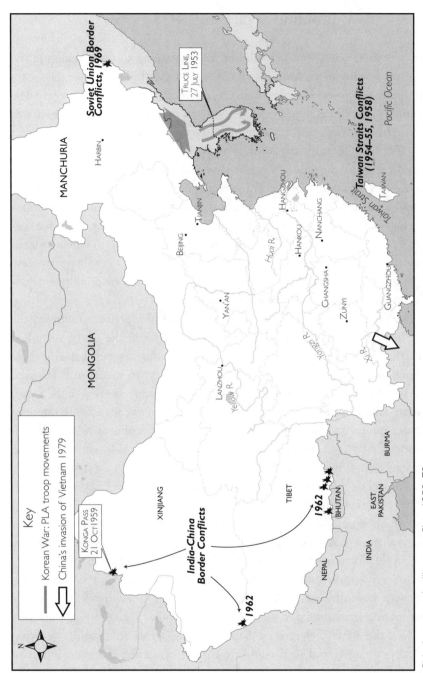

Key

Korean War: PLA troop movements

China's invasion of Vietnam 1979

MANCHURIA

Soviet Union Border Conflicts, 1969

Truce Line, 27 July 1953

HARBIN

MONGOLIA

BEIJING

TIANJIN

HANGZHOU

HANKOU

NANCHANG

Taiwan Straits Conflicts (1954–55, 1958)

TAIWAN

Taiwan Strait

Pacific Ocean

YAN'AN

Huai R

CHANGSHA

ZUNYI

GUANGZHOU

LANZHOU

Yellow R

Yangzi R

XINJIANG

Konga Pass 21 Oct 1959

India–China Border Conflicts

1962

TIBET

BHUTAN

1962

NEPAL

INDIA

EAST PAKISTAN

BURMA

N

China's wars and military conflicts, 1950–79.

革

Building Socialism, 1953–1956

The war in Korea played a significant role in shaping China's economic and political development, coming as it did at such a critical time after the CCP's assumption of power in China. Army recruitment for the war effort gave desperately poor young men in the villages and in the cities an opportunity to escape from poverty and alleviated China's thirteen percent unemployment rate. Former Guomindang soldiers and other men with political problems found refuge from political campaigns and an opportunity to transform themselves into politically acceptable people through army service. For the People's Liberation Army itself, the war helped with the problem of demobilizing soldiers after victory in the civil war by remobilizing them for service in Korea. The Korean War also provided the PLA with a chance to learn how to fight against a world-class mechanized enemy, to incorporate new technology (particularly air power), and to begin a program of military modernization in imitation of the Soviet Union.

The need to mobilize resources and organize production to support the war in Korea also gave an advantage to those within the party, including Chairman Mao Zedong, who preferred to take a more aggressive, radical approach toward the transition from market economy to socialism.[20] The goal was to establish a thoroughly socialist planned economy like that of the Soviet Union. This "Soviet model" of economic development called for the state to extract capital and raw materials from the vast agricultural sector through taxation and state control of prices and marketing, and invest them in the construction of heavy industry (machine tool plants, iron and steel works, cement works, military equipment, and so on), all in accordance with a series of five-year economic plans. China's first Five-Year Plan (for 1953–57) called for a doubling of industrial production. In order to carry out this plan, the government would need to eliminate the private market economy, which was responsible for more than two-thirds of China's production in 1953.[21]

Collectivization of the rural economy took place between 1953 and 1956. The state began by establishing state trading companies to assert complete control over prices and purchasing of grain and other agricultural goods. This enabled the state to ensure a reliable supply of grain to a rapidly growing urban population and to accumulate capital by setting the state purchase price of agricultural goods low and the sales price relatively high.[22] But the party wanted not simply to control prices and purchasing, but to transform China's mode of agricultural production from family farming to collectives in which farming families would pool their land, tools, labor, and other resources.

In 1951 and 1952, as land reform was completed, party cadres encouraged farming families to form "Mutual Aid Teams" to help each other on their fields. Next, farmers were urged to create "Agricultural Producers' Cooperatives" (APCs), in which their land, draught animals, and tools were surrendered to the collective.

Some farmers resisted collectivization, slaughtering and eating animals rather than surrender them and dragging their feet when assigned to perform collective labor. Many of the party leaders in Beijing, realizing the difficulties, advised a "go-slow" policy with regards to collectivization. But Mao Zedong disagreed. Convinced that only a high degree of collectivization would both boost agricultural production and prevent the re-emergence of an exploiting class of rich peasants and landlords, Mao insisted (against all the evidence) that people were clamoring to join the collectives. Mao's personal charisma and the support of provincial party cadres, who saw an opportunity to ingratiate themselves with the Chairman, enabled him to override the objections of Liu Shaoqi, Peng Zhen (1902–97), and other more cautious men in the Politburo. By the end of 1956, ninety-five percent of China's farming families were organized into collectives.[23]

While they were pushing the farmers into collectives, the Communist Party leaders were also forcing the pace of the socialization of the urban economy. State expropriation of major industries and banks and the Five-Antis Campaign of 1952 had broken the back of private enterprise. In the autumn of 1955, party leaders began to transform China's remaining large private businesses into joint state-private enterprises in which the state held the controlling interest. Smaller businesses were reorganized as collectives.

By the end of 1956, both China's rural and urban economies were well on the way to being completely socialist. Privately owned farms, handicraft shops, and factories produced less than three percent of China's total output.[24] China's society, too, had undergone fundamental changes. Women were incorporated into the work force outside the home more thoroughly than ever before. Urban and rural families had been investigated and had been assigned class labels like "landlord," "rich peasant," "capitalist," "bureaucrat capitalist," "poor peasant," "worker," "bad element," and so on. These labels had been the basis on which the party had carried out socioeconomic revolution, dispossessing the rich and redistributing land and other property to the poor. Now these labels would become a permanent feature of each family's and each individual's private and public life.

Power relationships in urban and rural society, too, had changed. The educated, landowning rural elites who had been local leaders and the interface between village China and Chinese governments for over two thousand years no longer existed: instead, villagers organized into collectives were led by local activists close to the Communist Party and by party members. The party-state controlled urban people through street committees in older established neighborhoods and through each individual's place of employment, or "work unit." Street committees were staffed by local people, not necessarily party members. They helped the elderly and the sick, organized folks to clean the streets, and kept tabs on suspicious individuals and activities, which they reported to the local Public Security (police) office.

Most Chinese were also connected to their current or (if retired) former work unit (that is, their place of employment). The best work units were those directly owned by the state: state-owned factories, government offices, research institutions, universities, and the like. A job in a state work unit was an "iron rice bowl"—that is, a guarantee of lifetime employment and a wide range of social services, which might (depending on the wealth of the work unit) include subsidized housing, subsidized shops and cafeterias, day care, schools, cultural activity, and health care. The work unit was also an instrument of social control: work-unit leaders had the power not only to award pay raises and promotions, but also to allocate scarce goods like housing and ration tickets for various commodities. Work-unit leaders maintained detailed personnel files which included information such as class background, political attitude, and attitude toward authority.

The work units, neighborhood committees, and rural collectives gave the agents of the party-state the ability to infiltrate all aspects of work, social, and private life in a way not achieved by any previous Chinese regime. Party leaders would soon use this power to push China's society, culture, and economy down uncharted and dangerous paths of development.

Radicalism and Disaster, 1957–1960

In September 1956, delegates to the Eighth National Congress of the Chinese Communist Party gathered in Beijing. The mood was largely celebratory. China had fought the United States to a draw in Korea, the transition to a socialist economy was nearly complete, and national income had been growing at a very respectable average rate of 8.9 percent.[25] Industrial output for 1956 was up by twenty-five percent over the previous year.[26] The strategies of the Five-Year Plan and alignment with the Soviet Union seemed to be working.

Resolutions passed at the Congress called for continued, steady progress along the lines already begun in the First Five-Year Plan, and de-emphasized the "cult of personality" which had grown up around Mao Zedong. The Congress also stated that with the victorious transition to socialism, the contradiction between the working class and the bourgeoisie in China had been basically resolved: the main task before the Chinese was not more class struggle, but to continue with economic development, build a stable legal system, and pursue a policy of openness with regard to writers, artists, and other intellectuals. All seemed quite optimistic. But below the surface, some leaders, including Mao Zedong, were deeply concerned about China's relations with the Soviet Union, about imbalances in China's economic growth, and about the social and political effects of China's having followed the Soviet model of economic development.

The Soviet Union had supplied China not only with a model of how to build socialism, but also with a significant degree of assistance. The Soviets and Eastern Europe supplied advisors, blueprints for factories, and substantial imports of machinery in what one economic historian describes as "one of the largest transfers of technology in world history."[27] Nonetheless, Mao had always had a fundamental distrust of the Soviet Union: in his dealings with the Chinese Communists both before and after 1949, Stalin had always seemed more concerned about advancing the Soviet Union's strategic interests in China than in the well-being of China or of the CCP itself.

Sino-Soviet tension increased when Nikita Khrushchev took over the Soviet leadership after Stalin's death in 1953. Khrushchev's denunciation of Stalin and the Stalinist cult of personality in February 1956 both surprised and disturbed Mao, who had assiduously cultivated his own cult of personality in China. The subsequent anti-Soviet political unrest and Soviet interventions in Hungary and Poland (October–November 1956) were both indications to the Chinese that internal unrest in China, too, might bring unwelcome Soviet intervention.

Internal unrest was a real possibility in China. Economic growth had not brought equal benefits to all. Under the First Five-Year Plan, investment in the urban industrial sector had far surpassed investment in agriculture. Agricultural production was not increasing as rapidly as expected. Since the agricultural sector was to generate surpluses for investment in industry, shortfalls in agricultural production would in turn make it impossible to meet China's targets for industrial growth. With farmers already unhappy as a result of collectivization and with some urban workers (particularly transient workers, temporary workers, and women workers) dissatisfied with their wages and conditions of employment, there was good reason for concern.

As Mao saw it, the problems with China's Soviet-style economic development extended to the Communist Party itself. The emphasis on planning and heavy industry required a large force of party bureaucrats. It also demanded trained "experts"—statisticians, lawyers, engineers, managers, scientists, and such. In factories, universities, research institutions, and in some government bureaus "white experts" with "bad" class background took precedence over politically reliable but less educated "red" party cadres and workers. Both "white experts" and the burgeoning ranks of party-state bureaucrats enjoyed power and privilege, higher pay, better living conditions, and many other perquisites. To Mao, this sort of privilege was the antithesis of socialism.

Many of China's leaders—not just Mao—were concerned about the character of the party and its relations with the Chinese people. In 1956, party leaders including Liu Shaoqi, Deng Xiaoping (1904–97), and Mao Zedong had decided that the best way to defuse tensions and to keep the party bureaucrats from becoming too removed from the people was to loosen up restrictions on the expression of opinion. In this spirit, they welcomed writers and intellectuals to be more creative with the slogan "let a hundred flowers bloom, let a hundred schools of thought contend."

Chinese writers were understandably cautious about expressing their ideas: restrictions on literature had been very tight. In 1955, the poet and literary theorist Hu Feng (1903–85) had been sentenced to fourteen years in prison on charges of counterrevolution simply because he and a circle of friends had exchanged correspondence in which they criticized the party's literary orthodoxy and the cadres who enforced it. Nonetheless, some authors responded with heartfelt critiques of the dark side of the "New China." Journalist Liu Binyan (1925–2005), for example, wrote cutting pieces of "reportage" on corrupt, callous party leaders. In his story "A Young Newcomer to the Organization Department," the twenty-two-year-old author Wang Meng (b. 1934) described an idealistic young party member running up against a brick wall of cynicism, laziness, and indifference on the part of his superiors in the Communist Party office of a gunnysack factory.

The initial results of the "Hundred Flowers" policy sparked intense debate among top Communist Party leaders. Many party members found works like those of Liu Binyan and Wang Meng deeply disturbing. They responded with increased control and a movement to criticize Wang Meng's story. Mao, on the other hand, believed that deepening the Hundred Flowers Campaign and encouraging more criticism from intellectuals would be the ideal way to carry out a thorough rectification of the bureaucratized Communist Party. Most of the rest of the party leaders disagreed with Mao. They would have preferred that the party itself conduct a careful review and criticism of party members and their work. But Mao and his supporters argued that the masses, including non-party intellectuals, should actively participate. Mao even suggested that intellectuals who voiced criticisms would be immune from political prosecution.[28]

As with the issues of going to war in Korea and moving ahead rapidly with collectivization, Mao again prevailed over his comrades. On 1 May 1957, the *People's Daily,* the newspaper mouthpiece of the Party Center, published a directive calling on the masses to criticize the party cadres' workstyle. Reluctant at first, intellectuals finally unleashed a torrent of heartfelt criticism. Lawyers and professors, writers and university students criticized particular party policies and even the Communist Party's monopoly on political power. Party cadres were required to leave their comfortable offices to perform part-time manual labor as a way of getting closer to the masses.[29] Workers joined in, staging strikes and protests.[30]

Party leaders—those who had opposed this sort of rectification and even Mao himself—watched with increasing concern. On 8 June 1957, they responded with a crackdown: the Anti-Rightist Campaign, directed by Deng Xiaoping. Any criticism of the party, of socialism, or of life in China in general was now unwelcome. Even party organizations were affected. The All-China Women's Federation (ACWF) laid aside plans for further improvement of women's rights when it became clear that even suggesting that socialism had not completely resolved women's problems was a "rightist" position. To be safe, the ACWF launched a new campaign to encourage women to "diligently, thriftily" build the country and manage the family—thoroughly traditionalist sentiments!

The need for caution was very real. In meetings held at work units, party members and intellectuals denounced those (including other party members and intellectuals) whose publications, remarks, or other behavior identified them as "rightists." Many work units apparently established a quota: five percent of their people were to be designated as "rightists."[31] Knowing that it was safer to accuse others than to wait to be accused oneself, people turned on each other, calling in old grudges or even slapping the "rightist" label on a coworker because he or she was unpopular or had simply failed to attend a meeting (and therefore was not present to defend him- or herself). Between three and four hundred thousand intellectuals were labeled "rightists."[32] Many spent most of the next thirty years in prisons and labor camps or were sent to the countryside to "learn from the farmers."[33] Among those sentenced or sent down were Liu Binyan, Wang Meng, and some of the leading lights of the older generation, including Ding Ling.

The Hundred Flowers Campaign had been as disastrous as Mao's opponents had predicted, but the problem that he had wanted to address remained—bureaucratic attitudes, corruption, laziness, and privilege among party cadres. So too did Mao's growing doubts about the efficacy of the Soviet model and its Five-Year Plans and reliance on "white experts" who, as a class, had given further evidence of their unreliability in the Hundred Flowers Campaign.[34] Not only Mao, but also Liu Shaoqi, Deng Xiaoping, and others believed that China needed to break out of the strictures of the Soviet model of economic development and create a distinctively Chinese path of economic development: to make a Great Leap Forward that would put China ahead of the West and allow it to "leap forward" from socialism to the ultimate Marxist goal of communist society.

The economic reasoning behind the Great Leap was simple (though fundamentally wrong): capital-poor China would fully mobilize its greatest resource, human labor power. The creativity and hard work of the masses would take the place of politically unreliable scientists and engineers. In order to make full use of the people's potential and to achieve economies of scale, production would be more highly collectivized than ever. Higher levels of collectivization would also help the Chinese people prepare psychologically for life in the communist society of the now near future, when all would be equal, and there would be no more distinctions between manual and intellectual labor.

The Great Leap began at the end of 1957. Chinese everywhere were urged to "produce more, better, faster" and to "overtake England in fifteen years and America in twenty years." In the countryside, the farmers, so recently forced into collectives, were now reorganized into "people's communes" during the summer of 1958. The average commune was five thousand households (around thirty thousand people).[35] All remaining privately owned agricultural land (small plots amounting to seven percent of arable land in 1957) was taken by the communes. So too, in some places, were any family-owned animals, pots, pans, furniture, watches, and other personal property.[36] Communes expanded rural elementary education and health care. They organized collective day care and communal kitchens in order to release more women for labor. In order to bring industrial development to the countryside, communes and local governments were encouraged to set up small-scale industries: coal mines, oil refineries, chemical and food-processing plants, machine tool factories, and so on.

In the countryside and in the cities, all Chinese were mobilized to "produce more, better, faster." Farmers were expected to improve grain production by applying pseudo-scientific practices like "deep plowing" (5-foot-deep [1.5 m] furrows) or "close planting" (12.5 million seedlings per 2.5 acres [1 hectare] instead of the usual 1.5 million).[37] Workers put in dangerously long hours as they competed to become labor heroes. Countless hours and resources were sacrificed when Mao encouraged Chinese everywhere to smelt steel in homemade steel furnaces. Enthusiastic amateur steelmakers left crops to rot in the fields while they threw tons of scrap iron (including many perfectly good pots, pans, and other implements) into the furnaces. Authors were recruited to churn out propaganda singing the praises of the Great Leap. In the words of a "new folk song":

> Work, work, work!
> We have exceeded the quota by a half!
> Yet when all are crying "Make a leap forward!"
> Still more ambitious will be our targets,
> For they'll be like heaven-soaring rockets![38]

The "heaven-soaring rockets" of the Great Leap Forward soon crashed to earth. Communes and factories had set utterly unrealistic production goals, which had then become quotas. Eager to please their superiors, local and provincial cadres falsely reported that they had fulfilled or overfulfilled their quotas. Mao and the party leaders greeted reports of record grain crops with enthusiasm, asking what should be done with all the expected surpluses. In some communes, people were allowed to eat all they wanted at the poorly managed, wasteful communal mess halls. The backyard furnaces produced nothing more than immense chunks of useless substandard "steel."

Many people were fully aware that what they were doing was insane. But knowing that any expression of criticism could be branded as "rightist," few had the courage to speak up. So while the Party Center received exaggerated reports of increases in the year's grain and steel production at the end of 1958, China's economy was spinning out of control. The government requisitioned grain in amounts based on the inflated production reports that were submitted to the government. Rather than reveal the truth, local cadres forcibly collected enough grain to meet their quotas, even when it meant leaving farmers without enough to survive. Bad weather in the spring and summer of 1959 contributed to a man-made famine.

As a crisis began to unfold, Communist Party leaders including Mao became aware that all was not well. In July 1959, the Central Committee met at the mountain resort of Lushan to discuss the situation. Some criticism of the exaggerated production estimates was expected: even Chairman Mao now favored a more careful, planned approach to economic development. But the meetings took an unexpected turn when Marshal Peng Dehuai, the minister of defense, decided to speak up.

A blunt, short-tempered man, Peng had worked with Mao since the early days of the Red Army at Jinggangshan and had been on the Long March. As minister of defense, he had no expertise in economic affairs. But Marshal Peng had toured villages in several provinces and seen for himself the insanity of the Great Leap policies and the suffering that they were causing. In a letter to the Chairman, he suggested that the errors were due to "a lack of realistic thinking" and "petty-bourgeois fanaticism."[39]

Peng had recently been to the Soviet Union: though there is no evidence to suggest it, Mao apparently feared that Peng's move was part of a Soviet plot against him.[40] A masterful politician, Mao now turned the Lushan Plenum into a denunciation of Peng Dehuai. Though some of them harbored doubts, the Central Committee members agreed to censure and demote Peng. Marshal Lin Biao, whose loyalty to Mao was beyond question, stepped in as minister of defense. Instead of critically discussing and revising the Great Leap, as originally planned, the Lushan Plenum reconfirmed it, thus extending the disastrous policies for another year.

The Great Leap was a major setback for the Chinese people and the Chinese economy. Wildly irrational economic policies combined with continued forced requisition of grain caused a man-made famine that lasted from 1960 through 1962. Starving farmers were forbidden even to talk about famine. Officials searched for and confiscated pitifully small stocks of grain that some families had illegally hidden. In some places, people starved to death while within walking distance of granaries full of grain to be delivered to the state. Perhaps as many as thirty to forty million Chinese died unnatural deaths during the famine years of 1960–62.[41] Despite the suffering, China continued to make its scheduled shipments of grain to the Soviet Union in payment for Soviet loans and technological assistance.

The fact that Chinese starved to death while grain was shipped to Russia was particularly ironic. Tension between the two great socialist countries had been building steadily since Stalin's death. In 1958, Mao rejected the Soviet Union's requests to build a Soviet military radio transmission center on Chinese soil and cooperate in a joint submarine fleet.[42] In August 1958, when Mao ordered the PLA to open fire on the Nationalist-held islands of Jinmen and Mazu (2 miles [3 km] off the Fujian coast) in order to whip up nationalist fervor for the Great Leap Forward, the Soviets offered their support only reluctantly. Since Mao was no more interested in causing a war with the United States than Khrushchev was, he suspended the bombardment in October, putting an end to the 1958 Taiwan Straits Crisis, but the Soviet Union's lukewarm attitude still rankled.[43]

In 1959, the Sino-Soviet relationship deteriorated further. When a group of Tibetans launched a revolt (with some supplies and training from the American Central Intelligence Agency) and the Dalai Lama escaped to India, China accused India of aiding the rebels. Instead of supporting the Chinese position, Moscow condemned China and supported India's position.[44] In July Khrushchev, apparently still annoyed about the way China had precipitated the 1958 Taiwan Straits Crisis and concerned about Mao's cavalier attitude toward the possibility of nuclear war, reneged on an earlier promise to share nuclear weapons technology. All Soviet experts and advisors in China were withdrawn, including over two hundred who had been working on nuclear programs.[45]

From Recovery to Cultural Revolution

From 1960 to 1965 the Communist Party stepped back from Mao Zedong's disastrous Great Leap policies. Central Committee members including State Chairman (President) Liu Shaoqi, Premier Zhou Enlai, Vice-Premier Deng Xiaoping, and Beijing mayor Peng Zhen (1902–97) took control of the day-to-day business of the party and government. These men believed that the causes of the disaster included both unrealistic economic policies and the devolution of power, which had put too much power in the hands of provincial and local officials. Their solution included a recentralization of state power. Decision-making, planning, and budgetary authority were once against to be concentrated at the top, in Beijing, in the hands of Liu and Deng: Mao was relegated to the sidelines. This did contribute to a restoration of order and control. It also brought reduced funding for the small rural enterprises, rural schools, and rural health care, which were among the projects that provincial and local cadres had funded.

The leaders in Beijing used their power to implement economic policies that involved fundamental departures from the radical egalitarianism and unrealistic goals of the Great Leap. In the countryside, the people's communes were scaled down from an average size of five thousand to two thousand households and subdivided into three levels of administration: commune, work brigade, and work team, with most accounting being done at the more manageable level of the twenty- to thirty-family work teams.[46] Many work teams experimented with a "responsibility system" under which farming families were given responsibility for cultivating particular fields and their compensation linked directly to their productivity.

The responsibility system was part of a larger pattern in which the party leadership now used material incentives to encourage production. Small private family plots, confiscated during the Great Leap, were restored and once again contributed a disproportionate percentage of total agricultural production. Markets were reopened. People were allowed, even encouraged, to open small businesses like teahouses, restaurants, shoe-repair stands, tailor shops, and so on. Factory workers could earn extra pay for overtime and bonuses for increased productivity.

These new policies led to the beginnings of an economic recovery. But the re-introduction of even very limited market reforms and financial incentives also sharpened social tensions. Those who benefited by making more money, earning bonuses, or opening successful small businesses often incurred the resentment of their fellow workers and neighbors—particularly when those who were successful had "bad" bourgeois or rich peasant class backgrounds, as some did.

In addition, while the Liu-Deng leadership team loosened restrictions on economic activity, they re-imposed tighter controls in other areas. As refugees fled famine in the countryside, the government responded by instituting a strict household registration, or *hukou,* system. With household members registered, and the register regularly checked against master files in the Public Security offices, migration from the villages to towns and cities or from smaller to larger cities became virtually impossible. Violators were rounded up, held in temporary jails, and then returned to their places of origin. Schooling, employment, social services, and ration coupons for daily commodities (grain, eggs, milk, oil, meat, fabric, and much, much more) were all tied to household registration. China became one of the most rigidly policed and immobile societies in the world.

The household registration system added to the mechanisms of control that had already become fundamental parts of life in China. People all lived within tight-knit, but often tension-filled collective neighborhoods, apartment blocks, work units, or schools. Everyone was conscious of their own, and of others', class background, political "behavior," and the fact that nearly anything that one said or did was subject to political interpretation, especially if one was unlucky enough to be from a "bad" class background or to have fallen victim to one of the earlier campaigns.

The party, too, was full of tension and contradictions. Liu, Deng, Zhou Enlai, Peng Zhen, and others had increased their power partly at Chairman Mao's expense. They regularly showed their respect for the Chairman, but their policies were not in line with his thinking. They also undermined him in subtle ways. For example, writers associated with Beijing mayor Peng Zhen published newspaper columns in which they indirectly attacked Mao and defended Peng Dehuai. One, for example, suggested that a person who thinks that he can be in charge of everything is suffering from a mental disorder, and that such a person "must promptly take a complete rest. . . . If he insists on talking or doing anything, he will get into a lot of trouble."[47]

Mao was not resting. His power was reduced, but far from eliminated. He still commanded respect (and perhaps fear) from the members of the Central Committee. He also played an important role in foreign policy issues, particularly in China's worsening relationship with the Soviet Union. As Khrushchev worked to improve the Soviet Union's relationship with the United States and to bring other socialist countries into line, Mao responded by attacking Khrushchev as a "revisionist." Soviet failure to support China during its border war with India in 1960 sharpened the contradiction. When Khrushchev's comrades in Moscow deposed him in 1964, Mao still had no cause for rejoicing. The new Soviet leaders were as "Khrushchevite" as Khrushchev himself. In Mao's opinion, the Soviet Union was sliding backward along the historical evolutionary scale, from socialism back toward capitalism.

Mao was concerned that China, too, was moving toward a capitalist restoration. At an expanded meeting of the Central Committee in 1962, he attacked his enemies in no uncertain terms, warning that people were using novels to create the ideological basis for anti-party activity and urging comrades who had "connections with foreign countries" or "belong to secret anti-party groups" to "spill the beans and tell the whole truth." He also told the assembled Central Committee members: "We can now affirm that classes do exist in socialist countries and that class struggle undoubtedly exists." The party must be constantly vigilant against "Chinese revisionism," lest the country slide backwards and the "reactionary classes" be restored to power. To tackle the problem of revisionism within the party would require yet another Rectification Campaign like that of 1942 in Yan'an.[48]

As he worked to restore the party to the correct path, Mao could draw on three sources of strength: his own role and image as party chairman and leader of the revolution; Lin Biao and the People's Liberation Army; and his wife, Jiang Qing (1914–91), and her connections with radical intellectuals in Shanghai. Mao's reputation and the cult of personality that he and the party had built around him beginning back in the Yan'an days still gave him tremendous respect—bordering on worship—among lower-level party members, in the army, and in society in general. The roles of Lin Biao and Jiang Qing, which intersected with each other and with the cult of personality, need brief explanation.

Lin Biao, a Long March veteran and a brilliant, though erratic, general, had become minister of defense in 1959 following Peng Dehuai's fall from grace at the Lushan Plenum. Lin left much of the day-to-day running of the PLA to his chief of staff, Luo Ruiqing (1906–78). But he did spearhead the drive to make the Mao's cult of personality into a central part of the PLA's military training. It was on Lin's orders that pithy quotations from Mao's four-volume *Selected Works* were compiled into the *Quotations of Chairman Mao,* a pocket-sized book bound in red plastic. Reading, discussing, and memorizing passages from the "Little Red Book" became an essential part of a Chinese soldier's indoctrination.

The PLA flattered Mao by inflating the cult of personality. Mao returned the favor by making the army into a role model for the country. All Chinese were encouraged to "Learn from the PLA" in a campaign carried out from 1962 through 1965. Young people, in particular, were given a role model in the person of Lei Feng (1940–62), a common soldier who died in an accident in 1962. In his diary (which some suggest is partly or entirely the creation of party propagandists), Lei Feng described his unselfish desire to serve the people, his faith in the party, and his undying loyalty to Chairman Mao. His ideal, he said, was to be a screw in the great machine of socialism, serving wherever the party wanted him. It was the kind of sentiment that any party leader, Mao, Liu Shaoqi, or any other, could appreciate.

Lin Biao's use of the PLA to inflate the cult of personality fit neatly with the political activities and ambitions of Mao's wife, the former movie actress Jiang Qing. Since her marriage to Mao back in Yan'an, Jiang Qing had endured the humiliation of being frozen out of any significant political power. After years of minor positions and multiple visits to the Soviet Union for medical treatment, she was determined to play a more significant role in the life of the nation, and particularly in the party's management of high culture. Even after more than ten years of Communist rule, traditional Beijing operas, with their stories of generals and heroes, scholars and beautiful women, were quite popular. Jiang Qing was incensed at this continued domination of "feudal" and "bourgeois" culture. In 1962, she began working with People's Liberation Army drama units to write, direct, and stage new "model operas" that would feature peasants denouncing landlords, PLA units conquering their enemies, and plenty of strong, independent female characters.

Through his own actions and his relations with Lin Biao and Jiang Qing, Mao was laying the groundwork for an intense political struggle for the soul of the nation—and control of the party-state. His first attempt to regain the control he had lost after the failure of the Great Leap came when he called for a "Socialist Education Campaign" in 1963. Liu, Deng, and the others (who evidently did not regard this as an attack on them) agreed that the party was in trouble and needed rectification. But Mao and Liu disagreed on how to carry out the campaign. Mao wanted to mobilize the people to criticize corrupt party cadres from the bottom up. Liu and the other party leaders, remembering the Hundred Flowers debacle and fearing that this campaign, too, might spin out of control, preferred a "top-down" approach. Work teams of a thousand or even several thousand party members would go to a rural county to investigate local cadres and recommend disciplinary action.

The campaign unfolded as a tug-of-war, with Mao and Liu issuing instructions and revised instructions, each man trying to guide the movement in the "correct" direction. Many base-level cadres were investigated and disciplined, some very severely. The blows fell most heavily on people who already had "bad" class background labels and on those who seemed to their neighbors to have become unreasonably rich since 1961. The campaign dragged on through 1965, but it was not achieving Mao's purpose, which was to undermine Liu and Deng's economic policies and engineer his own return to power. For his next attack, he would choose an arena in which he had a particular advantage: culture.

By 1965, Mao had already, with Jiang Qing's help, been making inroads on the party's cultural policies. Jiang had been working to "rectify" the theater and film worlds. Mao had ordered the Politburo to set up a "small group" to look into problems in the cultural realm, but the Politburo had put the group under Beijing mayor Peng Zhen's control, and only one member (secret police chief Kang Sheng) shared Mao's concerns. Understanding that Beijing and the Party Center's propaganda apparatus were out of his control, Mao launched a new movement: the Great Proletarian Cultural Revolution. To do so, he drew on his remaining sources of power: his own reputation, his ability to mobilize the masses, Lin Biao's PLA, and his wife Jiang Qing's connections with radical party members in Shanghai.

It was a pair of Shanghai intellectuals who helped Mao to fire the opening salvo of the Cultural Revolution: an attack on a historical drama called *Hai Rui Dismissed from Office*. The play told the familiar story of how the Ming official Hai Rui, concerned about the suffering of the common people under a corrupt government, criticized the Jiaqing emperor and was dismissed from office. The author, Wu Han, was a vice-mayor of Beijing and protégé of one of the men whom Mao so desperately wanted to topple: Mayor Peng Zhen. Mao had seen and praised the play in 1962. But now, convinced that it was a disguised attack on him, Mao instructed a Shanghai intellectual friend of Jiang Qing's to write an article criticizing Wu Han. As Mao put it later: "The damaging issue in *Hai Rui Dismissed from Office* is 'dismissed from office.' The Jiaqing emperor dismissed Hai Rui from office; in 1959 we dismissed Peng Dehuai from office. Peng Dehuai is indeed 'Hai Rui.'"[49] The article was published in Shanghai on 16 November 1965.

The Beijing party establishment initially resisted the call to criticize Wu Han and his play. Peng Zhen, who was obliged to lead the criticism, emphasized that the discussion must be purely academic—in other words, not political. Mao and his supporters continued to make linkages between seemingly abstruse academic issues and politics. Still traveling in the Yangzi Valley provinces, building support among provincial leaders, he engineered the criticism and dismissal of one key Central Committee member after another: Wu Han, Peng Zhen, and then PLA Chief of Staff Luo Ruiqing. But these were small fish. His real targets were Liu Shaoqi, Deng Xiaoping, "bureaucrats" throughout the party, and the policies that the party was carrying out under their leadership.

In order to build momentum for the movement, and to pass what he considered his revolutionary legacy directly to the younger generation, Mao called on students around the country to rise up and make revolution against feudal and bourgeois culture and, by implication, against party members and other authorities who were infected with feudal and bourgeois ideas and taking China down the "capitalist road." Mao was using an unofficial support base—lower-level party members and students—to circumvent the party that he had built. This added a new, violent, anarchic element to the Cultural Revolution. It also made a high-level factional struggle into a nationwide mass movement. In this way, criticism of an historical drama could be the beginning of a series of events that would send one of the most populous countries on earth into ten years of turmoil.

The Red Guard Generation: From Revolution to Disillusion

The middle school, high school, and college students of 1966 had grown up in the "New China." They had been taught that revolution was good, that the people, the motherland, and the party and, above all, Chairman Mao (who embodied those wonderful things) commanded their most fervent love and complete loyalty.

But how was one to express that love and loyalty? What was it to be revolutionary? Was it a matter of being "born red," the child of parents who were workers or poor peasants or, even better, who had joined the party before 1949 and fought in the Revolution? Or was being "revolutionary" a matter of one's beliefs and behavior? In other words, could you become revolutionary by serving the country, loving the people and the party, being loyal to Chairman Mao and the party, and studying diligently in order to be of service to party, people, and motherland? If so, then even children of "bad" class background could become part of the revolutionary masses by firmly rejecting their exploiting-class heritage.

In effect, there were two contradictory criteria for determining whether or not an individual was "revolutionary": class label, assigned by the party-state; and beliefs as demonstrated in public behavior. This contradiction was one of the many sources of tension in the lives of Chinese students. Other sources of tension included competition for grades, conflicts between students and teachers, conflicts between students and administrators, and conflicts between students from "good"-class high-ranking party cadre families and "bad"-class bourgeois intellectual families. Mao himself had criticized the elitist, high-stakes education system:

> At present, there is too much studying going on, and this is exceedingly harmful. There are too many subjects at present, and the burden is too heavy, it puts middle-school and university students in a constant state of tension.[50]

When Mao used students as the shock troops in his Cultural Revolution, the tension-filled world of the schools and colleges exploded in an orgy of violence and destruction. This was exactly what he wanted. According to Mao, only an explosive mass movement could break through and destroy the Communist Party bureaucracy, which he believed was taking the country in the wrong direction. And only by arranging for the students to temper themselves in the fires of revolutionary action could he create a generation of successors who would carry out his policies and pursue his dreams even after his death.

In late May 1966, Mao's supporters in Beijing encouraged Beijing University students to criticize the university administrators for being an "anti-party group." As they had done during the Socialist Education Movement, Liu Shaoqi, Deng Xiaoping, and the party leadership tried to give this movement direction by sending party work teams to the schools and colleges. Beginning in early June, with party work teams guiding them, students of "good" class background organized themselves into "Red Guard" units and rounded up the usual suspects: teachers, administrators, and fellow students unfortunate enough to bear "bad" class labels. Other students, acting with support from some of Mao's supporters in the Party Center, organized rival Red Guard groups in resistance against the work teams.

On 16 July 1966, with Beijing campuses in turmoil, Mao Zedong took a widely reported two-hour swim in the Yangzi River. It was a public declaration of his physical and political stamina. On 18 July, he returned to Beijing to take matters into his own hands. In private meetings, he lashed out at Deng Xiaoping and Liu Shaoqi. How dare they use their work teams to suppress the spontaneous revolutionary enthusiasm of the masses? The work teams were withdrawn. Now, the students could make revolution without being restricted by the Party Center, making Deng, Liu, and other party and government leaders direct targets.

What followed was three years of chaos that brought China to the brink of anarchy. In schools and colleges all over the country, students of varying class backgrounds formed their own "Red Guard" units to rise up in revolutionary struggle against bourgeois and "feudal" culture and to overthrow "revisionists," "reactionaries," "counterrevolutionaries," and "capitalist roaders" within the Communist Party. Interpreting Mao's directives into concrete application in their own schools, communities, and families, the Red Guards attacked teachers, administrators, and rival Red Guard units.

People were targeted for a variety of reasons. Teachers might be attacked because they had "bad" class background, because they were strict graders or disciplinarians, or because they were unpopular. Some were even attacked because their dress or behavior seemed bourgeois, because they were too good-looking, or because they were ugly. Many victims were labeled "cow demons and snake spirits." The rooms or buildings in which they were imprisoned were dubbed "cowsheds." With all inhibitions released and students competing with each other to be most "revolutionary," beatings and torture were common.[51]

Red Guard violence soon spilled beyond the confines of school and college campuses. Young people in many work units—factories, newspapers, government bureaus, and so on—also organized Red Guard units to attack their work-unit management. Called upon to "destroy the Four Olds" (old customs, culture, habits, and ideas), Red Guards attacked and sometimes destroyed churches, mosques, temples, imperial graves, and antiquities. Intellectuals (the "stinking Ninth" of the nine categories of reactionaries) were particular targets.[52]

"Study the 16 Articles," 1966. Propaganda poster depicting Red Guard passing out copies of the decision that launched the Cultural Revolution.

Red Guards raided intellectuals' homes repeatedly, confiscating furniture, collections of stamps, coins, art, phonograph records, musical instruments, books, jewelry—anything that could be considered "bourgeois" or "feudal." Some confiscated property was publicly destroyed. Some was warehoused. Some was hoarded by Red Guards who knew the value of what they were taking. Some later appeared in the shops of art and antiques dealers in Hong Kong.

Some of China's most well-known writers and artists were among the victims of the Cultural Revolution. Red Guards sought out Ding Ling, now living in a thatched hut on a remote commune, where she was kicked and beaten, imprisoned, and all her manuscripts destroyed.[53] Lao She, the left-wing author and playwright whose satirical attacks on the Nationalist government and sympathetic portrayals of working-class Beijing had been celebrated in the 1950s, committed suicide in August 1966 rather than face continued humiliation at the hands of Red Guards.

The modernist painters Lin Fengmian (1900–89) and Liu Haisu (1896–1994) were among the many artists who suffered. Many of their paintings were destroyed (Lin Fengmian tore his up and threw them down the toilet before the Red Guards could use them as evidence against him). Both men were imprisoned. But the Red Guards also attacked the residence, now a museum, of the late Xu Beihong, the staunch advocate of Realism and a bitter rival of Lin and Liu from the 1920s. Xu's status as a "leading authority," the obvious European influences in his work, and the fact that he had painted nudes all made his memory and his paintings "reactionary." The passion, spontaneity, and anger with which the Red Guards acted made it difficult to predict who or what might be attacked.

These attacks on teachers, other intellectuals, and culture, vicious as they were, were only one manifestation of a political struggle that extended to all levels of the party-state. By August 1966, Red Guards were actively attacking the Communist Party leaders of municipal and provincial governments, parading them through the streets, torturing them, and publicly humiliating them on stage in front of crowds of thousands of passionate onlookers whose shouted denunciations blurred the line between audience and participant in the political drama. The governor of Heilongjiang province, for example, was forced to stand precariously on a folding chair on stage, head bowed in defeat, a placard bearing his name and the label "counterrevolutionary" hanging around his neck while grim-faced Red Guards hacked off his hair.[54]

The Red Guards were responding to Mao's call to action with tremendous energy. As the revolutionary tide swept over the nation, Red Guards traveled across the country by foot (in imitation of the Long March) or by train (they were given free passage) to "exchange revolutionary experiences." For tens of thousands of these idealistic youth, the ultimate destination was Tiananmen Square, where they hoped to catch a glimpse of the Great Helmsman himself. Mao appeared before immense Red Guard rallies in the square on more than half a dozen occasions, waving from the Gate of Heavenly Peace, or from his motorcade as it cruised sedately along Chang'an Boulevard. Mao used these rallies and other occasions to encourage the Red Guards, praising them for overthrowing "reactionaries" and confirming that "internal rebellions are fine."[55]

By January 1967, Chairman Mao was well on his way to achieving his goals. Leading Central Committee members like Liu Shaoqi, Deng Xiaoping, and Peng Zhen had either been purged or were on the brink of falling under sustained verbal and physical attack. In January, Red Guard and revolutionary "rebel" worker groups, first in Shanghai, and then in other cities and provinces, carried out violent "seizures of power" in which they took control of municipal and provincial governments. As victory approached, Mao himself moved toward a restoration of order. He commanded that the violence be moderated and that new "Revolutionary Councils" made up of representatives of the party, the Army, and the people take over the tasks of city and provincial government.

But by this time, the movement had acquired a momentum that even Mao found difficult to rein in. In Beijing, struggle continued to unfold between more conservative party leaders and PLA generals on the one hand and radical factions led by Jiang Qing and Lin Biao on the other. When men from the "conservative" faction met to discuss a moderation of Cultural-Revolutionary struggle in February 1967, Jiang Qing and Lin Biao won Mao's support for a renewed struggle against their "February Adverse Current."

At the grassroots level, rival Red Guard units were now fighting each other in the streets of major cities in battles that often pitted groups composed predominantly of youth from "good"-class background against youth of "bad"-class intellectual families. In many of these battles, Red Guards used guns and even artillery pieces taken from the PLA. In the most serious incident, the city of Wuhan was paralyzed by fighting between the four hundred thousand members of the Cultural-Revolutionary "Workers' Headquarters" and the five hundred thousand–strong "Million Heroes" (mostly young workers) who defended the city government and party authorities from the Red Guards. When the regional PLA commander backed the "Million Heroes" and kidnapped one of the emissaries from the Party Center who had been sent to negotiate an end to the fighting, other PLA units had to be moved in to take over the city.[56]

At this point, even Mao Zedong had had enough of chaos and anarchy. In late July, he ordered an end to the Red Guard movement. The People's Liberation Army restored order to campuses and cities, played the leading role in the new "Revolutionary Councils," and firmly suppressed Red Guard organizations. Beginning in December 1967, Red Guard organizations were disbanded. The rebellious students were sent to the countryside where they were supposed to learn the values of hard work, self-sacrifice, and revolutionary struggle from the peasants.[57] Between 1968 and 1970, around 5.4 million urban youth were "rusticated" in this manner. Since their household registrations were transferred to the countryside, they faced the possibility of staying in the country for the rest of their lives.[58]

For many of the Red Guard generation, being "sent down" was the first step in a process that left them utterly disillusioned with the revolutionary values that Mao and the party had been trying to instill in them. Life in the villages was not what they had been taught it was. The work was hard, the living conditions primitive. The peasants were not interested in the Red Guards' political ideas and often resented and looked down on them as young, naïve city kids. Subject to the whims of arbitrary, often uneducated local cadres, former Red Guards began to wonder why they had been making revolution in the first place. Many also found that the farmers did not like socialism: they would prefer to own their own land, and they had liked the responsibility system and other policies that Liu Shaoqi and Deng Xiaoping had tried during the early 1960s.

The disillusionment of the former Red Guards and of many other Chinese, too, deepened as they negotiated the constantly shifting political sands of the 1970s. In 1969 the Ninth Party Congress declared that the Cultural Revolution had come to a victorious conclusion. Mao was reconfirmed as leader, Lin Biao as his successor, and Mao Zedong Thought reinstated as the guiding thought of the party and the people. But trouble lurked just below the surface. Mao was suspicious of Lin's ambitions. Lin, in turn, was keenly aware of the danger of being the designated successor to a man who had purged many of his closest comrades. What happened next is not clear. The official version is that Lin and his son were plotting a coup in which they would assassinate Mao. When they became aware that they were under suspicion, Lin, his wife, his son, and a few others hastily commandeered an airplane and fled toward the Soviet Union. The plane crashed over Mongolia, killing all on board.[59]

The news of Lin Biao's plot and death prompted a mass movement to dig out supporters of Lin everywhere: thousands were implicated, mostly on flimsy or entirely imaginary evidence. In the rush to denounce Lin, modern Chinese history was rewritten: Lin, formerly a hero of the revolution and loyal supporter of Mao, was now found to have been a counterrevolutionary all along. This blatant rewriting of history was too much to swallow, even for Chinese who had become accustomed to suspending their disbelief in the improbable propaganda which had filled their lives since 1949.

As the Lin Biao incident clearly indicates, power struggles within the Communist Party did not end with the overthrow of Liu Shaoqi and Deng Xiaoping. Mao used the Lin Biao affair to reduce the power of the PLA.[60] With Lin Biao gone, moderates including Premier Zhou Enlai struggled against radicals led by Jiang Qing. Mao, standing above the fray, gave each side a few victories to enjoy—but not enough to completely defeat their rivals.

The rival factions fought each other not simply for power (although this was clearly part of it) but also over fundamental political issues. One of the most significant of these was foreign policy. China faced two enemies: the "revisionist" Soviet Union to the north, with which China had an unresolved border conflict, and the "imperialist" United States, which was allied to Japan

Mao Zedong and Richard Nixon.

and Taiwan, China's enemies, and actively engaged in Vietnam. Over the course of three years, from 1969 through 1971, top-ranking PLA generals and Premier Zhou Enlai convinced Mao that rapprochement with the United States would help avert a possible war with the Soviet Union, whom they saw as a bigger threat. Thus Chinese diplomats were instructed to respond cautiously but positively when the American Nixon administration worked to open contacts. As President Richard Nixon (1913–94) and his national security adviser Henry Kissinger (b. 1923) were equally interested in "playing the China card" against the Soviet Union and laying the groundwork for an American withdrawal from Vietnam, Zhou knew that a deal was possible.

With Nixon's visit to China in 1972, the two countries built a new relationship based on their common enmity toward the Soviet Union. America and China entered into agreements on intelligence sharing and monitoring of Soviet nuclear tests. In the Shanghai Communiqué (27 February 1972), signed by Nixon and Mao Zedong, the two sides emphasized common interests. Areas of disagreement, particularly on the issue of Taiwan, were set to one side, with the Chinese side stating that "Taiwan is a province of China" and the United States acknowledging that "all Chinese on either side of the Taiwan Strait maintain there is but one China and that Taiwan is a part of China."[61]

The opening of unofficial relations with the United States in 1972 (formal diplomatic recognition did not come until 1979) brought with it a small amount of trade and cultural exchange between the two countries. But it did not indicate any significant change in China's domestic politics. Factional struggle continued unabated, with moderates, led by Zhou Enlai, coming under attack from what Mao once referred to as the "Gang of Four": his wife, Jiang Qing, and her allies, the radical intellectuals Yao Wenyuan and Zhang Chunqiao, and Wang Hongwen, a young worker from Shanghai whose revolutionary zeal had gained him promotion to the party Central Committee. Both sides employed teams of propagandists, so that when leftists started a campaign to "Criticize Lin Biao, Criticize Confucius" (in which "Confucius" was a stand-in for Zhou Enlai), the moderates joined in with propaganda designed to turn the campaign into an attack on arbitrary power. Jiang Qing, quite aware of Mao's ill health, was busily laying the foundations for herself to succeed her husband. Unpopular with the old generals who still dominated the PLA, she lined up support in the party propaganda apparatus and initiated a mass movement to celebrate the achievements of powerful women in Chinese history, notably Wu Zetian, the female Tang emperor.

The ten years of vicious factional struggle finally came to an end in 1976. On 8 January Zhou Enlai, age seventy-eight, succumbed to cancer. On 8 July Zhu De, the cofounder of the PLA and an open enemy of Jiang Qing, died at the age of ninety. On 28 July, an earthquake measuring 7.5 on the Richter scale hit the northern Chinese city of Tangshan (near Tianjin), killing an estimated two hundred fifty thousand people, China's largest disaster to date. Many interpreted the earthquake, which damaged buildings even in Beijing, in traditional terms as a sign of Heaven's anger, perhaps portending the end of an era.

The feeling that change was imminent carried through to April, when common folk in Beijing marked *Qingming* (5 April), the traditional grave-sweeping festival, by bringing wreaths and poems in honor of the late Zhou Enlai to lay at the martyrs' monument in Tiananmen Square. This public mourning for Zhou was a clear statement on the part of the politically astute Beijing people that they preferred Zhou (and, by implication, Deng Xiaoping) and his moderate policies to the radicalism of Jiang Qing and her faction.

The police quickly removed the wreaths, arrested protesters, and labeled the "April Fifth Movement" counterrevolutionary. The protests were easily suppressed, but immense public dissatisfaction remained. Life in China, and especially life since the Anti-Rightist Campaign, the Great Leap Forward, the Socialist Education Campaign, and the Cultural Revolution had been too miserable for too many, and the misery too obviously caused by the radical policies and cutthroat factional struggles that Mao had instigated. When Mao

Zedong himself died on 9 September 1976, people responded with shock, with emotion, and with tears, some genuine, some faked to fend off accusations of being counterrevolutionary.

The Legacy of the Mao Era

Mao Zedong played a dominant role in the lives of the Communist Party and the Chinese people during the chaotic first twenty-seven years of the People's Republic of China. For this reason, it is common to refer to those years as the "Mao era" and to speak of China's situation as of 1976 as "Mao's legacy." While acknowledging Mao's tremendous influence, and his responsibility for some truly disastrous decisions (the Great Leap Forward and the factional struggle of the Cultural Revolution), it is important to realize that the legacy of those twenty-seven years was not Mao's alone. Much of what the Chinese people and the party-state accomplished (for good or for bad) during those years was not Mao's doing, or even necessarily to his liking.

By some measures, the People's Republic of China had seen some significant achievements between 1949 and 1976. China had entered the nuclear age, with the PLA conducting its first successful test of an atomic bomb in 1964, and a hydrogen bomb in 1967.[62] The new China asserted control over its sovereign territory, even fighting brief military engagements with India and the Soviet Union over disputed boundaries. Chinese cooperation with the United States against the Soviet Union had made China a key player in the Cold War. After nearly thirty years of Communist rule, China had made considerable economic progress. The Chinese economy had grown by around three to four percent annually from 1953 to 1978, a rate of growth that compared well to other developing countries.[63] China had also seen gains in life expectancy, literacy rates, and per capita productivity.

But despite a respectable performance by many measures, the socialist economy had not improved the life of the average person as much as one would have expected. Economic growth had been strongly skewed toward heavy industry and military production, neither of which made any substantial contribution to ordinary people's daily well-being. Many economically unviable factories (automotive and machine tool plants, for example) had been constructed in remote western provinces on the theory that the extra industrial capacity would be needed in case an enemy should invade and occupy eastern China or Manchuria. All of this directed investment and labor into enterprises did little to raise incomes, productivity, or standards of living.

With resources disproportionately and inefficiently invested in heavy industry, little investment was made in development and production of consumer goods or in housing construction. The average available housing in China's major cities had dropped from about 15 square feet (4.5 sq m) per person in 1952 to about 12 square feet (3.6 sq m) per person in 1978.[64] Worker productivity in both agriculture and in industry was low, and the socialist organization of production gave workers no incentive to work harder or to innovate. Innovation was also held back by China's isolation from both the Soviet bloc and the capitalist world. By 1976, China had become a veritable working museum of 1940s-era cars and trucks, 1950s Soviet-style industrial machinery, 19th-century steam locomotives, and a hodge-podge of other Victorian-era or earlier technology.

Low productivity meant that Chinese lived simple lives and had very high savings rates. Wages, particularly for educated professionals, were kept artificially low. Housing, medical care, old-age care, and other social services were provided to urban people through their work units at deeply subsidized rates. In order to purchase items of daily use like rice, noodles, flour, eggs, meat, milk, cooking oil, and fabric, people needed not only cash, but also ration tickets, which were allocated through their work unit. Work-unit cadres (or work-brigade and commune cadres in the countryside) had the power to allocate housing and other scarce goods.

Chinese dealt with this scarcity and with the fact that cadres controlled access to goods and services by building networks of connections (*guanxi*) with useful people. Building and maintaining *guanxi* networks involved much flattery of superiors, giving and receiving of gifts and favors, invitations to dinner, and so on. With the right *guanxi,* one could "go through the back door" to get things done, avoiding the many layers of bureaucracy, and the rules and regulations that might stand in the way of achieving one's goal. This quiet subversion of the system allowed people to get things done without actually challenging the system itself. In fact, the use of *guanxi* reinforced the power of party cadres who had to be carefully cultivated precisely because they could provide access to goods and services.

In all of their dealings, Chinese had to develop and hone very sensitive political antennae. As mass movements from the 1957 Anti-Rightist Campaign onward attacked vaguely defined targets, everyone, whether of "good" or "bad" class background, party member, intellectual, student, or worker, had to be very careful in order to avoid being labeled a "class enemy," "reactionary," "bad element," or "counterrevolutionary." Most people's reaction was to determine the way the political wind was blowing and then conform to it:

attend the political study sessions, denounce whoever was the target of the day, shout the right slogans, and, in all things, be careful. Even an innocent mistake like getting mixed up while shouting slogans or writing the wrong character on a "big-character poster" could have serious consequences.

Artists, musicians, and writers, too, generally dealt with the oppressive atmosphere by trying to conform. All artistic and literary production, especially after the Anti-Rightist movement, was bound by a very narrow interpretation of Mao's "Talks at the Yan'an Forum on Art and Literature." Art and literature were expected to serve the people and the party. Cadres—not necessarily educated or artistically inclined—were the judges of political correctness. As a result, art and literature were intensely political. With Jiang Qing's encouragement, artists painting in the traditional *guohua* style churned out socialist realist celebrations of glowing, ruddy-faced masses and revolutionary heroes and, above all, Mao Zedong.[65] Many artists produced brightly-colored propaganda posters which portrayed a world of strong, determined male and female workers, farmers, and soldiers, fictional bumper crops, denunciations of class enemies, and celebrations of revolutionary triumph over the forces of revisionism, feudalism, and capitalism.[66]

The traditional arts of the old Qing scholar elite, too, survived, and were adapted to the new political circumstances of the People's Republic. Mao Zedong and many other high-ranking party leaders wrote poetry in the classical styles of the Tang and Song dynasties. Like the Chinese emperors and court officials of old, Mao Zedong and other party leaders bestowed examples of their calligraphy on buildings and other public places. Ordinary intellectuals also continued to practice traditional arts, but with care. Painting, calligraphy, and poetry, as much as anything else, needed to conform to the demands of constantly shifting political demands and the ways in which they were interpreted.

Life was difficult for those who sought to conform. For those who could not, or would not conform, life was hell. All urban intellectuals suffered to some extent. Nearly everyone had been, or knew someone who had been, victim of one campaign or another: denounced as a "Rightist," "struggled against" by Red Guards, or caught up in the wild purge of alleged co-conspirators of Lin Biao. Whole groups of intellectuals and party cadres were "sent down" to the countryside for terms ranging from months to years on the theory that extended periods of hard physical labor would help to wipe out their "bourgeois" thinking and habits.

People with what were deemed to be serious political problems could be taken into custody by the police, without a warrant, held indefinitely for "questioning," and sentenced to up to three years of "Re-education Through Labor" without formal charges or a trial. Those considered guilty of an actual crime (whether it be a common crime or a political offense) would be formally arrested, tried, and sentenced in court. The outcome was generally decided before the trial began; appeals were considered evidence of a bad attitude and might very well earn one a stiffer sentence. Those found guilty of serious offenses, including political offenses, could be sentenced to death, but the more typical punishment was a term of imprisonment in a "labor reform camp."[67]

The labor reform camps were prisons in which the party-state's theoretical intent was to reform offenders by forcing them to participate in a regime of intense collective labor, political study, and self-criticism. The hope was that this program would wipe out the selfish bourgeois individualism that was considered the fundamental root of all criminal behavior. The reformed offender could be returned to society, where he or she would now be "useful timber" for the construction of the socialist motherland.[68] The government also hoped that by forcing inmates to perform useful labor, the prison camps would pay for themselves and help to develop the economies of remote areas. Particularly large prison camps were constructed in the harsh areas of Qinghai Province and the Xinjiang-Uighur Autonomous Region—the latter a place where the Qing dynasty, too, had sent exiled prisoners.

In practice, the labor reform camps were brutal places. Overwork, overcrowding, vermin, unsafe working conditions, and violent punishment were common. Guards routinely used food deprivation as a technique of control, keeping the prisoners in a state of near-starvation.[69] By the 1980s, when more information about labor reform became available, researchers concluded that the labor camps generally failed to reform criminal or political offenders and that, rather than generate a profit, the system was "uneconomical and could not pay its own way."[70] Perhaps the same could be said of China as a whole: nearly three decades of socialist construction and political campaigns had neither made China a world-class industrial power nor made the Chinese people into Marxist-Leninist revolutionaries in the Maoist image. With Mao's passing from the scene, the way was open for a new leadership to try new styles of politics, new strategies of economic development, and new attitudes toward culture, society, and the capitalist world.

Notes

1. Denny Roy, *Taiwan: A Political History* (Ithaca: Cornell University Press, 2003), 76.

2. Maurice Meisner, *Mao's China and After: A History of the People's Republic,* 3rd ed. (New York: The Free Press, 1999), 63; Kenneth Lieberthal, *Governing China: From Revolution Through Reform,* 2nd ed. (New York: W.W. Norton, 2004), 55.

3. Lieberthal, *Governing China,* 78.

4. Dennis J. Blasko, "'Always Faithful': The PLA from 1949 to 1989," in David A. Graff and Robin Higham, eds., *A Military History of China* (Boulder: Westview Press, 2002), 250.

5. Yu-nan Chang, "The Chinese Communist State System Under the Constitution of 1954," *The Journal of Politics,* 18.3 (Aug. 1956): 520–46.

6. This and the understanding of the nature of campaigns throughout this chapter draw on Julia Strauss, "Morality, Coercion, and State Building by Campaign in the Early PRC: Regime Consolidation and After, 1949–1956," in Strauss, ed., *The History of the PRC (1949–1976)* (Cambridge: Cambridge University Press, 2007), 37–58.

7. Warren I. Cohen, *America's Response to China: A History of Sino-American Relations,* 4th ed. (New York: Columbia University Press, 2000), 167; U.S. Senate Committee on Armed Services and Senate Committee on Foreign Relations, "Policy Information Paper—Formosa," *[Hearings on the] Miltary Situation in the Far East,* 82nd Cong., 1st Sess., 1951, Part 33, 1667–68, cited in Claude S. Phillips, Jr., "International Legal Status of Formosa," *The Western Political Quarterly* 10.2 (June 1957): 279.

8. Mao Zedong, "Be a True Revolutionary," in *Selected Works of Mao Tsetung,* (Beijing: Foreign Languages Press, 1977), vol. 5, 39.

9. Julia Strauss, "Paternalist Terror: The Campaign to Suppress Counterrevolutionaries and Regime Consolidation in the People's Republic of China, 1950–1953," *Comparative Studies in Society and History* 44.1 (Jan. 2002): 80–105.

10. Vivienne Shue, *Peasant China in Transition: The Dynamics of Development Toward Socialism, 1949–1956* (Berkeley: University of California Press, 1980), 67.

11. Frederick C. Teiwes, "Establishment and Consolidation of the New Regime," in Denis Twitchett and John K. Fairbank, eds., *The Cambridge History of China, Vol. 14: The People's Republic, Part 1: The Emergence of Revolutionary China, 1949–1965* (Cambridge: Cambridge University Press, 1987), 87.

12. A. Doak Barnett, *Communist China: The Early Years, 1949–1955* (New York: Praeger, 1964), 140; Franz Schurmann, *Ideology and Organization in Communist China* (Berkeley: University of California Press, 1968), 318.

13. Mao Zedong, "Unite and Distinguish Between Ourselves and the Enemy," in *Selected Works,* vol. 5, 80.

14. Marriage Law of the People's Republic of China (1950), Chap. 2, Art. 3.

15. Elisabeth Croll, *Feminism and Socialism in China* (New York: Routledge, 1978), 235–7. See also Carma Hinton and Richard Gordon's documentary film *Small Happiness: Women of a Chinese Village"* (Wayne: New Day Films, 1994).

16. Neil J. Diamant, "Re-examining the Impact of the 1950 Marriage Law: State Improvisation, Local Initiative, and Rural Family Change," *China Quarterly* 161 (March 2000): 171–98.

17. The following discussion draws on Xi-aobing Li, *A History of the Modern Chinese Army* (Lexington: The University Press of Kentucky, 2007), 79–112.

18. Chen Jian, *China's Road to the Korean War: The Making of the Sino-American Confrontation* (New York: Columbia University Press, 1994), 160–1. The Soviet Union extended limited assistance to China during the Korean War.

19. Shu Guang Zhang, *Mao's Military Romanticism: China and the Korean War, 1950–1953* (Lawrence: University Press of Kansas, 1995), 29–30.

20. In building a strong state-run economy, the Communists drew not only on the Soviet example, but also on the wartime experience of Chiang Kai-shek's government. The Nationalist government's accumulation of state capital, establishment of state-run industries, and training of economic and industrial planners were all important legacies that contributed to the development of a planned socialist economy in the People's Republic. See William C. Kirby, "The Chinese War Economy," in James C. Hsiung and Steven I. Levine, *China's Bitter Victory: The War with Japan 1937–1945* (Armonk: M. E. Sharpe, 1992), 205–6.

21. Nicholas R. Lardy, "Economic Recovery and the First Five-Year Plan," in Twitchett and Fairbank, eds., *The Cambridge History of China, Vol. 14,* 156.

22. Shue, *Peasant China in Transition,* 214–27.

23. Lardy, "Economic Recovery," 157.

24. Ibid., 156.

25. Ibid., 155.

26. Immanuel C. Y. Hsu, *The Rise of Modern China,* 6th ed. (Oxford: Oxford University Press, 2000), 654.

27. Barry Naughton, "Economic Growth in the Mao Era," in Kenneth Lieberthal, Joyce Kallgren, Roderick MacFarquhar, and Frederic Wakeman, Jr., eds., *Perspectives on Modern China: Four Anniversaries* (Armonk: M. E. Sharpe, 1991), 233.

28. Timothy Cheek, *Mao Zedong and China's Revolutions: A Brief History with Documents* (Boston: Bedford/St. Martin's, 2002), 129.

29. Roderick MacFarquhar, *The Origins of the Cultural Revolution 1: Contradictions Among the People 1956–1957* (New York: Columbia University Press, 1974), 228. The following discussion draws on Mac-Farquhar's work.

30. François Gipouloux, *Les Cent Fleurs à l'usine: Agitation ouvrière et crise du modèle soviétique en Chine, 1956–1957* (The Hundred Flowers in the factory: worker unrest and the crisis of the Soviet model in China, 1956–1957) (Paris: École des Hautes Études en Sciences Sociales, 1986). Reviewed by Elizabeth J. Perry in *The Journal of Asian Studies* 48.1 (Feb. 1989): 134–5.

31. Merle Goldman, "The Party and the Intellectuals," in Twitchett and Fairbank, eds., *The Cambridge History of China, Vol. 14,* 257; Li Zhisui, *The Private Life of Chairman Mao* (New York: Random House, 1994), 216. The source of the five percent quota may have been Mao's remark on 8 June 1957: "Reactionary elements number no more than a few percent and the most frantic only one percent" (Mao Zedong, "Muster Our Forces to Repulse the Rightists' Wild Attacks," *Selected Works,* vol. 5, 448); or his remark on 27 February 1958 to the effect that somewhere from one to ten percent of Chinese might be counter-revolutionaries (Mao, "On the Correct Handling of Contradictions Among the People [Speaking Notes]," Roderick MacFarquhar, Timothy Cheek, and

Eugene Wu, eds., *The Secret Speeches of Chairman Mao: From the Hundred Flowers to the Great Leap Forward* [Cambridge, Mass.: Council on East Asian Studies, Harvard University, 1989], 147).

32. Merle Goldman and Timothy Cheek, "Introduction: Uncertain Change," in Goldman and Cheek, eds., *China's Intellectuals and the State: In Search of a New Relationship* (Cambridge, Mass.: Council on East Asian Studies, Harvard University, 1987), 15.

33. Jonathan D. Spence, *The Search for Modern China,* 2nd ed. (New York: W.W. Norton, 1999), 542–3.

34. MacFarquhar, *The Origins of the Cultural Revolution 1,* 314.

35. Meisner, *Mao's China and After,* 220.

36. Ibid., 223.

37. Jasper Becker, *Hungry Ghosts: China's Secret Famine* (London: John Murray, 1996), 72–3.

38. "On the Construction Site," translated by Li Yixie in Nankai daxue waiwenxi, ed., *New Chinese Folk Songs II,* Chinese-English ed. (Beijing: Shangwu chubanshe, 1959), 59.

39. Comrade Peng Dehuai's Letter to Chairman Mao (July 14, 1959), in *Memoirs of a Chinese Marshal: The Autobiographical Notes of Peng Dehuai (1898–1974),* trans. Zheng Longpu (Beijing: Foreign Languages Press, 1984), 518–9.

40. Chen Jian, *Mao's China and the Cold War* (Chapel Hill: University of North Carolina Press, 2001), 79.

41. Vaclav Smil, "China's Great Famine: Forty Years Later," *BMJ* 1999; 319: 1619–21 (18 December), online at http://www.bmj.com/cgi/content/full/319/7225/1619. Accessed 15 August 2008.

42. Chen, *Mao's China and the Cold War,* 73–4.

43. Ibid., 77–8; Li, *History of the Modern Chinese Army,* 178–9.

44. Li, *History of the Modern Chinese Army,* 156.

45. Ibid., 156–7.

46. Franz Schurmann, *Ideology and Organization in Communist China,* 2nd ed. (Berkeley: University of California Press, 1968), 492; Nicholas R. Lardy, "The Chinese Economy Under Stress, 1958–1965," in Twitchett and Fairbank, eds., *The Cambridge History of China, Vol. 14,* 389.

47. Quoted in Merle Goldman, "The Party and the Intellectuals: Phase Two," in Twitchett and Fairbank, eds., *The Cambridge History of China, Vol. 14,* 444.

48. Mao Zedong, "Speech at the Tenth Plenum of the Eight Central Committee (The Morning of 24 September 1962)," in Stuart Schram, ed., *Mao Tse-tung Unrehearsed Talks and Letters: 1956–71* (Harmondsworth: Penguin Books, 1974), 188–96.

49. Quoted in MacFarquhar, *The Origins of the Cultural Revolution 3: The Coming of the Cataclysm 1961–1966* (New York: Columbia University Press, 1997), 453.

50. Mao Zedong, "Remarks at the Spring Festival, Summary Record, 13 February 1964," in Schram, *Mao Tse-tung Unrehearsed,* 203.

51. Youqin Wang, "Student Attacks Against Teachers: The Revolution of 1966," paper presented at the conference "The Cultural Revolution in Retrospect," Hong Kong University of Science and Technology, 4–6 July 1996; presented at the Association of Asian Studies annual meeting, Chicago, 14–16 March 1997; online in China News Digest International, *Virtual Museum of the "Cultural Revolution,"* English version, at http://www.cnd.org/CR/english/

articles/violence.htm, accessed 28 December 2007.

52. The "Nine Black Categories" were: landlords, rich farmers, counterrevolutionaries, bad elements, rightists, traitors, spies, capitalist roaders, and intellectuals. All were loosely defined and all were fair game for attack.

53. Yi-tsi Mei Feuerwerker, *Ding Ling's Fiction: Ideology and Narrative in Modern Chinese Literature* (Cambridge, Mass.: Harvard University Press, 1982), 13.

54. Li Zhensheng, *Red-Color News Soldier: A Chinese Photographer's Odyssey Through the Cultural Revolution* (London: Phaidon Press, 2003), 74–5, 105–13.

55. Mao Zedong, "A Letter to the Red Guards of Tsinghua University Middle School" (1 August 1966), in Schram, *Mao Tse-tung Unrehearsed,* 260.

56. Meisner, *Mao's China and After,* 337; see also Wang Shaoguang, *The Failure of Charisma: The Cultural Revolution in Wuhan* (Hong Kong: Oxford University Press, 1995).

57. Harry Harding, "The Chinese State in Crisis," in Roderick MacFarquhar and John K. Fairbank, eds., *The Cambridge History of China, Vol. 15: The People's Republic, Part 2: Revolutions Within the Chinese Revolution, 1966–1982* (Cambridge: Cambridge University Press, 1991), 188–9.

58. Thomas P. Bernstein, *Up to the Mountains and Down to the Villages: The Transfer of Youth from Urban to Rural China* (New Haven: Yale University Press, 1977), 57–8.

59. Roderick MacFarquhar and Michael Schoenals, *Mao's Last Revolution* (Cambridge, Mass.: Harvard University Press, 2006), 333–6.

60. Ibid., 336.

61. "Joint Communiqué of the United States of America and the People's Republic of China," February 28, 1972, Articles 11 and 12. Text taken from CNN's Web site, http://edition.cnn.com/SPECIALS/cold.war/episodes/15/documents/us.china/.

62. John Wilson Lewis and Xue Litai, *China Builds the Bomb* (Stanford: Stanford University Press, 1988), vol. 1, 205–6.

63. Barry Naughton, "The Pattern and Legacy of Economic Growth in the Mao Era," in Lieberthal et al., eds., *Perspectives on Modern China,* 229–30. The following analysis of China's economy in the Mao era draws on Naughton.

64. Martin King Whyte and William L. Parish, *Urban Life in Contemporary China* (Chicago: The University of Chicago Press, 1984), 79.

65. Julia F. Andrews, "The Victory of Socialist Realism: Oil Painting and the New Guohua," in Julia F. Andrews and Kuiyi Shen, eds., *A Century in Crisis: Modernity and Tradition in the Art of Twentieth Century China* (New York: Guggenheim Museum, 1998), 233–4.

66. For examples, see Harriet Evans and Stephanies Donald, eds., *Picturing Power in the People's Republic of China: The Posters of the Cultural Revolution* (Lanham: Rowman & Littlefield, 1999); and Stefan R. Landsberger, *Stefan Landsberger's Chinese Propaganda Poster Pages* (Amsterdam: International Institute of Social History, n.d.), online at http://www.iisg.nl/~landsberger/, accessed 18 August 2008.

67. On the legal system, see Jerome Alan Cohen, *The Criminal Process in the People's Republic of China, 1949–1963: An Introduction* (Cambridge: Harvard University Press, 1968); and Harold M. Tanner, *Strike Hard! Anti-Crime Campaigns and Chinese Criminal Justice, 1979–1985* (Ithaca: Cornell East Asian Series, 1999).

68. Michael R. Dutton, *Policing and Punishment in China: From Patriarchy to "the*

People" (Cambridge: Cambridge University Press, 1992), 250–1.

69. For life in the labor camps see Bao Ruowang (Jean Pasqualini) and Rudolph Chelminski, *Prisoner of Mao* (Harmondsworth: Penguin Books, 1976); and Philip F. Williams and Yenna Wu, *The Great Wall of Confinement: The Chinese Prison Camp Through Contemporary Fiction and Reportage* (Berkeley: University of California Press, 2004).

70. James D. Seymour and Richard Anderson, *New Ghosts, Old Ghosts: Prisons and Labor Reform Camps in China* (Armonk: M. E. Sharpe, 1998), 199–201, 214.

Chapter 6   THE MARCH
                                                TOWARD
                                        WEALTH AND POWER

When Mao and the Communist Party came to power in 1949, they set out to transform the everyday lives of the Chinese people and to realize the dreams that had been the driving force behind Chinese reformers and revolutionaries from the late Qing Self-Strengtheners onward: to transform the old Qing Empire into a wealthy, militarily powerful nation-state that could stand proud and defend its territory in the modern world. During the twenty-eight years of Chairman Mao's leadership, the People's Republic of China did bring nearly all the former Qing territory (save Outer Mongolia, Taiwan, Hong Kong, and Macao) under its control. Although the People's Liberation Army (PLA) was still very backward in terms of technology, it did have an air force, nuclear weapons, and the beginnings of a guided missile program. But Mao's policies had not made China into a wealthy country or a country whose military could compare to those of the two superpowers of the Cold War world.

In the three decades after Mao's death, China's new leaders cast aside the "Great Helmsman's" policies, which they associated with chaos and economic mismanagement. Instead of constant mass movements and socialism, they instituted market-oriented reforms and engagement with the capitalist global economy as the most effective methods of moving China toward the goals of national wealth and power. Their reforms would fundamentally change China's role on the international stage and the lives of over a billion Chinese citizens.

The Reformists Take Power

When Mao died, three factions competed for control over China.[1] Jiang Qing, who commanded strong support from within the party's propaganda apparatus, had already begun to use her status as Mao's widow and close comrade-in-arms to cement her claim to be his political heir. Jiang's outspoken determination to continue Mao's revolutionary line put her in opposition to a group of party elders and PLA generals headed by Deng Xiaoping. These men, many of them Long March veterans who had suffered grievously during the Cultural Revolution, thought that China had seen quite enough of class struggle and harbored a strong personal animosity toward Jiang Qing. They believed that China needed to focus on achieving what the late Zhou Enlai had called the "Four Modernizations": agriculture, industry, science/ technology, and defense. But in 1976 their leader, Deng Xiaoping had, once again, been sent down to the countryside.

And then there was Hua Guofeng. Hua (1921–2008), a former minister of public security, had succeeded Zhou Enlai as premier. Before he died, Mao Zedong, whose hopelessly slurred speech nobody could interpret, had supposedly given Hua a handwritten note reading: "With you in charge, my heart is at ease." That, and the support of key elements in the PLA and the Ministry of Public Security, was enough to make Hua a serious contender for power. When Mao died, Hua's men quickly arrested Jiang Qing and the other members of the "Gang of Four." Hua now became party chairman as well as premier, and promised that "whatever policy Chairman Mao decided upon, we shall resolutely defend; whatever directives Chairman Mao issued, we shall steadfastly obey."[2]

In fact, Hua did not follow Mao's policies and instructions as blindly as his famous "two whatevers" slogan would suggest. His goal was to achieve rapid economic growth by returning to a 1950s-style regime of strong centralized planning and large-scale industry (an approach that Mao had rejected in 1958), but to combine that with a continued "Maoist" emphasis on unending class struggle. Hua's economic plans called for the simultaneous construction of one hundred twenty major projects, including fourteen major industrial projects and utterly unrealistic targets for steel and oil production.[3] Thus,

Hua proved himself to be as bad an economist as Mao: China simply did not have the capital, the foreign exchange, or the technical capacity to complete this ambitious plan. Hua's efforts to continue the class struggle and to create a new cult of personality around himself were equally ridiculous. Try as he would (he even began imitating Mao's hairstyle), no amount of propaganda could give Hua Guofeng the political genius, charisma, and personal connections of Mao Zedong.

Hua's attempt to play the "Wise Leader" fell flat not only because he was unsuited to the role, but also because the Chinese people were thoroughly tired of political campaigns. The sense of alienation, cynicism, and dissatisfaction was most vigorously expressed by the sent-down youth who were now returning in droves, legally or otherwise, to the cities. These young people in their twenties and early thirties had lost nearly a decade of their lives to political campaigns and re-education in the countryside. Now, some of them began using the propaganda techniques and rhetoric that they had learned during the Cultural Revolution to launch yet another round of criticism of the Communist Party and the cadres who seemed to control virtually every aspect of life. The center of the action was in downtown Beijing at the corner of Chang'an Boulevard and Xidan Street, just a mile or so west of Tiananmen Square. Beginning in December 1978, young people began gathering there, pasting "big-character posters" on the wall at this busy street corner, distributing their own self-published newspapers and magazines, making speeches, and networking. The content of their writings and discussions gave the place its name: Democracy Wall.[4]

The Democracy Wall activists included a wide range of people and opinions. Most of them, though, formulated and expressed their ideas using the Marxist-Leninist and Cultural Revolution–style concepts and rhetoric that they had grown up with: many criticized the Communist Party and its cadres for having become something like a bourgeois dictatorship.[5] But instead of recommending violent class struggle as the solution, they suggested that democracy was the solution to China's problems. For many of the participants, "democracy" was more like a moral value than a set of political institutions. Democracy was openness, freedom of discussion, and tolerance. Democracy would allow the voices of the people to be heard and prevent government from infringing upon people's human rights. Democracy, said Wei Jingsheng (b. 1950), a Beijing electrician and former PLA soldier, was the "Fifth Modernization" without which China would never be able to achieve the other "Four Modernizations" (agriculture, industry, science/technology, and defense).[6]

The Democracy Wall Movement flourished from December 1978 through the end of 1979 because it suited the needs of a factional struggle that was unfolding within the Communist Party's Central Committee. While party chairman and premier Hua Guofeng was trying to become a great leader, the irrepressible Deng Xiaoping and his supporters in the PLA were maneuvering themselves back into power. Deng's decades as a Communist Party member, his years of experience as a commissar in the PLA in the 1930s and 1940s, and his service as a key leading member of the Communist regime under Mao and Liu Shaoqi had given him a reputation and a network of *guanxi* (personal connections) far more powerful than anything that Hua Guofeng could muster.

The struggle came to a head in December 1978 at the Third Plenary Session of the Eleventh Central Committee of the Chinese Communist Party (CCP). At this meeting, Deng's supporters forced Hua to resign the post of party chairman and renounce his "two whatevers" slogan. In 1979 and 1980, Deng would place two of his younger protégés in key positions: Hu Yaobang (1915–89) was installed as party general secretary, and Zhao Ziyang (1919–2005) as premier. Deng reserved for himself the chairmanship of the Central Military Affairs Commission, but his real power came from his personal prestige: he was China's "paramount leader" because his peers recognized him as such. Deng relied on his relationships and his charisma to put together a delicately balanced reform coalition. Zhao Ziyang and Hu Yaobang were members of the party's liberal ("right wing" in Chinese Communist terms) faction. They favored aggressive pursuit of economic reform and more open political and cultural policies. Chen Yun (1905–95), who had worked on economic issues since the 1950s, party propaganda chief Deng Liqun (b. 1915, no relation to Deng Xiaoping), and other members of the conservative ("leftist") faction, though also supporters of reform, advocated a far more cautious approach than the "liberals."

There was much popular support in Beijing for Deng and the reform coalition. The Democracy Wall activists, too, were generally supportive of Deng and happy to attack Hua Guofeng and the "two whatevers." But in the spring of 1979, with Hua Guofeng on his way into forced retirement, Democracy Wall had served its purpose. As Deng saw it, the Democracy Wall activists, many of them former Red Guards, and their ongoing criticism of Communist Party rule as an undemocratic dictatorship were a potential source of social and political chaos. China, Deng said clearly, did not need more political chaos: it needed a stable atmosphere in which to pursue economic development. In order to realize the "Four Modernizations," Chinese must also respect the "Four Cardinal Principles:" upholding the socialist path, up-holding the people's democratic dictatorship, upholding the leadership of the Chinese Communist Party, and upholding Marxism-Leninism–Mao Zedong Thought.[7] The activities at Democracy Wall were incompatible with Deng's vision for economic development under strong party leadership. In the spring of 1979, the police began to move in on the Democracy Wall movement.

As the crackdown began, Wei Jingsheng wrote yet another essay. Praising Deng for his reform policies, Wei warned that if the political system re-mained unchanged, Deng, too, could become a dictator. Four days later, Wei was arrested. In October, he was put on trial and charged with giving for-eign reporters "classified" information about China's unsuccessful 1979 war with Vietnam and with "counterrevolutionary propaganda and incitement." Wei argued in his own defense that the information he had given to foreign reporters was freely available in the Chinese media and that dissemination of his ideas through public speech, "big-character posters," and unofficial pub-lications were all activities protected under China's constitution. The judges were not convinced: Wei spent most of the next eighteen years in prison be-fore being exiled to the United States in 1997.

In 1978–79, Wei Jingsheng had argued that without democracy, China's leaders, no matter how enlightened they might seem, would always have the power to suppress political dissidents. Over the next thirty years, Deng Xiaoping and his successors proved his point time after time. But Wei's belief that democracy—the "Fifth Modernization"—would be a prerequisite for economic growth and the modernization of agriculture, industry, science and technology, and national defense turned out to be mistaken. Authoritar-ian one-party rule and suppression of political dissidents turned out to be perfectly compatible with thirty years of rapid economic growth.

Building Socialism with Chinese Characteristics, 1978–89

Deng Xiaoping and the reform coalition came into power in 1978 promis-ing to shift the Communist Party's focus from class struggle to economic construction. Throughout the 1980s, the party leadership designed and im-plemented a series of economic reforms that reorganized agricultural pro-duction, restored markets, loosened restrictions on private ownership, and opened up the country to foreign trade, investment, and tourism. The reform policies did not come easily. Economic reforms and periods of economic

Deng Xiaoping as he leaves the White House, 1979.

growth were punctuated by bouts of inflation and by opposition from the more conservative elements within the CCP.[8] Some party members worried that the rebirth of a market economy and opening to the outside world was leading to a restoration of capitalism. The advocates of reform took a different view. They were not rebuilding capitalism: they were building "socialism with Chinese characteristics."

China's rural economy was one of the first areas to see significant economic reform. Back in the 1960s, Liu Shaoqi and Deng Xiaoping had allowed the People's Communes to experiment with household contract responsibility systems as a way of increasing production. In the 1980s, the contract responsibility system became the standard way of organizing Chinese agriculture. Under China's constitution, all land was owned by the state. But under the responsibility system, communes and work brigades assigned the "use rights" of land to families for a certain number of years. Each family would sign a contract in which they agreed to sell a set amount of their crop (such as grain, oil crops, or cotton) to the state at set prices. The family could then keep any overquota production for its own use or for sale on the open market, at market prices. As long as they could meet their commitments to the state, farmers might also decide to use some of their land to cultivate cash crops (vegetables, for example) to sell on the market, and/or to engage in "sidelines" like crafts, tailoring, small animal husbandry, food preparation, and so on.

The rural reforms also extended to the industrial sector. During the Great Leap Forward and, to a lesser extent, during the Cultural Revolution, communes and work brigades had been encouraged to build small-scale local industries such as metallurgy, fertilizers, and chemicals. In the 1980s provincial governments used low taxes, low-interest loans, and minimal regulation to encourage explosive growth of these local rural industries, now called Township and Village Enterprises (TVEs).[9]

By 1989, economic reform had brought significant increases in agricultural production and raised average rural incomes. The benefits, however, were not spread evenly. Rural people in southeastern and eastern China, particularly those with easy access to major urban markets, did far better than those in remote mountainous areas and in the western and southwestern provinces of the interior. Even within communities, families which were harder working, more talented, or perhaps had better networks of relations (*guanxi*) with the local leaders fared better than those who did not. As disparities in the distribution of wealth emerged, envy of one's neighbors (the "red-eye disease") caused new tensions, and sometimes increases in theft and violence in rural communities. Nonetheless, rural reform was relatively easy. China's long traditions of family farming and marketing and local leaders' experience with small industrial enterprises helped to smooth the way toward a very successful restoration of family farming, market activity, and small-scale rural industries. So too did the fact that the reforms offered both farmers and cadres palpable opportunities to make more money and improve their lives.

Reform of the urban economy was much more difficult. The employees of state-owned enterprises (SOEs), collectives, government organs, universities, and other urban work units enjoyed their "iron rice bowls." There was also an ideological problem: the state-owned enterprises were the core of the socialist-planned economy. How should one approach the question of reform of the socialist economy? Different leaders had different perspectives on this. Deng Xiaoping was favorable to relatively aggressive reform initiatives like removal of price controls, opening markets, and attracting foreign investment. However, he had no master plan. Making reform, he said, was like "groping for stones while crossing the river." Deng, and even more so Premier Zhao Ziyang and party General Secretary Hu Yaobang and other members of the party's "liberal" faction were determined to press forward with economic reform.

In contrast to Deng and the younger reformers there was Chen Yun, leader of the "conservatives." Chen had played a major role in designing the rural responsibility system. But he took a rather cautious view of reform, and even more so of opening to the capitalist world. Chen liked to say that the economy was like a bird. If you hold it tight in your hand, it will suffocate. You need to put it in a cage where it can fly around happily. You can argue about the size of the cage, Chen said, but without the cage—that is, state regulation and the Five-Year Plan—the bird will fly away, out of control.[10] Chen Yun and some of his younger protégés, including Li Peng (b. 1928, a Soviet-trained hydraulic engineer), were in favor of some urban economic reform, but only as a supplement to the socialist-planned economy and the state-owned enterprises.[11]

One approach to urban reform was to change SOEs and collectives from within through restructuring, tax incentives, and "responsibility systems."[12] The general idea was to make socialist industries behave more like capitalist enterprises by making them responsible for their own profits and losses. This transformation was pursued with great caution and met with considerable resistance. Too many people's jobs, housing, and social services were delivered through the socialist work units for the party to pursue enterprise reform with any real conviction. The reforms did allow SOEs and collectives to produce goods beyond their quotas under the state plan and to sell the above-quota goods on the market at market prices. Some of the better-managed and more competitive SOEs profited from these reforms. Many others continued to lose money and continued to impose a significant financial burden on the state.

Reforms that allowed individuals to go into business for themselves were more effective. In the mid-1980s, looser regulation allowed millions of Chinese to start their own small businesses—tailoring, bicycle and electronics repair, street vending, small restaurants and shops, and various services. Among the first and most enthusiastic of the new entrepreneurs were people who had no place in the socialist world of work units and iron rice bowls: returned "sent-down" Red Guards, unemployed youth, ex-convicts, and people who had been laid off or forced into "early retirement" as a result of restructuring of collectives and SOEs. The latter included a disproportionate number of women, who were often among the first to lose their jobs when work units were forced to reduce their payrolls. The unintended consequence was to produce a generation of successful women entrepreneurs.[13]

While carrying out rural and urban reforms on a nationwide basis, the Communist Party leadership also experimented with more radical ideas in the two provinces of Guangdong and Fujian. These two coastal areas, facing Taiwan and Hong Kong, were ideal laboratories in which to test (and to demonstrate the efficacy of) Deng's policy of "opening to the outside." In 1980, the Central Committee and the National People's Congress approved the creation of four "Special Economic Zones" (SEZs). Shenzhen, Shetou, and Zhuhai in Guangdong and Xiamen in Fujian would be open to foreign trade and foreign investment. In the SEZs, Chinese firms could produce goods for export, manufacture goods under contract for foreign companies, and go into joint ventures with foreign partners. The SEZs were intended to attract foreign investment and foreign technology. They also served as places in which China could experiment with Western management and financial techniques.

By 1989, the advocates of reform could point to some major success stories. Shenzhen, a small village just north of Hong Kong in 1978, had become a major city and center of manufacturing and trade. Foreign investment was flowing in from Taiwan, Hong Kong, Japan, the Americas, and Europe, and from overseas Chinese communities in Southeast Asia. China's economy had grown at an average of ten percent per year for a decade. But at the same time, critics could point to significant problems. Rapid economic growth and the regime's attempts (some of which had to be cancelled) to remove price controls on food and other commodities had caused inflation and market instability. After growing rapidly for several years, agricultural production had leveled off in 1984. Rural and urban Communist Party cadres, notably the sons and daughters of certain Central Committee members, used their political connections to conduct their own, very profitable businesses. Embezzlement, bribery, and kickbacks were common. Those in a position to do so bought goods at cheap state-subsidized prices and resold them at market prices for a tremendous profit. Both the successes and the problems of economic reform were leading to tension in Chinese society and within the ranks of the Communist Party leadership.

Political Reform, Legal Reform, and "Culture Fever"

China's 1980s economic reforms were intimately entangled with the question of political reform, legal system reform, and cultural policy. Both the "conservative" and "liberal" wings of Deng's reform coalition agreed that China's legal and political system had to be changed in order to prevent any repetition of the turmoil of the Cultural Revolution. Both wanted to back away from the extreme politicization of culture that had characterized the Cultural Revolution years. The trouble was that they had very different visions of China's future and different ideas as to how and how much to reform the political and legal systems and the party's cultural policies. The conservatives imagined limited reforms that would leave the party firmly in control and return China to what they imagined as the healthy norms that had governed political and cultural life prior to 1957. For the "liberals," legal, political, and cultural reform meant separating the party from the day-to-day business of government and law and loosening restrictions on journalism, art, literature, and people's daily lives in ways that would contribute to further economic reform.

Members of both factions agreed that China's legal system was in desperate need of reform. In the years when Mao's radical policies reigned supreme (1957–60, 1966–76), law and lawyers had been condemned as bourgeois. During the Cultural Revolution, Red Guards even attacked the Public Security (police) apparatus. In 1978, China still had no written codes of criminal law, criminal procedure, or civil law. Provincial and local party leaders controlled the courts, deciding cases on the basis of their sometimes arbitrary interpretation of party policy.

Deng and the reformists saw the lack of law as one of the causes of the chaos of the Cultural Revolution. One of their first priorities in 1979 was to have the National People's Congress approve China's first post-1949 Criminal Law and Criminal Procedure Law. Both were based on drafts begun in the 1950s which had taken Soviet laws as their model. A number of other laws followed during the 1980s, many of them designed to deal with the emerging market economy: the Inheritance Law (1985), Civil Law (1986), the Bankruptcy Law (1986), laws concerning private enterprises, joint enterprises, foreign investment, business taxes, and so on. The lawyers charged with writing these laws looked to the laws of the Soviet Union and other socialist states, Japan, the Western democracies, and even Chinese law from the era of Chiang Kai-shek as models to draw on.

By 1989 China's body of law, though still a work in progress, had grown impressively. Implementation of law, however, lagged far behind. Police, courts, and procuratorates continued to struggle with poorly educated and poorly trained staff and low budgets. Efforts to remove the Communist Party from the day-to-day practice of justice at the grassroots level met with some success, but party committees continued to control the appointment, assessment, and promotion of judges, procurators, and public security officers. Local and provincial party committees no longer intervened in legal work on a routine basis, but they continued to regard the legal system in instrumental terms as a tool or weapon in the hands of the party. Party leadership was most evident in a series of "Strike Hard" campaigns against crime, the

Democracy Wall. © DSK/AFP/Getty Images.

first of which was launched in 1983. In these campaigns, the Communist Party Center identified target offenses. Provincial and local party leaders coordinated the work of public security, courts, and procuratorates, and shortened up the criminal procedure in order to handle cases faster and impose harsher sentences than provided for by law. Legal defense of criminal defendants was still unwelcome and generally limited, confession was strongly encouraged, and police torture remained a serious problem.

Like the legal reforms, reforms of the political system were not meant as stepping-stones toward achievement of liberal multiparty democracy: the goal of reform was to preserve and enhance the stability of the single-party state. But with many in the leadership worried that any loosening of political restrictions would weaken the system, electoral and other political reforms proceeded very slowly. A 1980 experiment with more open rules for the election of representatives to the county-level People's Congresses failed when young candidates who questioned the CCP's understanding of Marxism-Leninism, socialism, and democracy stood for office in Changsha and Beijing, with some of the Beijing candidates, who had links to the Democracy Wall movement, actually winning. Local and central party authorities took steps to adjust the election lists and results in order to ensure a "correct" outcome.[14]

Although political reform made very little progress during the 1980s, there was a significant loosening of restrictions on speech, publication, and discussion of political issues. Struggle between conservative and liberal elements in the party leadership meant that party policy oscillated between periods of loosening and tightening, but in spite of periodic crackdowns on dissent, Party General Secretary Hu Yaobang and other "liberal" leaders tolerated the expression of a wider range of political ideas and criticism than China had seen since the Hundred Flowers Campaign. Restrictions were particularly loose in 1985–86. The reformers, led by Hu and supported by Deng Xiaoping, were actively pushing forward with economic reform, opening to the outside. They evidently believed that more lenient policies toward the media, art, and literature would enliven the atmosphere, allow the blossoming of new ideas, and challenge the more conservative opponents of rapid economic reforms. As it turned out, Hu Yaobang and the advocates of reform got more than they bargained for.

For many people, the more lenient cultural policies of the 1980s meant that they could return to the art, literature, music, and amusements that politics had forced them to abandon in the 1950s or 1960s. Beijing and other local operas, folk, Chinese classical, and Western classical music; ballroom dancing; Chinese, Soviet, and Western literature; *guohua* and oil painting;

stamp-collecting; and permed hair (for men and women) all enjoyed a strong resurgence.

The renaissance of prerevolutionary art, literature, and amusements caused little controversy. What bothered conservative, and sometimes even liberal, members of the party leadership was when artists, writers, and musicians pushed the envelope too far in terms of the aesthetic form and/or the political content of their work. One sensitive issue had to do with how far one could go in criticizing the Cultural Revolution. Artists and authors explored the physical and emotional trauma of the Cultural Revolution in "Scar Painting" and "Scar Literature," both of which were major genres in the early 1980s.[15] Painters also criticized the Cultural Revolution by celebrating Zhou Enlai and the April Fifth (1976) Movement in which Beijing people had honored Zhou and protested the Gang of Four. *Bitter Love,* a 1979 screenplay by People's Liberation Army writer Bai Hua (b. 1931), told the fictional story of a painter whose love of country brings him home from America in the 1950s, only to fall victim to the Anti-Rightist Campaign and the Cultural Revolution. In one of the most controversial lines of the screenplay, the protagonist's daughter asks her father, who has suffered so much: "You love your country—but does your country love you?"

For artists, writers, and musicians, it must have been difficult, at times, to know exactly where the line of aesthetic or political acceptability was. Rules were not written: they were defined in a constantly changing process of interaction between party leaders of different opinions, artists, writers, and musicians working in the party-state establishment, and unofficial artists, authors, and musicians. For example, in 1979 the "Star Group" of unofficial artists first showed their groundbreaking work in an illegal exhibit hung on the fence outside the National Art Gallery in Beijing. The police forced them to move, but within months and with the help of established artists, they were exhibiting their work in state-sanctioned venues. Among the works displayed was the sculptor Wang Keping's (b. 1949) *Idol,* which seemed to blend the massive head of a Buddhist statue with the features of Mao Zedong with one eye open (perhaps to keep an eye on the worshippers).[16]

Scar Literature, Bai Hua's *Bitter Love,* work like that of the Star Group, open debate about the value of "art for art's sake," and an influx of Western, Hong Kong, and Taiwanese popular culture provided party conservatives like Deng Liqun the grounds on which to launch periodic crackdowns on culture. In 1981, Scar Literature, and especially Bai Hua's *Bitter Love,* were targets of a campaign against "bourgeois liberalization." In 1983, party conservatives, with propaganda boss Deng Liqun in the lead, initiated a "Campaign Against

Spiritual Pollution." For several months, overenthusiastic local-level cadres disciplined women for wearing long hair and high heels and prohibited Taiwanese and Hong Kong pop music. Controversial artists found themselves demoted. Authors were asked to criticize themselves and each other.

Neither of these campaigns was anything like the Cultural Revolution. Deng Xiaoping was no friend of "bourgeois liberalization" himself, but he was aware that these campaigns in the cultural realm were closely linked to the party conservatives' opposition to further economic reform. As the Cultural Revolution itself had shown, criticism of "bourgeois" culture can easily pass into criticism of "bourgeois" economic policies. Deng made sure that the campaigns of 1981 and 1983 stopped before they reached that point.

By 1985, China's cultural scene was again pushing the boundaries of acceptability. The small but energetic Beijing rock-and-roll scene generated China's first rock star, Cui Jian (b. 1961), who combined electric guitars and traditional Chinese instruments with songs of rebellion and lost love, and on-stage shouts of "we're all hooligans" to his enthusiastic audiences. Artists began experimenting with one Western style after another: Surrealism, Dada, Pop, conceptual art. Authors worked with free verse and stream of consciousness. College students and intellectuals devoured translated works by Sigmund Freud, C. G. Jung, Friedrich Nietzsche, John Dewey, and a host of others. In a movement dubbed "Culture Fever," Chinese engaged in vigorous discussion on the relative values of Western and Chinese culture in relation to economic and political modernization.[17] Much of the debate involved criticism of elements of Chinese culture—such as filial piety—as a backhand way of criticizing China's single-party political system and its leaders.

Among those enjoying the more liberal policies of the mid-1980s were muckraking journalist Liu Binyan and Fang Lizhi (b. 1936), an astrophysicist and vice-president of the Chinese University of Science and Technology. Liu, who had been branded a "rightist" in 1957, was back in business in the 1980s, writing exposés of corruption in high places and arguing in print and in public talks that a free press was the best weapon against corruption and the basis of democracy. Fang Lizhi delivered talks to students at nine or more of China's elite universities in 1985–86. He thrilled his young listeners when he denounced corrupt officials, advocated freedom of speech and democracy, and argued that China's underpaid and underappreciated intellectuals should be the ones running the country. Fang also complained that students were too passive, asking rhetorically why students at his university did not show the slightest sign of "causing trouble."[18]

革

The skyline of contemporary Shanghai. Shanghai Skyline © Peter Morgan, 2008, http://www.flickr.com/people/pmorgan.

Chinese university students soon put Fang Lizhi's concerns to rest. In December 1986, students at the Chinese University of Science and Technology marched in protest when the Anhui provincial government refused to implement a more open electoral system. The protests spread to Shanghai and other cities and finally to Beijing, where as many as thirty thousand students demonstrated.[19] A variety of issues brought students into the streets: demands for more democracy and freedom of the press, protests against inflation and corruption, and even dissatisfaction with their cafeteria food.

Overthrow of the government or the Chinese Communist Party were not on the students' agenda. Still, the party leadership viewed any demonstrations with the utmost seriousness. A clear expression of party disapproval (aided by the bitterly cold Beijing weather) soon ended the protests. But repercussions within the Party Center continued on into the spring. Conservatives in the Central Committee blamed the trouble on Hu Yaobang, saying that his economic reforms and social policies had allowed corruption, inflation, and "bourgeois liberalization" to get out of control. With Deng Xiaoping's support, party conservatives launched a movement to criticize "bourgeois liberalization." Fang Lizhi and Liu Binyan, regarded as notorious peddlers of bourgeois liberal thought, lost their party memberships. Hu Yaobang lost his post as party general secretary.

The conservative backlash slowed the pace of reform, but did not stop it. Deng Xiaoping moved Zhao Ziyang from the premier's position to party general secretary, and political heir apparent. Li Peng, a younger (fifty-nine years of age) member of the party's conservative faction, was installed as premier. With Deng's support, Zhao overcame opposition from Li and other conservatives to move forward with another round of radical reforms in 1988. These included a "coastal strategy" of opening all major coastal cities and counties to overseas trade and investment and removal of price controls on many daily commodities, including meat, sugar, eggs, alcohol, and tobacco in 1988.[20]

The new round of reforms brought more economic growth, but it also increased social tensions, particularly in the cities. The price reforms of 1988 caused a buying panic and drove inflation to 18.5 percent.[21] Moves to reorganize SOEs, and experiments aimed at reducing social welfare benefits, gave workers cause for concern.[22] Blatant corruption on the part of high-ranking cadres, especially the sons and daughters of Central Committee members, made it clear that the politically powerful were reaping the greatest personal benefits from reform. By the spring of 1989, enthusiasm for reform among urban Chinese was low.[23] Anger at corruption and inflation ran deep among professionals, students, and workers, who had few legitimate avenues through which to express their concerns or to hold party and government leaders accountable.

The Student and Worker Demonstrations of 1989

Party factionalism and popular frustration together led to an explosive series of events in the spring of 1989. The trouble began on 15 April when Hu Yaobang died suddenly of a heart attack. Students and citizens in Beijing took to the streets and to Tiananmen Square to mourn for Hu and, by implication, to protest against inflation, corruption, and lack of freedom. Students from Beijing's many universities took the lead, occupying Tiananmen Square on 21 April. The next day, as the party leadership gathered in the Great Hall of the People for Hu's official memorial service, students carrying a petition addressed to Premier Li Peng knelt dramatically on the steps like humble officials presenting a memorial to a Qing emperor.

The students demanded that the party re-evaluate its criticism of Hu Yaobang's "bourgeois liberalization" from 1986, that party officials enter into dialogue with student representatives, and that restrictions on the press be loosened. When the party leaders refused to meet with the students and called for an immediate end to the "disturbance" in a *People's Daily* editorial on 26 April, the demonstrations grew even bigger.[24] Hundreds of thousands of students from Beijing's colleges and universities occupied the square, began organizing an independent student union, and began a hunger strike to force the regime to enter into dialogue with them. With the protests growing in intensity, workers, too, began to join the movement, some of them organizing an independent labor union. Citizens from all walks of life, including many ordinary Communist Party members, openly supported the students, even proudly marching to the square under the banners of their work units. Because the demonstrations coincided with Soviet leader Mikhail Gorbachev's historic visit to Beijing—the first by a Soviet leader since the Sino-Soviet split in 1960—the foreign press was there in force, giving the movement an unprecedented level of international publicity.

The student occupation of Tiananmen Square, the symbolic political heart of Beijing, stretched from late April into mid-May. Faced with this unprecedented challenge, the Communist Party leadership debated fiercely as to how to respond. Zhao Ziyang and the "liberal" faction hoped to use the student protests and the party's failure thus far to deal with them to discredit and

A protestor faces off against a column of army tanks near Tiananmen Square on 5 June 1989. © CNN/Getty Images.

weaken their conservative opponents on the Central Committee. Making a dangerous gamble, he argued that the party should step back from the 26 April editorial, meet with the students, and seek compromise on issues like democratization, transparency of cadre finances, and investigation of corruption.

Zhao's gamble failed. With the protests spreading to several provincial cities, Deng agreed with other party elders and Li Peng that the democracy movement must be firmly repressed. As the conservatives saw it, events had gotten out of hand precisely because for years the party had consistently failed to take a strong, unequivocal stance against "bourgeois liberalization." The student demonstrations and their rhetorical attacks on the party leadership reminded Deng and his generation of leaders of Mao's Red Guards and the chaos that they had caused. At this critical juncture, they said, there could be no compromise: it was a life-and-death struggle between the Communist Party and the "counterrevolutionaries."

The students, too, were divided and incapable of compromise. China's party leaders showed no signs of agreeing to a negotiated settlement with the students. Tiananmen Square, home to student protesters for nearly two months, was becoming increasingly filthy and unsanitary. As a result, some of the student leaders suggested that they return to their campuses and continue to work for democracy there. But the students' consensus-based style of decision-making and the constant influx of new, enthusiastic groups of students from outside of Beijing pushed moderate student leaders out of power and left the movement in the hands of those who were determined to stay in the square, even if it meant martyrdom at the hands of the PLA.

The possibility of violence hovered over all the students' deliberations. The Party Central Committee had declared martial law on 20 May. When army units tried to move peacefully into the center of the city to break up the demonstrations and take control of Tiananmen Square, workers and other citizens threw up roadblocks, stood their ground in the streets, and lectured soldiers on democracy. Unable to enter the center of the city, the army withdrew to the outskirts of Beijing in 23 May. On the night of 3 June, the army made a second attempt to retake the city center and Tiananmen Square, this time by force.

As they advanced along Chang'an Boulevard toward Tiananmen Square using tanks and armored personnel carriers (APCs), the soldiers were blocked by protesters and barricades made of buses and concrete blocks. Some protesters attacked APCs and tanks with iron bars and Molotov cocktails. Soldiers responded by firing at the few armed, and many unarmed, citizens. By 1:00 a.m. on 4 June, army units had surrounded Tiananmen Square. Negotiating a withdrawal with the soldiers, the students and their supporters left the square, peacefully but under gunpoint, at 5:00 a.m.[25] Shootings and a wave of arrests continued for many days afterward. Although there was no massacre of students in Tiananmen Square, anywhere from several hundred to a thousand Beijing citizens—students, workers, and others—were killed and an unknown number injured in the fighting along Chang'an Boulevard. The government also suppressed demonstrations that had broken out in many provincial cities including Shanghai, Changsha, Xi'an, Chongqing, and Chengdu.[26]

Deepening Reform, Transforming Everyday Life

The events of 1989 significantly weakened the Party Center's reform faction. Deng and the conservatives put Zhao under house arrest and appointed Jiang Zemin (b. 1926), formerly the party secretary of Shanghai, to serve in his place as party secretary general and Deng's third political heir apparent. Arguing that it was reform and opening that had led to corruption, inflation, and the "counterrevolutionary riots," conservatives opposed any further economic or political reform and even suggested that some of the reform measures of the 1980s, including the rural responsibility system, ought to be rolled back. The government strengthened protections for SOEs and discriminated against private enterprise and TVEs.[27]

As he had before, Deng Xiaoping supported the conservative clampdown on dissident students, workers, and intellectuals. But when it came to economic matters, he and the conservatives parted ways. It took more than two years, but in January 1992, the visibly ailing Deng, more than a little concerned about his legacy, restarted economic reform by taking a tour of the southern provinces, an act reminiscent of the Kangxi and Qianlong emperors' grand tours of the south during the Qing dynasty. Deng's own "Southern Tour" took him to the economically advanced areas of the Yangzi Valley, to Guangdong, Fujian, and the still-controversial Special Economic Zones. He finished the tour in Shanghai, urging that the city open further to foreign trade and development. The "Southern Tour," intense political bargaining within the party, and the opportune death of several of the octogenarian conservatives put the reforms back on track. Jiang Zemin, previously a fence-straddler, became an enthusiastic convert to the cause of market-oriented reforms.

As Deng's health deteriorated, Jiang consolidated his position as party general secretary, chairman of the Military Affairs Commission, and president of the People's Republic. When Deng passed away in 1997, Jiang's position as successor was secure. Remaining in power until his voluntary retirement in 2002, he presided over a deepening of economic reform and opening that saw a continued, vigorous growth of China's market economy, further restructuring of SOEs, and a rapid increase in exports. Economic growth, particularly of TVEs and private companies, continued under Jiang's successor, Hu Jintao (b. 1942), who took over the posts of president of the People's Republic and party general secretary in 2003.

The deepening of economic reform in the post-Deng era brought tremendous changes to rural and urban life, culture, the family, and the Chinese Communist Party itself. Underlying all of these changes was a fundamental economic fact. Reform had created in China a mixed economy of socialist and private enterprise. Both types of enterprise operated within a market economy, whose growth was spurred by a combination of domestic and foreign investment and by cheap, reliable labor that made China's products highly competitive in Western and Japanese markets. By the end of the first decade of the 21st century, the Chinese economy had been growing at an average annual rate of around ten percent for thirty years.

In China's rural areas, the responsibility system, markets, private enter-prise, and the explosive growth of township and village enterprises (TVEs) all contributed to significant increases in average family income, bringing two hundred million people out of poverty.[28] As their incomes increased, rural families built new houses and bought bicycles, motorcycles, television sets, cars, and other consumer goods. They also revived many traditions that had been suppressed during the Mao years, particularly lavish weddings and funerals.

While average rural incomes were rising, not all families or all parts of the country shared equally in the fruits of economic development. Rural com-munities saw increasing disparities between the rich and poor when village and county cadres dominated the local economy, running TVEs as their own private businesses. On the national scale, the east coast and Yangzi Valley, with their greater population density, higher educational levels, better infrastruc-ture, and access to foreign trade via ports and airports, grew at much higher rates than the western interior provinces. In 1978, the average rural indi-vidual's consumption was equivalent to 34.1 percent of that of an average ur-banite. By 2001, it had declined to 27.8 percent.[29] These regional inequalities and the growing gap between urban and rural incomes were in a sense a return to the conditions that had existed before 1949, and stood in strong contrast to Mao Zedong's attempt to combat income disparities through more egalitarian policies.

Unequal rates of economic development and the rising gap between the rich and the poor drove unemployed workers and young men and women from poor farming areas to China's booming coastal cities in search of jobs. By 2005 China had a "floating population" of over one hundred forty mil-lion migrants chasing primarily urban low-wage jobs in manufacturing, con-struction, and services.[30] This army of cheap labor helped to make Chinese goods extremely competitive on the international market. It also provided the workers who transformed China's cities and city life in the 1990s.

One of the most immediately obvious changes in urban China from the 1980s to the early 2000s was the appearance of the urban landscape itself. In the late 1980s and early 1990s, even major cities like Beijing and Shanghai were flat, often rather drab places with relatively little motor vehicle traffic and wide, heavily-used bicycle lanes. Shanghai, the epitome of modernity in the 1920s, had only one building higher than twenty stories in the late 1980s: the Park Hotel. Then, beginning in the 1990s, China went on a construction boom. Older buildings and neighborhoods, some of them with histories going back a hundred years or more, were razed to make room for wider streets, highway overpasses, and high-rise offices, apartment buildings, and shopping centers. Private cars, trucks, and motorcycles crowded bicycles off the city streets and clogged the new highways of Beijing and Shanghai. In 1999, Shanghai had 1,350 buildings over twenty stories high.[31] Beijing's signature buildings now include not only the Ming-Qing imperial palace, but also the National Stadium (the "Bird's Nest"), the "Water Cube," and the French-designed National Center for the Performing Arts, with its titanium and glass dome. Not only Beijing and Shanghai, but cities from Liaoning province in the north to Guangdong in the south have been remade, as have many of the major cities of the western interior, including Xi'an, the site of the Qin, Han, Sui, and Tang capital cities.

The striking changes in the urban landscape were accompanied by changes in urban culture and daily life. Construction of private (as opposed to work-unit) housing and office space created a market in housing and commercial real estate where none had existed before. The grim, understocked socialist shops and department stores of the 1970s and 1980s whose clerks so often treated customers as enemies, were gone: consumers now went shopping in brightly-lit malls stocked with name-brand Chinese, Japanese, and Western products, or bargained furiously with countless small private shops and vendors. The American Wal-Mart and French Carrefour chains offered the "big box" shopping experience, with groceries, clothing, electronics, and other consumer goods all under the same roof. The rapidly increasing ranks of millionaires and billionaires made China one of the best markets for Western luxury brands like Ferrari, Rolls-Royce, Cartier, Rolex, and many more.

As daily life in urban China changed, so too did art, literature, and music. In literature, the spirit of the 1990s was perhaps best captured by the iconoclastic Wang Shuo (b. 1958), whose stories, novels, television series, and films depicted the lives of Beijing's "hooligan" culture. The characters in Wang's fictional world were based on the experiences of Beijingers of his generation: born into cadre families, growing up in the chaos of the Cultural Revolution, schooling interrupted to "learn from the peasants" in the countryside or to join the army, and then drifting back to Beijing in the 1980s with nothing to fall back on but street smarts, fast talk, a certain criminal mischievousness, and a determination to enjoy life while working as little as possible.[32]

Wang Shuo and many of the other authors and artists who made their careers in the 1990s and beyond had little use for intellectuals or democracy movements. Working independently of the state and its framework of official writers' and artists' organizations, they were more interested in developing their craft and selling their work on the domestic and international markets. In the post-1989 era, the Chinese Communist Party had made a tacit deal with Chinese artists, writers, and musicians: do whatever you want, write, paint, sing, and live as you like, as long as you do not overtly criticize the party-state and its policies or cross the (often vague) line between art and pornography. Art and literature were not completely depoliticized, and censorship still existed, but the realm of freedom was considerably greater than it had been in the 1980s, and immeasurably greater than during the Cultural Revolution.

One reason for changes in the Communist Party's determination to press forward with reform and its more liberal attitude toward private enterprise, consumer culture, daily life, and the arts was that the party itself was changing. As the old guard retired and (more importantly) died off, China's new leadership was dominated by men and a few women whose average levels of education were much higher. Many were engineers, some of them trained in the Soviet Union. Their interest was not in making revolution, but in achieving continued economic growth. Both at the Party Center and in local and provincial governments, more and more party members, their spouses, and their children were involved in business enterprises. In a telling demonstration of the mutually supportive roles of business and the Communist Party, Jiang Zemin in 2001 officially permitted what had already begun: allowing private businesspeople to join the party.[33]

The Trouble with Reform

The reform policies and economic growth clearly brought benefits to ordinary Chinese and gave cities, provinces, and the central government new resources to invest in public projects. But reform and economic growth also generated new problems for citizens and for the party-state.

The process of economic reform itself created new difficulties for many people. As state-owned and collective industries tried to cut costs in order to be more competitive in the market economy, they reduced the social welfare benefits that workers had become accustomed to: medical care, child care, subsidized housing, free education, retirement plans—all these were areas in which work units could cut back. Lack of care for the elderly, lack of education for the poor, and inequities in the distribution of health care all emerged even as the economy boomed. Crime rates increased significantly in spite of the frequent anti-crime campaigns and the heavily publicized executions of thousands of serious offenders every year. China's opening to foreign trade brought with it the development of drug trafficking: opium and heroin from Southeast Asia and domestically manufactured methamphetamine. Intravenous drug use was the main factor in the spread of HIV/AIDS, with infection rates estimated at six hundred fifty thousand in 2005.[34] Contamination of blood products and prostitution, more or less openly carried out in karaoke bars, nightclubs, and massage parlors, also contributed to the spread of HIV/AIDS and other sexually transmitted diseases.

Workplace safety issues and tremendous deterioration of the natural environment added to the social problems that came along with reform and rapid economic growth. China's factories regularly flouted labor laws. Unsafe working conditions caused around a hundred thousand fatal accidents in 2007.[35] Chinese mines were the most dangerous in the world, with an average of well over six thousand miners dying in mine accidents each year.[36] The near absence of effective regulation of industry also helped contribute to a national environmental crisis. Tens of thousands of virtually unregulated TVEs spewed pollution straight into China's rivers, lakes, and skies. Coal-burning power plants and the growing number of trucks and private automobiles gave China sixteen of the world's twenty most polluted cities.[37] Desertification added to north China's pollution problems as winds whipped up massive clouds of dust from the desiccated plains of Inner Mongolia and blew them over Beijing and on to Korea and the American Pacific coast.

Looking forward to the mid-21st century, China also faced a demographic crisis. Improvements in sanitation and health care since 1949, lower rates of infant mortality, and longer average life spans helped to push China's population from 541 million in 1949 to 975 million in 1979.[38] In 1979 the party leaders, fearing that population growth would outstrip economic growth, issued a "one-child policy." This party policy, enforced as if it were a law, prescribed a number of measures intended to slow China's population growth: the legal age of marriage was raised (from eighteen to twenty for females, from twenty to twenty-two for males) and postponement of childbearing was encouraged. Each married couple was limited to one child.[39] The intense pressure to limit births, combined with the traditional emphasis on the importance of sons, led to the abandonment of girl babies, an increase in female infanticide, and the practice of using ultrasound scans to detect the gender of the fetus and then to perform an abortion if the child were found to be a girl. Abortion of girl fetuses gave China sex ratios at birth of 111.3 boys to

100 girls in 1990, and 116.9 boys to 100 girls in 2000. This imbalance in turn was expected to result in between thirty and forty million unmarried Chinese men by the year 2020.[40]

The one-child policy's social impact was more profound than any of Mao Zedong's failed social engineering projects. With exceptions and violations factored in, the result of the one-child policy was an average family size of around two children per couple from the 1980s onward. Differences in enforcement and differences in urban and rural preferences, work needs, and living spaces meant that one child was standard for urban Han Chinese. The change in family size had tremendous short-term and long-term effects. In the short term, new generations of urban Chinese grew up as only children: parents lavished tremendous attention and resources on their boy and (less likely) girl "little emperors." In the long term, China would face the challenges of a graying society as the "little emperors" would become responsible for the support of two aging parents and four elderly grandparents: the so-called "4–2–1" problem. Some experts predicted that as the population aged, China would go into a labor deficit around the year 2020.[41]

In addition to social problems, China's Communist Party leaders faced their own challenge: how to maintain power. In the years following 1989, China's leaders conducted a careful and sophisticated study of the circumstances that had led to the protests in Beijing, the downfall of the Eastern European socialist governments, and the collapse of the Soviet Union. They concluded that continued economic growth was only one of the factors necessary to the continued survival of the one-party system. The party would also need to demonstrate openness to the concerns of citizens, reduce corruption, exercise strict control over political information, expression, and organization, and put new emphasis on patriotic education in the school, in colleges, and in public propaganda.[42]

Dealing with social tensions developed into a major challenge in the decades after 1989. Workers, farmers, and the poor generally had little voice in what was becoming an atmosphere of "wild west" capitalism in which local and provincial party leaders and wealthy business people seemed to hold all the cards. Corruption, a weak regulatory structure, and a party-controlled legal system made it difficult to enforce laws on worker safety, environmental protection, or on the purity of foods and medicines. In the countryside, corrupt local officials often forced farmers to give up their land with little or no compensation in order to build dams, factories, or new commercial or residential districts. Urban residents had no recourse when local government forced them out of their homes to make way for new streets and new buildings.

When officials in Beijing tried to address problems like corruption, worker safety, and illegal transfers of land, they met with little success. Economic reform and political restructuring had decentralized both government decision-making and budgetary responsibility. County and township governments were responsible for their own budgets and reliant on local business and industry for tax revenue: they had no reason to enforce environmental or factory safety regulations or close unsafe illegal private coal mines. State-run labor unions gave little voice to workers. The fact that many Communist Party members and their families had one foot in the world of government and the other in the business world contributed to local governments' reluctance to enforce laws and policies emanating from faraway Beijing.

With few avenues of legitimate recourse open to them, farmers, workers, and citizens who felt that they had been wronged by powerful business or government interests took to the streets. Every year there were tens of thousands of public protests, many of them violent. Angry workers marched their bosses down the streets in Cultural Revolution style.[43] Urban residents marched when their houses or apartment buildings were slated for destruction to make way for a widened street or for a corporation or work unit's profitable high-rise office or apartment complex. Farmers rioted and attacked government offices when local authorities kept the cash that they were supposed to pay farmers for grain, invested it in TVEs, and then failed to repay the IOUs. Farmers also protested when local authorities confiscated their fields in order to build factories, apartments, or office buildings. Protests like these often led to violent clashes with local authorities. But these urban and rural protests—even when they turned violent—posed no direct threat to the Communist Party or the central government. The protestors were concerned about local issues and local leadership, not about the political system itself. In fact, it was common for local protestors to express the hope that the Party Center would heed their pleas and discipline corrupt local officials. In a sense, local protests operated as safety valves in a system that allowed few legitimate avenues for popular participation in politics.[44]

Communist Party leaders were aware of the causes behind the protests and did take some steps toward battling corruption and opening new avenues through which citizens might participate in the political process and voice complaints about local problems. China's legislative bodies, the National People's Congress and provincial and local People's Congresses, were no longer the rubber-stamp organs that they had been in the Mao era. Although they still did not actively draft laws, People's Congress representatives at all levels demanded (and won) revision of legislation that the Communist Party had sent forward expecting automatic approval.[45] Limited experiments were made with direct popular election of village cadres from slates of multiple candidates, including candidates who were not party members. People's Governments at all levels operated, for the most part, without micro-management from their corresponding party committees. Courts, procura-torates, and the police were all becoming more professional, the educational levels of their personnel improving.[46]

Changes in the political and legal system meant that in many respects, China in the early 21st century was far more democratic and the rule of law far stronger than it had been at any time previously in the history of the People's Republic (and, many might say, in the history of China, period). But the new policies and laws were designed to defuse social and political ten-sions: they were not intended as incremental steps toward the realization of Western-style multiparty democracy. Party leaders were concerned with preserving the political stability and strong leadership that, in their view, was essential if China was to advance further along the road to wealth and power. The country's newly emerging business-oriented middle class, too, put greater value on stability and on maintaining good connections with party and government leaders than in achieving democracy.[47] While determined to see China become a rich and powerful nation, neither Jiang Zemin, Hu Jintao, or the other Communist Party leaders were interested in extending freedoms to speech, action, or news that, in their view, might undermine China's social and political stability or call its territorial integrity into question.

The issue of territorial integrity was of particular concern. Ever since the fall of the Qing in 1911, Chinese governments had been struggling to forge the territory and multiple ethnic groups of the Qing Empire's vast territory into a cohesive nation-state, to give members of all ethnic groups an identity as Chinese. From 1949 through 1979, and particularly during the Cultural Revolution, the government had pursued a policy that might be described as assimilation through cultural genocide: repression of ethnic minority culture, language, and religion had fed strong feelings of alienation among some of the country's fifty-five ethnic minority groups, or "nationalities," as they are called in China. In the post-Mao era, minority people enjoyed a far greater degree of freedom to practice their own cultural traditions and religions, but tensions persisted. China's fifty-five minorities, concentrated in the less economically developed areas of the southwest and the interior western provinces, had lower educational levels and fewer economic opportunities than members of the Han Chinese majority.

Tensions were particularly strong in the Tibetan ethnic areas and among the Muslim Uighurs of Xinjiang. In Xinjiang, Uighurs became more assertive of their Turkic and Islamic identity and more openly resentful of Chinese political, economic, and cultural control. They expressed resistance to Chinese hegemony in literature, peaceful protests, and even through terrorist attacks on police stations and public buses. Some Uighur activists argued that Xinjiang should split off from China to become an independent state of "East Turkestan."

In the Tibet Autonomous Region and in culturally Tibetan areas of neighboring provinces (Qinghai, Yunnan, Sichuan, and Gansu), opposition to Chinese cultural and political domination was expressed in a resurgence of Tibetan Buddhism and in veneration (often surreptitious, sometimes open) of the Dalai Lama, Tibet's exiled spiritual leader and head of the Tibetan government–in-exile. Buddhist monks and nuns in Lhasa were at the forefront of protests against Chinese rule, leading protests in the streets of Lhasa in the 1980s. In March 2008, on the eve of the Beijing Olympics, violent protests took place in Lhasa and other areas. Monks were joined by young Tibetans who turned their anger on businesses owned by Han Chinese and Hui (Chinese Muslims).

The government handled Tibetans and Uighurs involved in movements for increased autonomy or independence with the utmost severity. Police and soldiers fired on protesters in Lhasa in 1987, 1988, 1989, and 2008.[48] Tibetan dissidents, particularly monks and nuns, faced brutal beatings, imprisonment, and torture. In Xinjiang, Uighur poets and authors whose work expressed Uighur nationalist sentiment were arrested.[49] Beijing's strict suppression of Tibetan and Uighur dissidents drew criticism from Western governments, but the Chinese public, including Chinese communities overseas, generally agreed that any demands for greater Uighur or Tibetan autonomy were tantamount to moves toward independence for these territories, and thus were generally supportive of the Chinese government's actions.

Strict suppression and refusal to compromise with Uighur or Tibetan dissidents[50] was directly related to the Communist leaders' conviction that if they showed weakness in the political realm, the floodgates of criticism might open, sweeping the Chinese Communist Party away, just as they had the Communist regimes of Eastern Europe and the Soviet Union. As a consequence, expressions of political dissidence were also severely punished. Ding Zilin (b. 1936), a woman whose son was shot in the back on 4 June

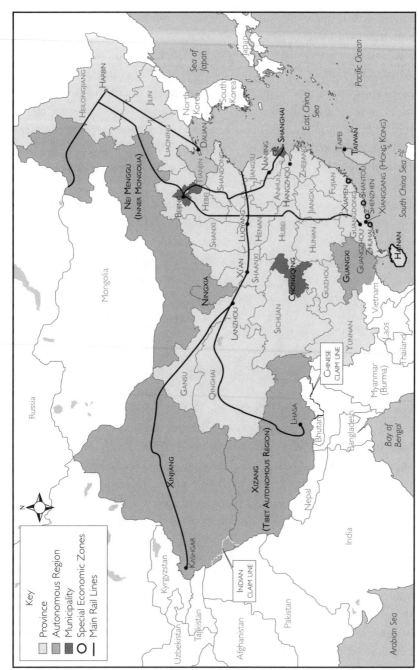

China in the era of reform.

1989, worked to organize other women whose children had been killed in the army's suppression of the student and worker protesters in Beijing. She often found herself under surveillance or house arrest.[51] In 2006, when Chen Guangcheng (b. 1971), a man from rural Shandong, tried to file charges against local party cadres who had used forced abortions to enforce the one-child policy (a clear contravention of law on the cadres' part), he was arrested and sentenced to four years in prison for "damaging property and organizing a mob to disrupt traffic."[52] Wang Xiaoning (b. 1950), a former participant in the 1989 protests in Beijing, published his writings on democracy, including a call for an independent political party, on the Internet. In 2003, he was sentenced to a ten-year prison term, partly on the basis of evidence of his online activities supplied by his Internet service provider, Yahoo!.[53]

Religious practitioners and organizations, too, were kept under careful scrutiny. From the Daoist rebellions of the Han dynasty to the Taiping rebellion, Muslim uprisings, and Boxer movement of the Qing, religions had played a significant role in domestic unrest. More recently, in Eastern Europe, the Catholic Church had helped to undermine Poland's Communist Party regime. In China, the practice and teaching of religion was permitted only in official, state-registered, and carefully monitored churches, mosques, and temples. While independent Protestant and Catholic church networks operated underground, their leaders and members faced arrest and prosecution. Authorities reacted with particular ferocity to the growth of "Falun Gong," an unregistered religious sect whose tens of thousands of followers practiced martial arts and meditation exercises derived from a pastiche of Buddhist and Daoist traditions as patched together by the charismatic cult leader. When thousands of practitioners quietly and peacefully surrounded Zhongnanhai, the Communist Party's central office and residential complex in Beijing, to demand the freedom to practice their religion, the government responded by banning Falun Gong. Mass arrests, torture, and imprisonment of Falun Gong practitioners followed.[54]

The continued repression of dissident voices was reinforced with control of information and a concentrated effort to inculcate the Chinese people with strong feelings of nationalism and with the belief that the Chinese Communist Party was the most effective defender of Chinese national pride and sovereignty. Party leaders took strong action to control not only political dissidents, but any organizations, individuals, or sources of news that, in their view, could lead to social unrest or undermine or even embarrass the government and/or its leaders. Tens of thousands of police supervised China's over one hundred million Internet users, blocking access to overseas Web sites with undesirable political (and pornographic) content and censoring Web sites and blogs.[55] A plainclothes security apparatus numbering in the millions, using the latest in listening, photographic, and computer technology, kept tabs on foreign diplomats, scholars, and journalists as well as Chinese dissidents.[56] The press and the educational system systematically emphasized that China had been humiliated by foreign powers for a hundred years from the mid-19th to the mid-20th centuries, and that the Chinese Communist Party alone had been able to stand up to the outside world and make China strong once again. Propaganda, control of information, and the undeniable material progress of the post-Mao decades were quite successful. In 2008, public opinion polls showed that although Chinese were generally not satisfied with their personal income, they were optimistic about the future, with more than eighty percent believing that the economy was good and the country heading in the right direction.[57] Around three in four believed that people in other countries liked China, but at the same time, more than thirty percent considered Japan and the United States of America as China's enemies.[58]

China on the Global Stage

While a large majority of the Chinese public was sure that the world in general liked China, the reality was far more complex. China's increased interaction with the developing and developed nations of the world was inextricably linked to its economic vitality. In order to grow, China needed foreign investment and foreign markets. In order to keep growing, it needed raw materials and energy. To assert its interests on the global stage and to defend its territory, China needed to invest part of its new wealth in its military. All three brought the Chinese government and Chinese companies into more and more complex economic, diplomatic, and strategic relations with the countries of both the developed and the developing world.

China's demand for timber, cement, uranium, minerals, and, above all, oil and gas, brought Chinese businesses (state, collective, and private) to Latin America, Africa, South and Southeast Asia, and the Middle East. China's approach to business relationships in the developing world was pragmatic: Beijing did not concern itself with a trading partner's environmental record, workers' rights, social problems, or politics. This attitude helped to gain China a warm welcome, particularly in African and Latin American states whose interaction with the West had been fraught with tension over political issues. China incurred particularly strong criticism from Western governments and Western public opinion for its close relations with Sudan and Myanmar, both important producers of oil and gas, and both ruled by regimes known for serious human rights violations.[59]

China's relations with African and Latin American nations were based primarily on economic interest. Its relationships with India, Pakistan, Russia, the Central Asian republics, Japan, and the West were based on a combination of economic and strategic concerns. In the final analysis, China's relations with these powers were centered on one issue: territorial sovereignty. China's close relations with Pakistan were clearly designed as a check on India, with whom China still had a serious border dispute as of 2008. The need for energy and water resources and a desire to build a network of strategic alliances on its Inner Asian border inspired China to bring the Central Asian republics and Russia together into the Shanghai Cooperation Organization (SCO) in 2001.[60]

Not an alliance (there are no mutual defense commitments), the SCO's stated goals are to ensure "cooperation among the member states in political, economic and trade, scientific and technological, cultural, educational, energy, communications, environment and other fields; devoting themselves jointly to preserving and safe-guarding regional peace, security and stability; and establishing a democratic, fair and rational new international political and economic order."[61] While many of the organization's activities revolved around regional security issues including terrorism, and its official external policy was one of "nonalignment, nontargeting anyone and openness," foreign policy analysts in the West believe that one of China's major goals with the SCO is to reduce American influence in Central Asia and thus to prevent the United States from encircling China with strategic partners and military bases.[62]

The relationship with the United States of America was indeed the most important, and perhaps the most complex, of China's relations with the Western nations. As established by Presidents Richard Nixon and Jimmy Carter (b. 1924) in 1972 and 1979, respectively, the Sino-American relationship was based on the two countries' shared suspicions of the Soviet Union. With the fall of the Soviet Union in 1991, the relationship became more difficult. On the one hand, business interests in both China and the United States saw opportunities: China wanted to attract American investment and technology and to export its products to the United States. American companies hoped to take advantage of China's cheap labor as a way of reducing production costs, and held hope that they would be able to sell American products and services to the growing number of Chinese consumers. On the other hand,

political relations could be tense. Americans criticized China regularly on issues of human rights, freedom of religion, arms sales to countries unfriendly
to the United States, and trade issues ranging from misleading labeling of
farm-raised fish to toys contaminated with lead.[63] Chinese responded to virtually any criticism with the countercriticism that the United States was
attempting to intervene in China's internal affairs. The major point of con-
tention between the two powers was the status of the island of Taiwan.

As we saw in Chapters 1 and 2, the island of Taiwan first became a part of
an empire ruled from the mainland of China in the early 18th century, only
to be lost to Japan in 1895. In 1949, Chiang Kai-shek fled to the island after
his defeat on the mainland. Then, before the People's Liberation Army could
prepare an assault on the island, the Korean War broke out, leading the
United States to prepare to defend Chiang Kai-shek. Virtually an American
protectorate since 1950, Taiwan under Chiang's government was a deeply divided society. "Mainlanders" who had accompanied Chiang and the Guomindang held a monopoly on political and military power. Under Chiang's iron
hand, the heavily censored press, the educational system, government cultural
policy, and government propaganda all emphasized the inculcation of Chinese
identity and unconditional loyalty to Chiang and his government. As Chiang
saw it, this was required in order to make Taiwan a bastion of Chinese culture and power from which he would eventually recover the mainland.

Many native Taiwanese people—descendants of Han Chinese who had
migrated from Fujian province during the Qing—responded by asserting
their own identity. They insisted on speaking the Taiwanese dialect and questioned their status as Chinese, pointing to the fact that the island had been
administered from the mainland only during the Qing. Taiwanese activists
demanded political freedom, democracy, and an end to martial law. Chiang
Kai-shek kept a tight lid on this sort of activity. The police spied on, harassed,
and arrested dissidents. Some Taiwanese dissidents served years in the notorious "Green Island" prison.

In the meantime, Taiwan's economy grew by leaps and bounds. Once on
Taiwan, the Guomindang regime pursued a policy of rural land reform: land
confiscated from the Japanese or taken from Taiwanese landlords (who were
financially compensated) was redistributed to farming families, creating a vibrant rural economy and a strong reserve of goodwill among rural residents.
The Korean War brought new American investments. Then, beginning in the
mid-1950s, Taiwan began to manufacture products for export, particularly
to the American market. Just as it did later in post-1979 China, the combination of a strong single-party state, a market economy, and an export-driven

development strategy led to explosive economic growth in Taiwan from the 1960s through the 1980s.[64]

On Taiwan, economic development was accompanied by political change. When Chiang died in 1975 his son and successor Chiang Ching-kuo (1910–88) began to remove restrictions on the press and to allow political parties and local elections. When Chiang Ching-kuo passed from the scene in 1988 the new Guomindang leader and president of the Republic of China (ROC), Lee Teng-hui (b. 1923), a native Taiwanese himself, continued to move the is-land's politics toward democracy. Lee subtly but clearly associated himself with the idea that Taiwan should eventually declare its formal independence from China. Pro-independence sentiment also found political expression in the formation of a new opposition political party: the Democratic Progres-sive Party (DPP), which was founded with the explicit goals of denouncing Guomindang corruption, pushing for further democracy, and achieving Taiwanese independence. From 2000 to 2008, Taiwan's president and DPP leader Chen Shui-bian (b. 1950) pushed Taiwan further in the direction of formally declaring independence from China.

In practical terms, Taiwan had been independent of the mainland ever since 1949. But Beijing regarded any talk of making the island's de facto in-dependence into an internationally recognized de jure independence with the deepest concern. One of the Communist Party's claims to legitimacy was that it, unlike the Qing and Republican regimes, was willing and able to de-fend China's territory. In 1984, China had successfully negotiated the return of the British colony of Hong Kong, which Britain returned to China in 1997. Mindful of Hong Kong's importance to China's economy and to the policy of opening to the outside, Deng Xiaoping proposed the formula of "one country, two systems." Hong Kong would be returned to Chinese sover-eignty and put under a Chinese-appointed chief executive, but its capitalist economy, banking system, legal system, civil service, and educational system would remain unchanged for fifty years.[65] China's hope was that the example of Hong Kong would serve as a model for a negotiated recognition of Beijing's authority over Taiwan. But whereas Hong Kong, a small British colony, was not militarily defensible, Taiwan had its own government, a natural defense in the form of the Taiwan Straits, and its own military.

Taiwan also had a peculiar defense relationship with the United States. The island had been essentially an American military protectorate since 1950, enjoying American support when tensions with the mainland erupted in the Taiwan Strait crises of 1954–55 and 1958. But as the United States built re-lations with the People's Republic, it downgraded its relationship with the

Republic of China on Taiwan. In 1972, President Nixon formally acknowledged that "all Chinese on either side of the Taiwan Strait maintain that there is but one China and that Taiwan is part of China" without saying whether the American government agreed or disagreed. When President Carter opened official diplomatic relations with the People's Republic in 1979, the United States ended diplomatic relations with the Republic of China, cancelled its defense treaty, and withdrew troops from Taiwan.

From that time on, the American government maintained a deliberately ambiguous stance on the question of whether or not, or under what circumstances, it would use military force to defend the island. The Taiwan Relations Act, passed by the American Congress in 1979, required the United States to consider any threat to Taiwan with "grave concern," to sell defensive weapons to Taiwan, and to maintain the capacity to defend the island against any threats. On the other hand, the Taiwan Relations Act did not legally bind the United States to commit its own forces to the defense of the island.

With American support, and with its own military capable of fending off an attack from the mainland, Taiwan's government had no particular incentive to accept any deal that submitted the island in any way to Beijing's authority. Negotiations on cross-straits relations in the 1980s and 1990s made no significant headway. When Lee Teng-hui or other Taiwanese political leaders made remarks that could be interpreted as advocating independence, China reacted with harshly worded denunciations. American support for Taiwan elicited even stronger reactions. In June 1995, the United States granted President Lee a visa to attend his class reunion at Cornell University. China responded with live-fire exercises, missile tests, and naval maneuvers in and around the Taiwan Straits. The PLA held more exercises in 1996 when Lee competed as the Guomindang candidate in Taiwan's first democratic presidential elections. China accompanied the exercises with warnings to the Taiwanese people not to vote for Lee. American president Bill Clinton (b. 1946) reacted by sending American navy ships toward the Taiwan Strait.

The Taiwan Straits Crisis of 1996 ended with an electoral victory for Lee Teng-hui and a reduction of tensions, but no reduction in Beijing's insistence on its right to bring the island under its control by peaceful or, if necessary, military means.[66] Acutely aware of the fact China was not ready to fight Taiwan, let alone the United States, President Jiang Zemin of the PRC initiated an ambitious program of military modernization in the late 1990s. Advances in airpower, submarine warfare, missile technology (nuclear and nonnuclear), cyberwarfare, and asymmetrical warfare were designed to enable the PLA to defeat Taiwan quickly while holding American power off.[67] By 2008, China had made substantial progress—foreign military analysts disagreed on when China would be able to launch a successful attack on Taiwan—but it was clear that the PLA had the ability to inflict serious damage on American aircraft carriers, spy satellites, and the computer-based American command and control system.

Chinese citizens generally supported their government's strong stance on Taiwan. On Taiwan itself, growing pro-independence sentiment in the 1990s contributed to the victory of Democratic Progressive Party candidate Chen Shui-bian, who served as president of Taiwan from 2000 to 2008.[68] The United States continued to balance delicately between the two sides, maintaining, for the most part, its policy of "strategic ambiguity." President George W. Bush (b. 1946) reduced the level of ambiguity in April 2001 when he remarked that the United States would "do whatever it took" to defend Taiwan.[69] American policy changed after the terrorist attacks of 11 September 2001. Desiring Chinese cooperation in the "war on terror" and China's support in negotiating a suspension of North Korea's nuclear weapons programs, the American president worked behind the scenes and publicly to dissuade Taiwanese president Chen Shui-bian from moves that would increase cross-straits tension. In 2003, when Chen Shui-bian proposed a referendum on a new constitution for Taiwan, which observers in both Beijing and the West understood as an implicit move toward a formal declaration of independence, President Bush declared: "We oppose any unilateral decision by either China or Taiwan to change the status quo. . . . [T]he comments and actions made by the leader of Taiwan indicate that he may be willing to make decisions unilaterally, to change the status quo, which we oppose."[70] The referendum ultimately failed.

Conclusion

History has traditionally been written as a story whose ending is the present: the status quo. At the same time, historical writing offers a commentary on the status quo and points the way toward the future. A history that has a happy ending suggests that the decisions and trends that got us to where we are today are good and should be continued on into the future. A history that is critical of where we are and how we got here suggests the need for new directions, new ideas, or new leadership.

革

People write different histories because they have very different assessments of the status quo, because they have different visions of the future and how to get there, and because the status quo itself changes every generation, or even more often. Our understanding of the past changes constantly because our understanding of the present and the future changes. History, in other words, is characterized by a high degree of instability. During the May Fourth/New Culture Movement, iconoclastic Chinese thinkers saw their own history as having led to weakness and defeat. The past was something to be rejected. In the words of Chinese Communist Party founder Chen Duxiu: "Smash the Confucian family shop!" During the Cultural Revolution, Red Guards literally smashed the material heritage of the Chinese past in their attempt to turn a new page to the future. In the early 21st century, China's Communist Party government lavishly funded the renovation of Confucian temples and established "Confucius Institutes" in major cities around the world to serve as centers for the teaching of Chinese culture and language.

The instability of history makes it difficult to bring the story of China to a satisfactory conclusion. Will China's economic growth continue for decades, making it the largest economy in the world? Or will the graying of Chinese society, the rising cost of energy, environmental degradation, or war slow or even stop the Chinese economy? Will economic growth or other factors lead China's farmers or its growing urban middle class to push for a more open society and democratic representation in the style of Taiwan, Japan, South Korea, or the Western democracies? Or will the next generation of Chinese Communist Party leaders initiate further and more daring experiments with democratization? Will an economic slowdown lead to social unrest and pressure for political change? Or will the combination of market economics, freedom of consumption, and repressive single-party politics continue to be as successful in the next thirty years as it has been since 1978?

Will the Western nations, particularly the United States, wrangle with China over human rights, trade, and energy, or even go to war over Taiwan? Or will China and the West cooperate on issues like global warming, the world economy, and nuclear proliferations? The book must come to an end, but the story goes on. If you would know what happens next, wait and see; then write the next chapter for yourself.

革

Notes

1. For the account of factional struggle in the years immediately following Mao's death and for the general narrative of political developments in the years from 1976 to 1997, I am much indebted to Richard Baum's excellent overview *Burying Mao: Chinese Politics in the Age of Deng Xiaoping* (Princeton: Princeton University Press, 1994).

2. Roderick MacFarquhar, "The Succession to Mao and the End of Maoism," in Roderick MacFarquhar and John K. Fairbank, eds., *The Cambridge History of China, Vol. 15: The People's Republic, Part 2: Revolutions Within the Chinese Revolution 1966–1982* (Cambridge: Cambridge University Press, 1991), 372.

3. Ibid., 377.

4. The following description and analysis of the Democracy Wall Movement follows Andrew J. Nathan, *Chinese Democracy* (Berkeley: University of California Press, 1985).

5. For example, see Chen Erjin, *China: Crossroads Socialism,* trans. Robin Munro (London: Verso, 1984).

6. Wei Jingsheng, "The Fifth Modernization: Democracy," in Wei Jingsheng, *The Courage to Stand Alone: Letters from Prison and Other Writings* (Harmondsworth: Penguin Books, 1997), 201–12.

7. Deng Xiaoping, "Uphold the Four Cardinal Principles," in *Selected Works of Deng Xiaoping (1975–1982)* (Beijing: Foreign Languages Press, 1984), 166–91.

8. For more detailed discussion of the relationship of economic cycles to the political cycles of liberalization and tightening (*fang* and *shou* in Chinese), see Baum, *Burying Mao,* 5–9.

9. Hongyi Lai, *Reform and the Non-State Economy in China: The Political Economy of Liberalization Strategies* (New York: Palgrave Macmillan, 2006), 34–9.

10. Baum, *Burying Mao,* 152.

11. Dwight Perkins, "The Lasting Effect of China's Economic Reforms, 1979–1989," in Kenneth Lieberthal, Joyce Kallgren, Roderick MacFarquhar, and Frederic Wakeman, Jr., eds., *Perspectives on Modern China: Four Anniversaries* (Armonk: M. E. Sharpe, 1991), 355.

12. On reform of state-owned enterprises, see John Hassard, Jackie Sheehan, Meixiang Zhou, Jane Terpstra-Tong, and Jonathan Morris, *China's State Enterprise Reform: From Marx to the Market* (London: Routledge, 2007).

13. Carrie Liu-Currier, "Bringing the Household Back In: The Restructuring of Women's Labor Choices in Beijing," *American Journal of Chinese Studies* 14:1 (2007): 71.

14. Baum, *Burying Mao,* 107–10.

15. Yang Jiang, *Six Chapters from My Life "Downunder"* (Seattle: University of Washington Press, 1983) is one easily accessible example of the "scar literature" genre. Many others, particularly first-person accounts of former Red Guards, are also available in English. For "scar painting," see The Asia Society, *New Chinese Art Inside Out: Chronologies* (New York: The Asia Society 1998–99), online at http://www.asiasociety.org/arts/insideout/chronologies.html, accessed 30 August 2008.

16. Michael Sullivan, *Art and Artists of Twentieth-Century China* (Berkeley: University of California Press, 1996), 215–24.

17. See the discussion in Jing Wang, *High Culture Fever: Politics, Aesthetics, and Ideology in Deng's China* (Berkeley: University of California Press, 1996).

18. "Excerpts from Fang Lizhi's Talk at Zhejiang University," (March 1985) in an internally circulated collection of Fang Lizhi's speeches. Document issued in 1987, in the possession of the author.

19. Julia Kwong, "The 1986 Student Demonstrations in China: A Democratic Movement?" *Asian Survey* 28.9 (Sept. 1988): 970–85.

20. Hongyi Lai, *Reform and the Non-State Economy,* 49, 72; Baum, *Burying Mao,* 233.

21. Lai, *Reform and the Non-State Economy,* 72.

22. Martin King Whyte, "The Changing Role of Workers," in Merle Goldman and Roderick MacFarquhar, eds., *The Paradox of China's Post-Mao Reforms* (Cambridge, Mass.: Harvard University Press, 1999), 188.

23. Ibid.

24. "It Is Necessary to Take a Clear-Cut Stand Against Disturbances," *People's Daily* editorial, 26 April 1989; English version online in *Tiananmen: The Gate of Heavenly Peace: Chronology* (Brookline: Long Bow Group, n.d.) at http://tsquare.tv/chronology/April26ed.html, accessed 3 September 2008.

25. On the democracy movement in Beijing, see Nora Chang et al., *Tianmen: Gate of Heavenly Peace* (Brookline: Long Bow Group, n.d.), online at http://tsquare.tv/. For an account of the retreat from Tiananmen Square, see Robin Munro, "Who Died in Beijing, and Why: Remembering Tiananmen Square," *The Nation* 250.23 (11 June 1990): 811–22.

26. Jonathan Unger, ed., *The Pro-Democracy Protests in China: Reports from the Provinces* (Armonk: M. E. Sharpe, 1996).

27. Lai, *Reform and the Non-State Economy,* 72.

28. Joydeep Mukherji, "The Causes of Differential Development: Beyond Regime Differences," in Edward Friedman and Bruce Gilley, eds., *Asia's Giants: Comparing China and India* (New York: Palgrave Macmillan, 2005), 59.

29. Lai, *Reform and the Non-State Economy,* 247–8.

30. "China's floating population tops 140 mln," *People's Daily Online,* 27 July 2005; online at http://english.peopledaily.com.cn/200507/27/eng20050727_198605.html, accessed 24 September 2008.

31. Hanchao Lu, "Nostalgia for the Future: The Resurgence of an Alienated Culture in China," *Pacific Affairs* 75.2 (Summer 2002): 169.

32. Yusheng Yao, "The Elite Class Background of Wang Shuo and His Hooligan Characters," *Modern China* 30.4 (Oct. 2004): 431–69.

33. Bruce J. Dickson, *Red Capitalists in China: The Party, Private Entrepreneurs and Prospects for Political Change* (Cambridge: Cambridge University Press, 2003), 61.

34. "Beijing Estimated Too High on HIV/AIDS," *International Herald Tribune: Asia Pacific,* 26 Jan. 2006, online at http://www.iht.com/articles/2006/01/25/news/aids.php, accessed 24 Sept. 2008.

35. "China crackdown on work accidents," BBC News, 22 January 2008, online at http://news.bbc.co.uk/2/hi/asia-pacific/7201875.stm, accessed 24 September 2008.

36. "The World's Most Dangerous Job?" News release, China Labor Watch, 22 Feb. 2005, online at http://www.chinalaborwatch.org/en/web/article.php?article_id=50344, accessed 24 September 2008.

37. Elizabeth C. Economy, *The River Runs Black: The Environmental Challenge to China's Future* (Ithaca: Cornell University Press, 2004), 72.

革

38. Data from China Population and Information Research Center, *1949–1998 Total Population of China* (Beijing: CPIRC, 2000), online at http://www .cpirc.org.cn/en/totpope.htm.

39. There were some exceptions. For example, parents of a disabled child were allowed to bear a second child.

40. Paul Wiseman, "China Thrown Off Balance as Boys Outnumber Girls," *USA Today*, 19 June 2002, online at http:// www.usatoday.com/news/world/2002/ 06/19/china-usat.htm, accessed 24 September 2008.

41. Derek Scissors, *People, Growth, and Reform: China's Uncertain Future* (Washington: The Heritage Foundation, 2008), online at http://www.heritage.org/ Research/AsiaandthePacific/wm2032. cfm, accessed 1 September 2008.

42. The process is described and analysed in David Shambaugh, *China's Communist Party: Atrophy and Adaptation* (Washington: Woodrow Wilson Center Press, 2008).

43. Jean Oi, "Realms of Freedom in Post-Mao China," in Wiliam C. Kirby, ed., *Realms of Freedom in Modern China* (Stanford: Stanford University Press, 2004), 267–8.

44. On protests, and their possible function as "safety valves," see Oi, "Realms of Freedom in Post-Mao China," 264–84.

45. Murray Scot Tanner, "The National People's Congress," in Merle Goldman and Roderick MacFarquhar, eds., *The Paradox of China's Post-Mao Reforms* (Cambridge, Mass.: Harvard University Press, 1999), 100–28.

46. Susan Trevaskes, *Courts and Criminal Justice in Contemporary China* (Lanham: Lexington Books, 2007), 202–6; Murray Scot Tanner, "Campaign-Style Policing in China and Its Critics," in Børge Bakken, ed., *Crime, Punishment and Policing*

in China (Lanham: Rowman & Littlefield, 2005), 171–85.

47. Bruce J. Dickson, *Red Capitalists in China: The Party, Private Entrepreneurs, and Prospects for Political Change* (Cambridge: Cambridge University Press, 2003).

48. Lee Feigon, *Demystifying Tibet: Unlocking the Secrets of the Land of the Snows* (Chicago: Ivan Dee, 1996), 196–200.

49. For example, Rebiya Kadeer, a successful Uighur businesswoman and advocate of women's rights, was thrown in prison for five years because she had sent clippings from Xinjiang newspapers to her husband, a Uighur dissident, while he was visiting Washington, D.C. Amnesty International USA, "Rebiya Kadeer, Prisoner of Conscience – GOOD NEWS!" in *Special Focus Cases* (New York: AIUSA, 17 March 2005), online at http://www .amnestyusa.org/individuals-at-risk/ special-focus-cases/special-focus-cases/ page.do?id=1101237&n1=3&n2=34 &n3=53, accessed 8 September 2008. See also English PEN, "Uighur Rights and Writers," in *China Campaign 2008* (London: English PEN, 2008), online at http://www.englishpen.org/writersin prison/campaigns/chinacampaign2008/ uighurrightsandwriters/, accessed 1 September 2008.

50. By contrast, the government was willing to compromise when ethnic minority communities made demands that did not imply any challenge to China's territorial sovereignty. For example, when Hui (Chinese Muslim) activists staged public marches in Beijing and Lanzhou in 1989 to protest the publication of a book that they deemed insulting to Islam, police protected the marchers and the government even agreed to the protesters' demands: the offensive book was banned and its authors were arrested. Dru Gladney, *Muslim Chinese: Ethnic*

Nationalism in the People's Republic (Cambridge, Mass.: Council on East Asian Studies, Harvard University, 1996), 1–7.

51. Ding Zilin's efforts have resulted in an online map indicating the names of known victims of the crackdown and the places where they were killed. See Ellen Bork, Tian Jian, and Philip Chalk, "The Tiananmen Massacre Map," online at http://www.massacremap.com/, accessed 10 October 2008.

52. Joseph Kahn, "Chinese Court Upholds Conviction of Peasants' Advocate," *The New York Times,* 13 Jan. 2007, online at http://www.nytimes.com/2007/01/13/world/asia/13beijing.html?_r=1&oref=slogin, accessed 2 September 2008.

53. Victoria Kwan, "Prisoner Profile: Wang Xiaoning" (New York: Human Rights in China, n.d.), online at http://hrichina.org/public/PDFs/CRF.3.2006/CRF-2006-3_WangXiaoning.pdf, accessed 31 August 2008.

54. Barend ter Haar, *Falun Gong* (Leiden: Sinologisch Institut, Universeit Leiden, 2002–5), online at http://website.leidenuniv.nl/~haarbjter/falun.htm, accessed 31 August 2008.

55. Xiao Qiang, "The Development and the State Control of the Chinese Internet," testimony before the U.S.–China Economic and Security Review Commission, *China Digital Times* (Berkeley: Berkeley China Internet Project, Graduate School of Journalism, University of California, 26 April 2005), online at http://chinadigitaltimes.net/2005/04/xiao-qiang-the-development-and-the-state-control-of-the-chinese-internet/.

56. Jerome A. Cohen, "State of Surveillance: Big Brother on the Mainland Has Become More Efficient at Watching Your Every Move," *South China Morning Post,* 7 Aug. 2008.

57. Pew Global Attitudes Project, "The Chinese Celebrate Their Roaring Economy, As They Struggle with Its Costs" (Washington: Pew Research Center, 22 July 2008), online at http://pewglobal.org/reports/display.php?ReportID=261, accessed 1 September 2008. See also Rajesh Srinivasan and Nicole Naurath, "Urban Optimism," *China Business Review Online* (Washington: U.S.–China Business Council, 2008), online at http://www.chinabusinessreview.com/public/0807/gallup.html, accessed 1 September 2008.

58. Global Attitudes Project, "The Chinese Celebrate Their Roaring Economy, As They Struggle with Its Costs."

59. To note Chinese behavior in this respect is not to deny the fact that the United States and other Western governments have consistently supported, and continue to support, brutal, undemocratic regimes when they believe that it is in their national interest to do so.

60. Shanghai Cooperation Organization, English-language Web site: http://www.sectsco.org/home.asp?LanguageID=2, accessed 1 September 2008.

61. "Declaration on Establishment of Shanghai Cooperation Organisation" (Shanghai: SCO, 15 June 2001), online at http://www.sectsco.org/html/00088.html, accessed 1 September 2008.

62. "Brief introduction to the Shanghai Cooperation Organisation" (Shanghai: SCO, 2004–2005), online at http://www.sectsco.org/html/00026.html, accessed 8 September 2008; Lionel Beehner and Preeti Bhattacharji, "The Shanghai Cooperation Organization" (New York: Council on Foreign Relations, 8 April 2008), online at http://

www.cfr.org/publication/10883/, accessed 8 September 2008.

63. While it was not without basis, much of the criticism of Chinese exports and the Chinese human rights record in the first decade of the 21st century, and particularly in the year or so prior to the Beijing Olympics, was sensationalized and taken out of context: Stephen Mihm, "A Nation of Outlaws: A Century Ago, That Wasn't China—It Was Us," *The Boston Globe,* 26 Sept. 2007, online at http://www.boston.com/news/globe/ideas/articles/2007/08/26/a_nation_of_outlaws/, accessed 2 September 2008; Jeffrey N. Wasserstrom, "Getting Real About China," *The Nation,* 10 Oct. 2007, online at http://www.thenation.com/doc/20071022/wasserstrom, accessed 2 September 2008.

64. Thomas G. Rawski, "Economic Influence in China's Relations with the West," *Footnotes: The Newsletter of the Foreign Policy Research Institute's Wachman Center* 13.9 (Aug. 2008): 14–15.

65. The Portuguese colony of Macao was returned under similar arrangements in 1999.

66. Denny Roy, *Taiwan: A Political History* (Ithaca: Cornell University Press, 2003), 196–7.

67. Xiaobing Li, *A History of the Modern Chinese Army* (Lexington: The University Press of Kentucky, 2007), 284–94.

68. Popular frustration with the open corruption of Guomindang officials also contributed to the DPP's electoral victory. Pro-independence sentiment is only one of many factors that drive Taiwanese voter behavior.

69. "Bush Pledges Whatever It Takes to Defend Taiwan," CNN, 25 April 2001, online at http://archives.cnn.com/2001/ALLPOLITICS/04/24/bush.taiwan.abc/, accessed 24 September 2008.

70. Brian Knowlton, "Bush Warns Taiwan to Keep Status Quo: China Welcomes U.S. Stance," *International Herald Tribune,* 10 Dec. 2003, online at http://www.iht.com/articles/2003/12/10/policy_ed3_.php, accessed 2 September 2008.

Further Readings

Full citations for the various sources consulted in writing this book can be found in the notes for each chapter. Readers who want to explore a particular topic in depth are advised to look to the endnotes to locate books and articles that may be of interest. The following list of selected further readings is far from exhaustive: its purpose is to provide readers with a basic list of easily accessible secondary works and/or primary sources relevant to a particular topic or time period.

Atlases

Caroline Blunden and Mark Elvin, *Cultural Atlas of China*. Checkmark Books, 1998.

Stephanie Hemelryk Donald and Robert Benewick, *The State of China Atlas: Mapping the World's Fastest Growing Economy*. University of California Press, 2005.

Unesco World Heritage Atlas: China. Long River Press, 2008.

General Overviews

K. C. Chang, ed., *Food in Chinese Culture: Anthropological and Historical Perspectives*. Yale University Press, 1977.

Craig Clunas, *Art in China*. Oxford University Press, 1997.

Joanna Waley-Cohen, *The Sextants of Beijing: Global Currents in Chinese History*. W. W. Norton, 1999.

Patricia Buckley Ebrey and Kwang-ching Liu, *The Cambridge Illustrated History of China*. Cambridge University Press, 1999.

Bruce A. Elleman, *Modern Chinese Warfare, 1795–1989*. Routledge, 2001.

Mark Elvin, *The Retreat of the Elephants: An Environmental History of China*. Yale University Press, 2004.

John King Fairbank and Merle Goldman, *China: A New History*. Harvard University Press, 2006.

Jacques Gernet, J. R. Foster, and Charles Hartman, *A History of Chinese Civilization*. Cambridge University Press, 1996.

David A. Graff and Robin Higham, eds., *A Military History of China*. Westview Press, 2002.

Valerie Hansen, *The Open Empire: A History of China to 1600*. W. W. Norton, 2000.

Immanuel C. Y. Hsu, *The Rise of Modern China*, 6th edition. Oxford University Press, 2000.

Donald S. Lopez, Jr., *Religions of China in Practice*. Princeton University Press, 1996.

Victor H. Mair, ed., *The Columbia History of Chinese Literature*. Columbia University Press, 2001.

James A. Millward, *Eurasian Crossroads: A History of Xinjiang.* Columbia University Press, 2007.

W. Scott Morton and Charlton M. Lewis, *China: Its History and Culture.* McGraw-Hill, 2004.

F. W. Mote, *Imperial China, 900–1800.* Harvard University Press, 1999.

Joseph Needham, *Science and Civilization in China.* Cambridge University Press, 1986.

Conrad Schirokauer and Miranda Brown, *A Brief History of Chinese Civilization.* Wadsworth Publishing Company, 2006.

Edward L. Shaughnessy, ed., *China: Empire and Civilization.* Oxford University Press, 2000.

Jonathan D. Spence, *The Search for Modern China,* 2nd edition. W.W. Norton, 1999.

Peter Worthing, *A Military History of Modern China: From Manchu Conquest to Tian'anmen Square.* Praeger Security International, 2007.

Primary Sources

Patricia Buckley Ebrey, ed. *Chinese Civilization: A Sourcebook,* 2nd edition. The Free Press, 1993.

Pei-kai Cheng and Michael Lestz with Jonathan Spence, eds., *The Search for Modern China: A Documentary Collection.* W. W. Norton, 1999.

Chapter 1 – The Qing Dynasty to 1799

Tonio Andrade, *How Taiwan Became Chinese: Dutch, Spanish, and Han Colonization in the Seventeenth Century.* Columbia University Press, 2008.

Beatrice S. Bartlett, *Monarchs and Ministers: The Grand Council in Mid-Ch'ing China, 1723–1820.* University of California Press, 1991.

Thomas M. Buoye, *Manslaughter, Markets, and Moral Economy: Violent Disputes Over Property Rights in Eighteenth-Century China.* Cambridge University Press, 2000.

Pamela Kyle Crossley, *The Manchus.* Blackwell Publishers, 1997.

Benjamin A. Elman, *A Cultural History of Civil Examinations in Late Imperial China.* University of California Press, 2000.

R. Kent Guy, *The Emperor's Four Treasuries: Scholars and the State in the Late Ch'ien-lung Era.* Council on East Asia Studies, Harvard University, 1987.

Philip A. Kuhn, *Soulstealers: The Chinese Sorcery Scare of 1768.* Harvard University Press, 1990.

Melissa Macauley, *Social Power and Legal Culture: Litigation Masters in Late Imperial China.* Stanford University Press, 1998.

Ichisada Miyazaki, *China's Examination Hell: The Civil Service Examinations of Imperial China.* Yale University Press, 1981.

Susan Naquin and Evelyn S. Rawski, *Chinese Society in the Eighteenth Century.* Yale University Press, 1987.

Peter C. Perdue, *China Marches West: The Qing Conquest of Central Eurasia.* Harvard University Press, 2005.

Bradley W. Reed, *Talons and Teeth: County Clerks and Runners in the Qing Dynasty.* Stanford University Press, 2000.

Edward J. M. Rhoads, *Manchus and Han: Ethnic Relations and Political Power in Late Qing and Early Republican China, 1861–1928.* University of Washington Press, 2000.

Jonathan D. Spence, *Emperor of China: Self-Portrait of K'ang-Hsi.* Vintage Books, 1975.

Jonathan D. Spence, *Treason by the Book.* Penguin Putnam, 2001.

Frederic Wakeman, Jr., *The Great Enterprise: The Manchu Reconstruction of Imperial Order in Seventeenth-Century China.* University of California Press, 1985.

Chapter 2 – The Qing Dynasty's 19th-Century Crisis

Marie-Claire Bergère, *Sun Yat-sen.* Stanford University Press, 1998.

Hsin-pao Chang, *Commissioner Lin and the Opium War.* Harvard University Press, 1964.

Paul A. Cohen, *History in Three Keys: The Boxers as Event, Experience, and Myth.* Columbia University Press, 1997.

Mark C. Elliott, *The Manchu Way: The Eight Banners and Ethnic Identity in Late Imperial China.* Stanford: Stanford University Press, 2001.

Joseph Esherick, *The Origins of the Boxer Uprising.* University of California Press, 1987.

Robert D. Jenks, *Insurgency and Social Disorder in Guizhou: The "Miao" Rebellion 1854–1873.* University of Hawaii Press, 1994.

Hodong Kim, *Holy War in China: The Muslim Rebellion and State in Chinese Central Asia, 1864–1877.* Standford University Press, 2004.

Robert B. Marks, *Tigers, Rice, Silk and Silt: Environment and Economy in Late Imperial South China.* Cambridge University Press, 1998.

Robert B. Marks, *The Origins of the Modern World: A Global and Ecological Narrative from the Fifteenth to the Twenty-first Century,* 2nd edition. Rowman & Littlefield, 2007.

Kenneth Pomeranz, *The Great Divergence: China, Europe, and the Making of the World Economy.* Princeton University Press, 2000.

Douglas R. Reynolds, *China, 1898–1912: The Xinzheng Revolution and Japan.* Council on East Asian Studies, Harvard University, 1993.

Edward J. M. Rhoads, *Manchus and Han: Ethnic Relations and Political Power in Late Qing and Early Republican China, 1861–1928.* University of Washington Press, 2000.

Jonathan D. Spence, *God's Chinese Son: The Taiping Heavenly Kingdom of Hong Xiuquan.* W. W. Norton, 1996.

Frederic Wakeman, Jr., *The Fall of Imperial China.* The Free Press, 1975.

J. Y. Wong, *Deadly Dreams: Opium, Imperialism, and the Arrow War (1856–1860) in China.* Cambridge University Press, 1998.

Zhou Xun, *Narcotic Culture: A History of Drugs in China.* The University of Chicago Press, 2004.

Zheng Yangwen, *The Social Life of Opium in China.* Cambridge University Press, 2005.

Chapter 3 – The 1911 Revolution and the Early Republic, 1912–26

Marie-Claire Bergère, *Sun Yat-sen.* Stanford University Press, 1998.

Lucien Bianco, *Origins of the Chinese Revolution 1915–1949.* Stanford University Press, 1971.

Sherman Cochran, *Big Business in China: Sino-Foreign Rivalry in the Cigarette Industry, 1890–1930.* Harvard University Press, 1980.

Ono Kazuko, *Chinese Women in a Century of Revolution, 1850–1950*. Stanford University Press, 1989.

E. Perry Link, Jr., *Mandarin Ducks and Butterflies: Popular Fiction in Early Twentieth Century Chinese Cities*. University of California Press, 1981.

Hanchao Lu, *Beyond the Neon Lights: Everyday Life in Shanghai in the Early Twentieth Century*. University of California Press, 1999.

Brian G. Martin, *The Shanghai Green Gang: Politics and Organized Crime, 1919–1937*. University of California Press, 1996.

Elizabeth J. Perry, *Shanghai on Strike: The Politics of Chinese Labor*. Stanford University Press, 1993.

Edward J. M. Rhoads, *Manchus and Han: Ethnic Relations and Political Power in Late Qing and Early Republican China, 1861–1928*. University of Washington Press, 2000.

Kristin Stapleton, *Civilizing Chengdu: Chinese Urban Reform, 1895–1937*. Harvard University East Asian Center, 2000.

Michael Sullivan, *Art and Artists of Twentieth Century China*. University of California Press, 1996.

Chow Tse-tsung, *The May 4th Movement: Intellectual Revolution in Modern China*. Harvard University Press, 1960.

Guoqi Xu, *China and the Great War: China's Pursuit of a New National Identity and Internationalization*. Cambridge University Press, 2005.

Ernest P. Young, *The Presidency of Yuan Shih-k'ai: Liberalism and Dictatorship in Early Republican China*. University of Michigan Press, 1977.

Wang Zheng, *Women in the Chinese Enlightenment: Oral and Textual Histories*. University of California Press, 1999.

Chapter 4 – China Under Chiang Kai-Shek's Guomindang Government

Hsi-sheng Ch'i, *Nationalist China at War: Military Defeats and Political Collapse, 1937–45*, University of Michigan Press, 1982.

Jonathan Fenby, *Chiang Kai-shek: China's Generalissimo and the Nation He Lost*. Carroll & Graff Publishers, 2003.

Joshua A. Fogel, ed., *The Nanjing Massacre in History and Historiography*. University of California Press, 2000.

Emily Honig, *Creating Chinese Ethnicity: Subei People in Shanghai, 1850–1980*. Yale University Press, 1982.

Honda Katshuichi, *The Nanjing Massacre: A Japanese Journalist Confronts Japan's National Shame*. M. E. Sharpe, 1999.

Diana Lary and Stephen MacKinnon, eds., *Scars of War: The Impact of Warfare on Modern China*. University of British Columbia Press, 2001.

Leo Ou-fan Lee, *Shanghai Modern: The Flowering of a New Urban Culture in China, 1930–1945*. Harvard University Press, 1999.

Stephen R. MacKinnon, *Wuhan, 1938: War, Refugees, and the Making of Modern China*. University of California Press, 2008.

Dai Qing, *Wang Shiwei and Wild Lilies: Rectification and Purges in the Chinese Communist Party 1942–1944*. M. E. Sharpe, 1994.

Tony Saich, ed., *The Rise to Power of the Chinese Communist Party: Documents and Analysis*. M. E. Sharpe, 1996.

Harrison E. Salisbury, *The Long March: The Untold Story*. Harper & Row Publishers, 1985.

Jay Taylor, *The Generalissimo: Chiang Kai-shek and the Struggle for Modern China*. Belknap Press of Harvard University Press, 2009.

Hans Van de Ven, *From Friend to Comrade: The Founding of the Chinese Communist Party, 1920–1927*. University of California Press, 1991.

Hans Van de Ven, *War and Nationalism in China: 1925–1945*. Routledge, 2003.

Frederick Wakeman, Jr., *Policing Shanghai 1927–1937*. University of California Press, 1995.

Frederic Wakeman Jr., and Richard Louis Edmonds, eds., *Reappraising Republican China*. Oxford University Press, 2000.

Odd Arne Westad, *Decisive Encounters: The Chinese Civil War, 1946–1950*. Stanford University Press, 2003.

Maochun Yu, *The Dragon's War: Allied Operation and the Fate of China 1937–1947*. Naval Institute Press, 2006.

Margherita Zanasi, *Saving the Nation: Economic Modernity in Republican China*. The University of Chicago Press, 2006.

Chapter 5 – The Mao Era

Julia F. Andrews and Kuiyi Shen, eds., *A Century in Crisis: Modernity and Tradition in the Art of Twentieth Century China*. Guggenheim Museum, 1998.

Jasper Becker, *Hungry Ghosts: China's Secret Famine*. John Murray, 1996.

Timothy Cheek, *Mao Zedong and China's Revolutions: A Brief History with Documents*. Bedford/St. Martin's, 2002.

Warren I. Cohen, *America's Response to China: A History of Sino-American Relations*, 4th edition. Columbia University Press, 2000.

Yi-tsi Mei Feuerwerker, *Ding Ling's Fiction: Ideology and Narrative in Modern Chinese Literature*. Harvard University Press, 1982.

Chen Jian, *China's Road to the Korean War: The Making of the Sino-American Confrontation*. Columbia University Press, 1994.

Yang Jiang, *Six Chapters from My Life "Downunder."* University of Washington Press, 1983.

Xiaobing Li, *A History of the Modern Chinese Army*. The University Press of Kentucky, 2007.

Kenneth Lieberthal, *Governing China: From Revolution Through Reform*, 2nd edition. W. W. Norton, 2004.

Roderick MacFarquhar and Michael Schoenhals, *Mao's Last Revolution*. Belknap Press, 2008.

Maurice Meisner, *Mao's China and After: A History of the People's Republic*, 3rd edition. The Free Press, 1999.

Denny Roy, *Taiwan: A Political History*. Cornell University Press, 2003.

⸍ Ruo-wang (Jean Pasqualini) and Rudolph Chelminski, *Prisoner of Mao*. Penguin Books, ⸍6.

James D. Seymour and Richard Anderson, *New Ghosts, Old Ghosts: Prisons and Labor Reform Camps in China*. M. E. Sharpe, 1998.

Philip F. Williams and Yenna Wu, *The Great Wall of Confinement: The Chinese Prison Camp Through Contemporary Fiction and Reportage*. University of California Press, 2004.

Shu Guang Zhang, *Mao's Military Romanticism: China and the Korean War, 1950–1953*. University Press of Kansas, 1995.

Chapter 6 – The March Toward Wealth and Power

Richard Baum, *Burying Mao: Chinese Politics in the Age of Deng Xiaoping*. Princeton University Press, 1994.

Bruce J. Dickson, *Red Capitalists in China: The Party, Private Entrepreneurs and Prospects for Political Change*. Cambridge University Press, 2003.

Elizabeth C. Economy, *The River Runs Black: The Environmental Challenge to China's Future*. Cornell University Press, 2004.

Lee Feigon, *Demystifying Tibet: Unlocking the Secrets of the Land of the Snows*. Ivan Dee, 1996.

Merle Goldman and Roderick MacFarquhar, eds., *The Paradox of China's Post-Mao Reforms*. Harvard University Press, 1999.

John Hassard, Jackie Sheehan, Meixiang Zhou, Jane Terpstra-Tong, and Jonathan Morris, *China's State Enterprise Reform: From Marx to the Market*. Routledge, 2007.

Wei Jingsheng, *The Courage to Stand Alone: Letters from Prison and Other Writings*. Penguin Books, 1997.

William C. Kirby, ed., *Realms of Freedom in Modern China*. Stanford University Press, 2004.

Andrew J. Nathan, *Chinese Democracy*. University of California Press, 1985.

David Shambaugh, *China's Communist Party: Atrophy and Adaptation*. Woodrow Wilson Center Press, 2008.

Michael Sullivan, *Art and Artists of Twentieth-Century China*. University of California Press, 1996.

Susan Trevaskes, *Courts and Criminal Justice in Contemporary China*. Lexington Books, 2007.

Jing Wang, *High Culture Fever: Politics, Aesthetics, and Ideology in Deng's China*. University of California Press, 1996.

Index